MY SEARCH FOR REVOLUTION

MY SEARCH FOR REVOLUTION

And how we brought down an abusive leader

CLARE COWEN

Copyright © 2019 Clare Cowen

The moral right of the author has been asserted.

Cover design: Brian Eley

Photographs in this book are scanned from the daily newspapers *Workers Press* (Socialist Labour League, 1969-1976) and *News Line* (Workers Revolutionary Party, 1976-1985) and retain the appearance of their source newspapers, which were an integral part of the author's life. Other pictures are the author's or were provided by Durham Miners Gala Brochure, Dot Gibson, Dave Bruce, and Sandra Baker for the photograph of Phil Penn.

Apart from any fair dealing for the purposes of research or private study, or criticism or review, as permitted under the Copyright, Designs and Patents Act 1988, this publication may only be reproduced, stored or transmitted, in any form or by any means, with the prior permission in writing of the publishers, or in the case of reprographic reproduction in accordance with the terms of licences issued by the Copyright Licensing Agency. Enquiries concerning reproduction outside those terms should be sent to the publishers.

Matador
9 Priory Business Park,
Wistow Road, Kibworth Beauchamp,
Leicestershire. LE8 0RX
Tel: 0116 279 2299
Email: books@troubador.co.uk
Web: www.troubador.co.uk/matador
Twitter: @matadorbooks

ISBN 978 1838590 987

British Library Cataloguing in Publication Data.
A catalogue record for this book is available from the British Library.

Printed and bound by CPI Group (UK) Ltd, Croydon, CR0 4YY
Typeset in 11pt Adobe Garamond Pro by Troubador Publishing Ltd, Leicester, UK

Matador is an imprint of Troubador Publishing Ltd

For Aileen Jennings

And for all Healy's victims

– they know who they are

ACKNOWLEDGEMENTS

Many people have helped me with research, remembering details, refining the text, and giving me permission to include their story.

Colleagues on my Creative and Life Writing MA at Goldsmiths, University of London, originally convinced me to change tack to write a memoir and commented on early drafts; my tutors, Blake Morrison and Francis Spufford, encouraged me.

My university friends Sue Branford and Helen O'Riain commented on several early drafts; Rosie Barron improved the text with a late, detailed reading.

Countless former comrades, some mentioned by name in the book, gave me assistance, encouragement and confidence to continue. Bridget Leach advised me from the beginning. Martin Westwood and John Spencer read it with lawyers' eyes. Sue Hunter checked the text from a literary angle. Liz Leicester, Dave Temple, Hilary Horrocks, Terry Brotherstone, Simon Pirani and Martin Mayer encouraged me, as did many others. Brian Eley shored up my confidence in bleak moments and designed the cover. Steve Drury gave me incomparable assistance and advice with the pictures and allayed my panic.

I'm particularly grateful to those – comrades and others – who encouraged me in moments of doubt about the wisdom of revealing Healy's sexual abuse.

I'm grateful to Mary Russell and John Manix who contacted me of their own accord.

The moral support of the four others in our group of five – Aileen Jennings, Dave Bruce, Dot Gibson and Charlie – has been essential.

I appreciate the encouragement and patience of my wider family.

CONTENTS

2016	**THIRTY YEARS ON**	**1**
1961	**RIOTS IN RHODESIA**	**8**
1964	**PARIS**	**15**
1965	**BRISTOL**	**27**
	Unilateral Declaration of Independence	27
	The Socialist Labour League	33
1967	**SHEFFIELD**	**42**
	Marriage	45
	May-June 1968	50
1969	**LONDON AND *WORKERS PRESS***	**53**
	Launch of the daily paper	60
	My husband, T	68
	1972 the Right to Work Marches	74
	Dagenham and the docks	85
	Work at the Centre	90
	1974 Three-day week	98
	Cowley	105
	Workers Press ends	111

1976 NEWS LINE — 115

- Firemen's strike — 124
- Runcorn printshop — 128
- A revolutionary daily paper – pictures — 133
- My parents — 149

1982 FINANCE OFFICE — 157

- International Committee — 166
- Twenty thousand dollars — 169
- Volume 38 — 174
- Finances deteriorate — 178

1984 MINERS' STRIKE — 182

- South West Africa — 182
- My secret flat — 185
- *News Line* circulation — 190
- M1 motorway — 196
- Political Committee meeting — 200
- My mother visits London — 202

1985 CLARITY — 208

- The revelation — 212
- My confusion — 217
- We prepare to act — 221
- The letter — 230
- Alexandra Pavilion — 231

1ST JULY TURNING POINT — 236

- The following days — 241
- Central Committee — 242
- The bookshops — 251
- Political discussion — 256
- August heat — 258

SEPTEMBER CRACKS APPEAR	**266**
News Line report	271
Challenges	276
Brixton riots	282
Finance report	285
The boil bursts	287
OCTOBER RUNCORN STRIKES	**291**
A stormy Central Committee	294
The charges	300
Two London aggregates	302
Expulsion	313
Congress confirms	318
The Minority splits	321
1986 AND BEYOND THE WOMEN'S QUESTION	**328**
Loose ends	332
Afterword	335
GLOSSARY	**337**
Political terms	337
Party publications	338
Party premises and companies	338
Party members who recur	340
Brief bibliography	341
Historical and political figures	342
Chronology 1964-87	343
INDEX	**347**

2016
THIRTY YEARS ON

I last glimpsed Gerry Healy in 1986, near Stockwell station: an elderly man, short, round, bespectacled, accompanied by my former comrade Corinna. He seemed disconcerted at seeing me but I looked at him unflinchingly, amused, quietly triumphant. An image from *The Wizard of Oz* film suddenly came to mind: the erstwhile power of the mighty wizard exposed as a few tricks of fire and smoke when a curtain flapped open to reveal an ordinary, bald old man.

'You have to be careful of this kind of thing,' Healy said, pointing to my baby in his buggy.

I smiled and said nothing. You can no longer frighten or intimidate me, I thought. Your ability to harm anyone has been reduced to almost nothing. We rose up and expelled you and I'm proud of my role in your downfall.

Thomas Gerard Healy, longtime leader of the Workers Revolutionary Party, was expelled by a unanimous vote of the Party's Central Committee on Saturday 19th October 1985. If he had attended the meeting to defend himself the vote would not have been unanimous as he had supporters on the committee. But he scuttled into hiding and his supporters didn't turn up either.

The Party's daily newspaper, *News Line*, reported his expulsion: Healy, a leader of the International Committee of the Fourth International, member of the Trotskyist movement for 49 years, had been charged with violating comrades' constitutional rights, establishing 'entirely non-communist and bureaucratic relations' inside the Party and abusing his power 'for personal gratification'.

Reports of sexual abuse caught the attention of the Fleet Street press, their interest heightened because well-known actors Vanessa and Corin Redgrave were Party members. 'Red in the bed – Sex scandal of sacked Trot chief and 26 women,' said the *Mirror*. 'Exit left the two Redgraves – Stars face purge in "Reds in bed" storm,' proclaimed the *Daily Mail*. The *Daily Express* declared 'fears for the safety of the secretary whose sex allegations ousted founder Gerry Healy'.

Some in the labour movement regretted the fall of an important leader; others felt vindicated in their disagreements with him over Trotsky's political legacy. Yet others felt Healy's overthrow and the Party's spectacular implosion were long overdue because of what they considered his crazy, extreme, left-wing politics. Healy's supporters formed a breakaway party, which split further. The Party majority continued for several years afterwards; groups split off and individuals left. The turbulent 1970s and 1980s gradually faded in memory and interest in the Workers Revolutionary Party receded.

For the first 20 years of my adult life Gerry Healy was a major influence. I had been impelled into political activity in the 1960s by events in apartheid South Africa, where I was born, and in white-controlled Southern Rhodesia, where I spent my teens. At university in Bristol I joined the Trotskyist Young Socialists and Socialist Labour League, later the Workers Revolutionary Party. My life was exhilarating, if exhausting. I felt in tune with major class struggles in Britain and worldwide, I had a purpose in life and I believed my actions in the working-class movement were making a difference.

Two things ended this phase. The first was the major explosion within the Party. The second was the birth of my first son.

Conversation round the supper table with a visitor turned to our shared past in the Party. Our teenage sons were mystified.

'You just let him smash you in the face?' the older one said to his father.

'He broke your glasses? Was he bigger and stronger?' asked the younger.

'Not at all. He was short, podgy and quite old.'

'I'd have hit him back really hard.'

'It wasn't quite like that,' I said. 'He had great authority as the leader of a big political organisation …'

'That's stupid.' They were already bored.

'Will our sons ever grasp anything about our lives?' I sighed as they left the table.

'Why not write something for them?'
'To read when they're about 40? Maybe.'

From time to time I met up with former comrades socially, after a political event or at a regular gathering in a pub near Victoria. Discussion inevitably turned to our time in the Workers Revolutionary Party. When I mentioned that I might write about my experiences reactions were mixed.

'Well, yes, someone should write a proper evaluation of what happened. But who has the energy?' said one. 'We were just a footnote to history and who would want to read it anyway?'

'It's all best forgotten,' said another. 'Come on, we were nothing but a sect – why couldn't we see it at the time?'

Others disagreed.

'During the miners' strike I found that dozens of local leaders had been recruited to the Young Socialists when they were 15 and 16,' said miner Dave Temple. 'I meet them every year at the Durham Miners' Gala and they tell me that whatever was wrong with the Party it gave them a basic education which changed the course of their lives.'

'Thousands of young people learned about socialism because of us.'

'Yeah, discos, football, coach trips. Very political.'

▼ Durham Miners' Gala 2018

▲ Audience at a 1983 Young Socialists' conference

'Come on, we organised demonstrations, meetings, conferences, classes. We gave them a perspective of defending their rights, fighting the government's attacks.'

'Have you read Kevin Flynn'*'s online oral history interview?' asked someone else. 'He started work at 15 in the shipyards and later met the Young Socialists there.'

I had read the interview.

'He says his introduction to politics was a wonderful education. He remembers Gerry lecturing in Wallsend to 50 or 60 ordinary working class people on philosophical questions. Kevin was very interested in the Portuguese revolution in 1974, Vietnam, the collapse of the Spanish fascist regime in 1975. And he says 300 people came to see Vanessa's film *The Palestinian*.'

'He also had bitter experiences and he says the Party had some ludicrous, barmy positions.'

'Yes, of course, and a lot of our policies were wrong.'

'Look, workers read our daily paper because they wanted an alternative to the capitalist press,' countered another. 'Where else could they find that?'

---

* http://nelh.net/resources-library/oral-history/oral-history-political-organisations/oral-history-political-organisations-kevin-flynn/

◀ Vanessa Redgrave's film, directed by Roy Battersby

'True. We supported working-class struggles that everybody else ignored or attacked, we defended workers who were victimised, suffered racist attacks or faced deportation.'

'And the sports pages were very popular.'

'*News Line* was a very interesting paper,' I said. 'It had reviews of books, films, theatre, scientific developments. It reported international events from a Marxist viewpoint.'

'Don't forget the endless articles on Gerry's philosophy … the fight against revisionism … "Security and the Fourth International", incomprehensible, boring, day after day, month after month.'

Some laughed, others groaned. We became more thoughtful.

'The plays and huge theatrical events we ran were stunning, written, produced and performed by top people from the entertainments industry. They conveyed complex historical and political ideas to audiences of thousands at our rallies. No one else did that.'

'We had impressive events, but selling and distributing the daily paper dominated our lives. It exhausted us.'

▼ News Line's back pages reported on many different sports and were called Sports Line

▲ April 1973 Young Socialists' conference in Blackpool's sumptuous Winter Gardens

'I don't discount the negative aspects, but I had interesting experiences in the Party and I think the 1985 explosion is worth recording and evaluating,' I insisted.

'All the websites dealing with the 1985 split discuss only what leading members did. None consider the role of ordinary members, particularly beyond London.'

'Maybe that's because the political uproar embroiling the Party was unfathomable from the outside,' I pointed out. 'The only account of what really happened is Norman's book, *Staying Red**, because it was written by a participant.'

'Healy's supporters claim his downfall was the work of MI5 or other agents of the state. Ken Livingstone says so explicitly in his foreword to Corinna's book** and so does Vanessa in her autobiography***. Alex Mitchell**** insinuates it was the work of state-paid "plants" in the Party.'

'I want to write about my own experiences and include Healy's sexual abuse because that's what galvanised the Party members against him,' I said.

'But that's not really a political question. There would just be prurient interest in it.'

---

* *Staying Red, Why I remain a Socialist*, by Norman Harding. Index Books, 2005. https://stayingred.wordpress.com/
** *Gerry Healy: A revolutionary life*, by Corinna Lotz and Paul Feldman, Lupus Books, 1994. pvii
*** *Vanessa Redgrave - An Autobiography*. Arrow Books, 1992. p250-2
**** *Come the Revolution*, Alex Mitchell, UNSW Press 2012. p482-3

◀ Our long-running and widely discredited 'Security and the Fourth International' investigation into Stalinist penetration of the Trotskyist movement charged veteran US Trotskyist leaders Joe Hansen and George Novack as accomplices of both Soviet intelligence and the United States' FBI in Trotsky's assassination.

'Nonsense,' I persisted. 'It's deeply political. And what other organisation has taken action against a sexual abuser in the way we did?'

'The salacious nature of the revelations might do damage. You'd be taking a risk.'

'Go ahead and write it,' encouraged a comrade who was on the women's committee of her trade union.

'But please don't mention me,' said another woman. 'I just want to forget about it.'

The bitter tone of her remark took me by surprise and I had to stop and think. Some considered the Party had been so unimportant that it was best forgotten – I disagreed with them – but I also knew that a number had suffered very dark events and bitter experiences which continued to affect their lives. In her case it seemed she wanted to consign these experiences to the depths of discarded remembrance. I would have to be sensitive to this if I wrote my own account.

The detailed preparations that ultimately led to Healy's expulsion were known only to five of us in the Party's inner administration. I consulted the other four. Two were not opposed to my writing about it but questioned whether it was worth the effort. The third said she had previously decided not to write anything, 'because it could bring the movement as a whole into disrepute'.

The fourth saw it completely differently.

'I'm with you all the way,' she said. 'I couldn't write about it myself but I'll give you any help you need. The sexual abuse story has to be told, warts and all. Yours will be the only voice we ever have.'

1961
RIOTS IN RHODESIA

I heard men shouting and cheering in the Drill Hall grounds as I reached the top of Blakiston Street. Opposite me and round the corner to the school gates hundreds of soldiers were leaning over the long fences, whistling enthusiastically and calling out as we schoolgirls cycled past. Worried that my stocking suspenders would show under my knee-length gymslip, I rode purposefully across the road as the men whistled at me too. It was very exciting.

Boarders from the hostel opposite were relishing the excitement, giggling and blushing. But Sandra from 4G, the 'general' class, sauntered in confidently, smiling brazenly at the men's appreciative leers. She had St Trinian's glamour and we knew that she had 'done it', but was it once behind the hockey shed or a more sustained affair?

The State of Emergency had been on the radio all day yesterday and this morning. We dawdled along the driveway, obscured from the Drill Hall grounds by a dense bank of conifers, past the tennis courts and the swimming pool, chattering excitedly.

'Why are the soldiers there?' someone asked.

'Come on! They're the army reserves. The *muntus* are causing trouble in Harare township,' said Kay. Like most boarders she was a farmer's daughter.

'And why does that surprise you?' said Reggie, the newly arrived daughter of the Italian consul, who often saw things differently.

We reached the brilliant green kikuyu grass in the quadrangle between the new block and the main buildings just as the bell rang at 20 to eight. I fetched the piano music for assembly, my thoughts in ferment. The soldiers had whistled at me too and some were quite good looking. Surely this Emergency couldn't be that serious? Perhaps it would all be over in a few days. The classes filed into the hall amid a flutter of excited whispers, first form at the front, sixth at the back, prefects and teachers along the side benches. The Calvinist Scottish gym mistress stood on the stage, feet apart, hands behind her back, seeking out miscreants.

Everything was calm when the headmistress mounted the stage from the back. Her black academic gown swept behind her; the head girl carried her bible and hymnbook. I played the introduction to 'Awake, my soul, and with the sun' from *Hymns Ancient and Modern*, a mundane hymn, sung without enthusiasm. A bible reading and other notices followed, but there was no mention of the Emergency or the soldiers. After the Lord's Prayer, I played a rousing march to speed the return to classes under the gym mistress's ever-vigilant gaze, but I felt deflated.

We had double Maths, followed by Latin. Break was our first chance to discuss the day's excitement.

'The *muntus* are just trying it on,' said Kay contemptuously.

'Africans, please,' chided Adrien.

'OK, OK. The "Africans". But they're stupid. All they know is how to burn things and make a lot of noise. The army will sort them out.'

'Will the soldiers be there when we go home?'

They were not. We saw people near the buildings but everything was quiet.

'There were soldiers at the Drill Hall,' I told my parents over lunch of salad and cold tongue, my favourite.

'Mmm. Yes, they have called up some of the army reserves.'

'What are army reserves?' asked my seven-year-old brother Allan. He went to Blakiston School opposite our house.

'They're extra soldiers. There have been riots in one of the townships and the government thinks they might need help to get it under control,' said my father.

'What are riots?' asked Allan.

'We won't talk about it when Candy brings in the fruit salad,' said my mother.

My afternoon was busy, with lots of homework and two hours of piano practice for my Grade VII exam. The piano was in my bedroom along with the upstairs telephone. At 4 o'clock I went down for tea, a daily ritual. Molly Robinson, one of our favourite Quakers, had called in. She was gloomy.

'More arrests, detentions, bannings – it just never stops. They say the townships are like tinder boxes.'

'This morning I spoke to Mrs Whitehouse, headmistress of Chirodzo school,' said my mother. 'They found piles of stones stacked along the school's fences so she organised the pupils to lay them on a pathway and the caretaker poured concrete over them.'

'Why were the stones there?' asked my sister, Norah.

'Someone had made them ready to throw at the school buildings.'

'Why?'

'Because they don't like what the government is doing.'

'What is it doing?' asked Allan.

'Well … they're bringing in a new constitution, a new way of running the country, to make sure most Africans won't ever be allowed to vote.'

Allan considered this information.

'But throwing stones might hurt children … How will that stop the government?'

'It won't. And I hope they wouldn't throw them at children.'

I tried to visualise the 'tinder box' atmosphere in the townships. Surely schools were very important to the Africans? Surely they would want to protect them?

'The Prime Minister said on the radio that outside trouble-makers are stirring things up in the townships,' I ventured.

'They always say that,' Molly sighed. 'They refuse to recognise how frustrated and desperate people are.'

I felt restless. Just before supper I went next door to see my friend Sue, who was in the sixth form at my school. Her father was Secretary to the Treasury, and I hoped she would have some inside knowledge about the Emergency.

'What does your father think?'

'I don't know. He doesn't say much, but I think he's worried.'

Just then the sound of the clanging bell in our house summoned me to supper at 7 o'clock. As I hurried home, I felt the residual warmth of the tarred road underfoot. It was unusual to be out on the street in the dark – white girls did not go out alone at night – and I felt heightened anxiety about the events playing out in the townships.

Family supper was a comforting, formal routine I had known all my childhood. We were allowed to come barefoot, but the big mahogany table was laid with table mats and coasters under our glasses of water. My mother served the shepherd's pie and Candy, wearing his white jacket, brought round the serving dishes with peas and cauliflower.

'Shall I help you, Master Allan?'

'Lots of peas, please Candy.'

'You'll turn into a pea yourself, Chippy!' my father said with a big grin. Chippy was his pet name for my brother, short for 'chip off the old block'.

After Candy had returned to the kitchen Allan looked at my mother.

'Mummy, Candy and Rowzhi sometimes tease me. They call me Chippy, and they laugh. It hurts my feelings.'

'I'm so sorry, darling. I'll speak to them.'

Anger surged inside me.

'But Mum, they're grown men and Allan is just a little boy.'

She looked thoughtful.

'I'll still talk to them.'

I felt dissatisfied. My mother and the Quakers worked hard to challenge Rhodesia's daily inequalities and I usually agreed with her more than with my father. He and I sometimes had gentle arguments at mealtimes when I would point out how low African wages were, and he would counter by asking who would employ them if we didn't. The African leader, Mr Nkomo, might become a good politician, I would say. Dad would smile and agree, and of course more Africans should have the vote. But his refrain was always: 'These are simple people, they're not ready to govern themselves.' I was frustrated at having no counter-argument and I felt his Sunday tennis club members influenced him, even though he didn't agree with them.

Tonight I let the family conversation wash over me. As the meal ended my father headed to the front door.

'I'm going to a meeting at Allan's school to hear some information from the government.'

'About the State of Emergency?'

'That sort of thing.'

I was shocked. My father never went to evening meetings. He and my mother went out only to unavoidable social obligations. In my bedroom I phoned my friend Judy, whose parents went out all the time. We mulled over what was happening.

'Do you think they'll sort it all out?' Judy asked.

'*Ag man*, I don't know. They didn't seem to last year in the Belgian Congo.'

'*Ja*, when all those people arrived … what were they called?'

'Refugees.'

'*Ja*, refugees. Hundreds of them, in tents in the fairground.' She thought a while. 'My father reckons the Belgians just panicked.'

'Did they all go back?'

Neither of us knew.

'What will happen now?'

'I don't know. My father's gone to a meeting.'

'Oh, so has mine!'

I tried to relax in the bath. Every night I washed my bra and pants and hung them to dry over the towel rail because I felt underwear was very personal. I also felt it was wrong for a grown man like Candy to have to wait on a 16-year-old. I made my own bed each morning, but I still left it to Candy to wash and iron my dresses and school shirts, and to change the sheets once a week.

The next day started at half past six with its usual strict routine. I drew the curtains and looked across at the green expanse of Blakiston School's playing field and the tall trees on its far side; I dressed quickly and practised piano scales for 20 minutes. My brown lace-up shoes, newly polished by Candy, were outside my door. I was always the first downstairs and I found him, tall, with round glasses, dusting the living room.

'Good morning Candy. Will it rain today?' We were in the unreliable time between the wet and dry seasons but I didn't want to lug my plastic raincoat to school unnecessarily. He went out on to the front lawn and looked up at the clear blue sky.

'No, Miss Clare. No rain today.' His weather forecasts never failed.

The cook, Rowzhi, was chopping vegetables in the kitchen. He came from Mozambique and spoke limited English, unlike Candy, who was educated to Standard Six and could read and write competently.

'Good morning, Miss Clare. I bring your porridge,' he said. 'Sure you want a cheese omelette? I make omelettes verry, verry good.'

'I know, Rowzhi. I know,' I laughed. 'But I'm not that hungry.'

I ate my mealie-meal porridge with milk and sugar and called goodbye to my parents. At the gateway, I looked right towards the cycle path that ran perpendicular to our short cul-de-sac of five houses. The early sun sparkling through the dew on the high grass always gave me a frisson of pleasure. When the grass became long enough to conceal thieves they mowed it.

Everything seemed normal at the Drill Hall, apart from armoured vehicles parked outside the buildings. We were trying to decide which subjects to select for A-level, which was very difficult because I wanted to do them all. Not one teacher mentioned the Emergency but they seemed more distracted than usual. In the afternoon I went back for tennis at 2 o'clock, unenthusiastic, resenting the waste of time.

Cycling home down jacaranda-shaded Blakiston Street, I saw Costa's green Volkswagen Beetle, waiting for me. He was a plump, young Greek man who wore dark glasses and worked in his father's business. I asked how his sister's wedding had gone and he told me all his relations from Mozambique and South Africa had come. His interest in me was flattering if inexplicable, but today I didn't feel like small talk so I didn't stay long. As I turned into our road I was shaken to see that the long grass on the cycle path had been cut. Why today?

At supper we were all on our best behaviour for a boring guest from Umtali, near the Mozambique border. We even wore shoes. She talked a lot.

'These journalists come from England for two weeks, they think they grasp everything and they start telling us how we should run Rhodesia. They just don't understand the blacks like we do. You have to live here to understand it, don't you?'

My parents were politely non-committal.

'I mean, what do these people know? They haven't lived through the Mau Mau terror in Kenya. And then look at the Belgian Congo. Am I right, or am I wrong, Betty?'

'Oh, yes,' said my mother while my father and I looked down at our plates. She hadn't lived in Kenya or the Belgian Congo either.

I escaped from the dinner table as soon as I could, aware of a gnawing worry that I couldn't articulate. I phoned Debbie from the Young Quakers to talk it over. Her father worked for the American Friends' Service Committee and had met all the African politicians. He was much more radical than the local Quakers.

'We had a riot drill in school today,' she said.

'A what?' I hooted with laughter. 'What on earth is a "riot drill"?'

'The teachers said if we're outside when rioters arrive we must immediately come into the buildings and if people start throwing things through the windows we must get down on the floor, under desks if possible.'

'Who would the rioters be? Africans?'

'That's what they meant. My mom was very cross when I told her. And the radio talks of *agents provocateurs* inciting people to burn buildings. Mom thinks it's just propaganda and makes things worse.'

'What does your father say?'

'He's away at the moment.'

I had my bath, lad out my clothes ready for the next day, and packed my homework into my school case, my thoughts a confused jumble. When I went downstairs for a glass of water, I found my father bolting the kitchen door from the inside.

'Dad, how will Candy and Rowzhi get in tomorrow morning?' I asked.

When he turned I saw a reflective armband on his left arm. He was holding a helmet and a truncheon and his expression was grave.

'At the meeting last night we arranged patrols in the sanitary lanes, taking turns in a rota to ensure no trouble-makers come and try to incite violence.'

I just looked at him.

'Go to bed. We'll make sure there's no trouble.'

I watched from the stairs as my mother in her dressing gown locked and bolted the front door behind him.

'It's just a precaution, Clare-lee,' she said.

I lay in bed feeling terrified, listening for any unusual sound in the night. Would we all be murdered in our beds? Would we hear the rioters when they came? Surely Candy and Rowzhi wouldn't attack us? True, they weren't paid very much, but they were part of our family, Candy had been with us for 12 years. My mother was a good, generous employer …

But this is about more than just Candy and Rowzhi, I thought. I am part of an oppressive, arrogant white society that is fundamentally wrong. What to do? I had no idea. My father's ideas about how things must change didn't seem right, and the Quakers didn't seem to be able to stop the terrible government. How could the Africans have a better life? As I drifted off to sleep I faced a painful conclusion: the Africans are justified in rising up. This is the only way to achieve their rights.

But Daddy, please, please keep us safe tonight …

I woke next morning and jumped up to look out of the windows. Blakiston's green field was still there. The sun was filtering through the trees along the cycle path. I opened my bedroom door. My clean, polished shoes were in place.

1964
PARIS

My older brother Howard and I celebrated New Year's Eve 1963 in the London embassy of soon to be independent Zambia. It seemed that every Zambian student in Britain was there, wearing glistening suit and colourful tie. I danced all night, delighted to be part of the brightly lit festivities.

'So you're from Southern Rhodesia,' said one partner, a very good dancer. 'And how does it feel to dance with a black man?' We were jiving so there was no close clutching, but he knew that even this could never have happened at home.

'Oh, fine, absolutely normal,' I said, trying to sound nonchalant. But he was probing beneath my multi-racialist exterior and I felt I had been found out.

Howard was studying at Cambridge. My mother and I had spent Christmas with him as a prelude to my joining 800 foreign students on the *Cours de Civilisation Française* at the Sorbonne University in Paris.

Each morning we had lectures on every aspect of French culture, with language classes in the afternoon. I spent my spare time in museums, galleries, concerts, theatres, the opera. I listened to haunting songs in smoke-filled *caves à chanson,* explored boulevards and narrow streets, drank sweet, black coffee in pavement cafés and watched Paris pass by. I tried to acquire some French glamour and avoided English-speaking students.

My lodgings were above Duroc Metro station in the sixth-floor apartment of the Montgolfier family, now in reduced circumstances. I experienced

◀ Caught by a street photographer on the Boulevard Saint-Michel

spring for the first time ever when masses of pink and white flowers burst out on the majestic chestnut trees lining the boulevards, softening the dominant, seven-storey, soot-blackened buildings. An acquaintance with a suburban garden brought me mauve and white lilacs which perfumed my room for days.

The patrician Gauthier-Lathuiles, mining contacts of my father, invited me to lunch, cooked by their maid Edmonde. We had five courses with two wines. Their apartment was furnished with Louis XVI furniture and wall-to-wall carpeting, devoid of any personal touch. The Beatles were performing in Paris and Madame offered to take Edmonde and me. We sat one behind the other in the stalls on *strapontin* seats that folded down at the end of each row. The capacity audience erupted enthusiastically when the Beatles appeared on stage: four young men in dark suits, no turn-ups on their trousers, long ties and softly long hair, masters of their instruments, relaxed. They seemed charmingly confused by the French fans' shouts. Only the sprinkling of English fans displayed the hysteria I had heard about. I thrilled to the harmonies, the rhythm, the melodies; I wanted them to go on all night. Edmonde seemed a bit bemused and goodness knows what Madame made of it, but I was captivated and I could hardly sleep that night. I wrote in my diary: 'This is the music of *my generation*! I LOVE IT!'

Alice was the daughter of another mining contact at a Belgian company with interests in the Congo. She was a few years older than me, lived in Paris and invited me to the family home in Belgium. Her father told me about Katanga province, which had broken away from the newly independent Congo.

'The Katangan leader Tshombe is a man we can work with,' he said. 'He's the most impressive politician in Africa.'

I felt reassured. Things appeared to have gone badly wrong during the Congo's independence settlements in 1960.

Alice's sister and young children were also staying in the house.

'She's separated from her husband and has to bring the children to Belgium to see their father,' Alice told me.

'Why can't he see them in Paris?'

'There's a warrant out for his arrest in France. He's a member of the OAS, the terrorist movement that opposed Algerian independence.'

I was surprised that Alice's gentle sister could be married to someone who sounded so unsavoury. He came to collect the children in a flashy black car, a huge hulk of a man with an excessively loud voice and what sounded to my foreign ear like a coarse accent. He wore a black leather jacket, a gold watch and gold bracelets, and was quite unlike Alice's cultured family. I disliked him instantly.

'He's no longer welcome in my father's house,' she told me as he drove off.

Like many before me I experienced the loneliness of Paris. Why couldn't we get to know the handsome young men in elegant suits who strode along the Boulevard Saint-Germain, totally uninterested in us foreign students? North African men sometimes followed us, making lewd remarks, which could be a nuisance. And on the morning Metro, crammed with unwashed bodies, wandering hands were unpleasant. I learned to stop them with an umbrella spike positioned forcibly on the offender's foot.

I was introduced to a posh family whose son Marc, a slight, sallow-faced young man, strolled with me through Paris's lawless parks. We sat on a bench and he kissed me, slipping his hand under my jacket to fondle my breast.

'Is it normal for a 25-year-old not to have made love?' he asked.

I had no idea. White Rhodesian schoolgirls led a very chaste existence. I enjoyed his tentative explorations and got used to the idea that it was all right to kiss in public, but I found him rather colourless.

Then I met Jadranko, a tall, blonde tennis player from Zagreb, studying post-graduate economic planning. I was delighted to stroll along the River Seine with this handsome, athletic Yugoslav who rolled his Rs and ran his fingers attractively through his wheat-coloured hair. His kisses in secluded, dark corners were quite different from Marc's. He slipped his hands inside my blouse to explore my breasts with a passion that was thrilling; this was my first experience of a man's aroused body pressing against mine.

'Sex outside marriage is OK, isn't it?' he suggested one day.

'Oh yes,' I said, without grasping where the discussion was heading.

The day before he left Paris, we went to his student residence. His roommate had already gone home so he locked the door, laid the key visibly on the table and led me to the sofa-bed. He kissed me and began intimate caresses, but without the magic I had felt under the Seine bridges. I suddenly realised that this was a carefully planned scenario. I pulled away from him. Somehow I wasn't ready.

'Are you scared you'll have a baby?' he asked desperately. 'Because you won't.'

'No, no, it's not that,' I said, feeling very confused.

His face was bitterly disappointed as he waved goodbye at the train station. We exchanged a few letters, but he didn't return to Paris in September and I regretted my reluctance.

I arranged summer holidays through the student travel service, starting with a student centre in Saint-Aygulf on the Côte-d'Azur and ending with a tour of Greece and Turkey in a group of French students, which improved my spoken French dramatically. In the lounge of the overnight ferry from Piraeus to Istanbul I came upon a scene that evoked the ancient world: a philosopher holding forth to a circle of admiring disciples. The fleshy Greek artist, speaking in French to members of my group, looked up as I entered and stopped in mid-sentence.

▲ On a beach in Saint-Aygulf

▲ On the Nice seafront with my father when he passed through on a business trip

'I can see you're English, and you're a missionary,' he said switching language.

'Wrong,' I said. 'I'm Rhodesian and I'm certainly not a missionary.'

'Aah, but you fight for your beliefs.' He abandoned the French students and escorted me up on deck. 'The French are all peasants,' he said with a contemptuous wave. 'Look at them, they're like cattle.'

I laughed, rather shocked. He acknowledged a woman with two children on the other side of the deck. 'The mother of my children.'

The evening sky was darkening. He stepped back to look me up and down. I felt awkward because my trousers – not common in those days, but practical for the overnight journey – were made of stretch fabric that emphasised every contour of my body. He leered appreciatively.

'Very nice,' he said, moving closer. I acceded hesitantly as he kissed me, pushing his tongue deep into my mouth. Then we went our separate ways. I supposed that the 'mother of his children' was used to this behaviour. Lechery or art – I didn't care. I was exhilarated by his assessment.

I arrived at Bristol to begin my chemistry degree. My 17-year-old roommate in the women's hall of residence had scarcely travelled beyond Llandudno. I found the adjustment difficult and longed for cosmopolitan Paris.

At Christmas I flew home to Salisbury. All my school friends were away, except Margaret who, to my astonishment, was now married. Our conversation was awkward. Was she trying to escape something? After a few days my father and I flew to South Africa to join the rest of the family on the Cape peninsula. The mountains and sparkling blue waves in False Bay were familiar from childhood holidays, but the daily indignities endured by black South Africans and newspaper reports about Rhodesia were depressing.

My intellectual schoolfriend Sharon was living in nearby Muizenberg. Not only was she married, but she had a tiny baby, a floppy, wriggling little animal, and she seemed rather confused by it. It was just 12 months since we had left school, and I had experienced Paris, art, music, theatre, university in England. She and Margaret, who both shared my liberal views, were … trapped, it seemed to me, in marriage – and southern African politics.

I floated on the waves in the sea, gazing at the towering mountains, realising my childhood had slipped away.

▲ Christmas 1964: with my mother, sister Norah, brother Howard and younger brother Allan at Fish Hoek, Cape Peninsula, after my first year in Europe

Back in Bristol the Anti-Apartheid group asked me to address a meeting, billed as 'Eye-witness Report on Apartheid', in preparation for a national demonstration the following weekend. The meeting room was packed. I described the poverty in Alexandra township, the Pass Laws for Africans, the 'Whites Only' park benches, buses, trains, the visible horrors. But I couldn't say much about the unseen atrocities because I knew very little. On the march in London it rained throughout the dreary, silent procession, which was quite unlike the muscular exuberance of Africans living and suffering under apartheid. I decided the Anti-Apartheid Movement was not for me.

I escaped to Paris for the Easter holidays and registered for a short French language course near the Sorbonne. I felt confused; I needed to find a direction. But what was I looking for? It wasn't that I didn't like Bristol and chemistry, but I had some other longing. For what? I wrote to my parents suggesting I might change to studying languages in Paris. They sent me a long telegram, which ended:

'THINK CAREFULLY. WILL SUPPORT WHATEVER YOU DECIDE.'

In the meantime my father's mining company had asked him to set up an office in Australia and my family was preparing to move there. Do I still have a home, I wondered?

Into this confusion stepped Fabrizio Cavaterra, a fellow-student in the language class.

The tall, slim Italian next to me in class wore a zipped jacket and open-necked shirt. His near-black hair waved softly above his broad forehead, ending in neat sideburns. His smooth skin was pale, with a delicate blush on the cheekbones, his eyes were an intense blue. As we sauntered along the Boulevard Saint-Michel to a cheap lunch bar I told him I was from Southern Rhodesia. He knew a lot about Africa because he had a degree in journalism from Rome University.

'Look at this,' Fabrizio said, pulling out a Communist Party membership card.

'Interesting.'

'I thought you'd be horrified.' He lit up a Gauloise.

I knew little about communism, but the Soviet Union seemed to offer some hope in the harsh politics of southern Africa. He took me to the Père Lachaise cemetery.

'This is where the Communards were shot.'

'Communards?'

'You studied French history on your course and they didn't tell you about the Paris Commune of 1871?' He was scornful. 'A revolutionary government in the city for more than two months. They shot thousands when it was defeated and you can still see the bullet scars.' He indicated the long cemetery wall.

Fabrizio's ideas were unfamiliar and interesting. We went to the cinema to see Fellini's film, *La Dolce Vita,* and Russian films about the second world war. We went to a large bookshop on Boulevard Saint-Germain.

'Pablo Neruda is a really good Chilean poet … You'll like this music from the

▲ Fabrizio Cavaterra introduced me to Trotskyism

Mexican revolution … Tchaikovsky always has rich melodies … Wilhelm Reich is important.' I bought everything he suggested, oblivious to his lack of money.

When we parted he kissed me on both cheeks. But one night he kissed me on the lips. I felt a surge of excitement and opened my mouth to receive his tongue. The taste of Gauloise tobacco was curiously attractive.

'I want to show you something,' he said next afternoon. He took me to a room on the seventh floor of a building off the Boulevard Saint-Michel, the kind often occupied by French students, empty except for a bed, paint brushes, tins of white paint, and some cloths.

'I'm decorating it for a friend,' he said as I peered out of the dormer window at the Paris skyline.

We went back down to the boulevard, talked, laughed a lot, ate in a brasserie and walked until sunset. As we climbed the seven flights my whole body pulsed with anticipation. He closed the door. The sky glowed red through the window. He extinguished his Gauloise and undid my blouse slowly, then my skirt. I fumbled awkwardly with the buttons on his shirt. He smelled masculine, mixed with tobacco. He undid my suspenders and slipped the stockings down my legs but struggled with the elasticated girdle that stopped my bottom wobbling.

'I can't take this off,' he muttered. I had to wriggle it off myself.

I returned to Bristol for the final term, but hurried back to Paris straight after the end-of-year exams. I felt alive; I had a new interest; I couldn't wait to see Fabrizio. I found a cheap hotel near the Sorbonne where he joined me at night.

'I'm working in the Renault car factory.'

'But you're a journalist.'

'I'm doing political work among the Italian immigrant workers.'

'Do you enjoy it?'

He laughed.

'No one *enjoys* working in a big factory – low wages, long hours, noise, boring, repetitive tasks.'

I waited to meet him for lunch outside Renault's massive plant on the outskirts of Paris. An Arab worker began talking to me, diffident but friendly. He shyly shook my hand when Fabrizio arrived and I wondered if chatting to a young woman had been an unusual experience.

We ate couscous in a small Algerian restaurant.

'North African workers earn very little and live in crowded hostels, away from their country, without women,' Fabrizio said. 'They're lonely and it's very frustrating for them. You must understand this and be careful.'

With only half an hour for lunch he barely had time to eat. I realised ruefully that I hadn't grasped the realities of factory life.

Fabrizio stirred my deepest feelings of guilt as a white from southern Africa.

'The blacks in Rhodesia have no rights. You beat them. You treat them with brutality.'

'Not me,' I protested, though I recognised a general truth. I repeated what Alice's father had told me: 'Tshombe is the most impressive politician in Africa.'

He hooted with derision.

'Tshombe? He's a puppet of imperialism. What about the Congo's real leader, Lumumba? Murdered by the CIA – and you supported that.'

I certainly hadn't paid much attention to Lumumba's death.

'I'm working inside the Communist Party as a Trotskyist.'

I struggled to understand. He told me that Stalin was responsible for the degeneration of the Soviet Union and for terrible crimes.

'Trotsky wanted to extend the Russian Revolution to other countries and that's why Stalin assassinated him. I did my military service willingly because workers will need to know how to use weapons in a revolution.'

When Fabrizio went inside the hostels for Italian workers I waited nearby, trying to read his news-sheet, using my knowledge of Latin and of Italian in music. He took me home one day to his room in the north-east of Paris on Avenue Jean-Jaurès to meet his brother Enrico, recently arrived from Rome. They shared a cold-water tap and squat toilet with everyone on the seventh floor. Enrico had cooked a stew of meat, tomatoes and chickpeas on the single gas ring. He was a bit older, gentle, without Fabrizio's education.

'I've never tasted chickpeas before. They're delicious.'

'The staple food of half Europe's poor,' said Fabrizio dismissively.

One evening we got talking to a well-dressed Italian student in a café. I met him the next day while Fabrizio was at work.

'I don't believe he's been to university,' said the smart student as he stubbed out his Marlboro cigarette. 'He speaks Italian like an ordinary worker.'

I was becoming aware of Europe's subtle class distinctions. Rhodesia's only expression of class difference was skin colour.

Bastille Day, 14th July. To celebrate the holiday, bands were scheduled to play all day and night in Place Saint-André-des-Arts. I met my Belgian friend Alice and her fiancé in one of the cafés.

'Fabrizio has another commitment, but he'll join us afterwards.' I was dying to show him off.

We danced late into the hot night and joined the crowds in snaking congas between the tables of all the cafés, but Fabrizio didn't show up. I wondered what Alice thought. We were all young and tolerant but I had a glimmer of realisation that Fabrizio and Alice came from opposing classes and it might not have been a successful combination.

I went back to my nearby hotel, disappointed, knowing the music would continue until six in the morning. Fabrizio arrived around 2 o'clock.

'Sorry, my meeting was very long. This is what happens in political struggle.'

Coming down the stairs from Fabrizio's room we met a young French woman on her way up. She had long wavy hair and dark eyes, very attractive in a quiet way. Fabrizio greeted her warmly.

'This is Michèle, one of the comrades.'

'I came to borrow the typewriter,' she stuttered, seeming upset to see me. He fetched the typewriter and we all travelled together on the Metro. Fabrizio sat next to her, talking comfortingly, but she couldn't hide her distress.

'Did you see how beautiful she was?' he said afterwards.

'Is she a student?'

'No, she works in an office. She's middle class, but she's a dedicated comrade.'

What exactly did he mean by 'middle class'? She wasn't like the Montgolfier daughter, nor Alice.

Rather to my surprise, I didn't feel jealous. Other worries were uppermost in my mind: a letter had reached me confirming that I had failed organic chemistry and I would have to resit the exam. As Paris emptied for the August holidays I wasn't too regretful about leaving.

'I'll travel with you,' said Fabrizio. 'When the English comrades were in Paris I arranged to discuss with them in London.'

I helped him find the address at Clapham Common for his appointment. As we came out of the tube station a petite young woman wearing an attractive floral dress hurried into a public phone box.

'She's one of them,' he said. 'I met her in Paris.'

I was surprised. She didn't fit my picture of a revolutionary. The address was above a butcher's shop, diagonally opposite the tube station. The office on the first floor was tidy and austere, with pamphlets and books on display, economical but business-like. Two large sash windows with frosted lower panes overlooked the noisy Clapham High Street. Fabrizio had a short discussion in French with Cliff, a tall man in his 30s. They planned further meetings and a woman in the office arranged where he would stay. At Fabrizio's suggestion I paid for a subscription to *The Newsletter*, weekly paper of the Socialist Labour League. Then I left to catch my train to Bristol.

The two chemistry tutors, middle-aged men in tweed jackets and corduroy trousers, greeted me kindly.

'Your maths results were very good. You could change your course or you could repeat the year.'

'I've found these last few months very upsetting ... elections in Rhodesia ... fear of riots. I would really like to stay on the course.'

'All right, but you'll need to resit the organic chemistry exam in three weeks.'

I found a temporary room and ensconced myself in the chemistry library. Fabrizio visited for just one day. I showed him around the university area, but we were both tense and he didn't want to come to my room.

'The discussions with the comrades were very worthwhile but I need some money for political work. Can you help?'

We stopped at the bank and I drew £70 in cash. On the way to the station Fabrizio stopped to stroke a black cat sitting on a wall, murmuring sweet words in Italian as it purred its enjoyment. At the ticket barrier he kissed me on both cheeks. I sensed our relationship had cooled.

For three mournful weeks I swotted up on organic reactions in the deserted chemistry department and discouraged the advances of a lone doctoral student with a scruffy mane of red hair and a bushy beard who persisted in putting his hand on my knee however many times I removed it. I had meals in the near-empty refectory, and returned each night to my dreary accommodation.

A letter arrived from Fabrizio, written on one of the paper table-mats used in some cafés. After several sentences it ended, '… and so I will no longer sleep with you.' That was how our relationship finished.

After my exam, not much of the holiday was left and I had little reason to go to Paris so I flew to Czechoslovakia to see a Soviet bloc country. I shared a room in an empty student residence in Prague with three French tourists. I met young people in the student restaurants which doubled as canteens for army conscripts, hitch-hiked to České Budějovice and Pilsen, and met kind people who accommodated me. On the train through Germany I was castigated for having no visa. I passed through Paris and, as expected, found Fabrizio and Michèle were now a couple. I was sad, but I didn't bear Michèle any grudge. Perhaps I had always known that my relationship with Fabrizio would be short term.

I looked ahead to sharing a flat in Bristol with four friends. There was much to be positive about.

1965
BRISTOL

Unilateral Declaration of Independence

A letter arrived from the Rhodesian High Commission on the Strand in London:

'Owing to events of 11/11/65, there will no longer be a Student Support Service. Address all enquiries to the British Council.'

Ian Smith's government had made a Unilateral Declaration of Independence from Britain. So white minority rule will continue, I thought bitterly. We white Rhodesians were now pariahs and I was thoroughly ashamed. I felt betrayed and bereft.

I read the newspapers. The African opposition parties, ZANU and ZAPU, demanded Britain suspend the Smith government with force. Prime Minister Harold Wilson recalled the British High Commissioner, ceased aid, banned Rhodesian tobacco imports, but would not send troops. The United Nations Security Council called for economic sanctions. How would my father's two cousins who had tobacco farms be affected? I suspected they supported Ian Smith. Rhodesia seemed to be on the edge of a precipice. Would it collapse? Would Smith give way? But South Africa, now a republic and no longer in the Commonwealth, continued trading with Rhodesia and so did Portugal and its colonies, Mozambique and Angola.

I had no direct news because my parents were in Australia. As the dark winter evenings drew in I felt disturbed and depressed. My flatmate Sue and

I hitch-hiked through Somerset. A car stopped as darkness gathered and the driver, a black man, told us where he was going.

'Thank you, but that's no good for us,' I said.

'Come on, Clare, it's perfect. Thank you very much,' said Sue, pushing me firmly into the car.

I had reacted instinctively: 'Don't get into a car with a black man'. I sat in the back seat near to tears while Sue chatted to the kind, fatherly driver.

'It's not wise for you young girls to be hitch-hiking on these dark afternoons.'

I felt bitterly ashamed, and thanked him over-profusely when he dropped us.

'What was wrong with you?' Sue asked.

'Oh dear, I thought I had no racialist prejudice. I still have a long way to go.'

Would I ever escape the curse of white colonialism? Deep down, was I the same as all the Rhodesian racialists?

Sue and I won the second round in a debating competition against two northerners, Steve Hammond and Peter Read, on the silly subject: 'The United Nations is more splendid than a sunflower'. We invited them downstairs for tea afterwards and they were keen to hear about South Africa, telling me they were socialists, whatever that meant. They won my eternal friendship by listening with great interest to my records of traditional African music, scorned by everyone else.

At one of the subsequent debates, a contestant who spoke like the Queen treated his subject melodramatically.

'Our children go to bed cold and hungry, they have no shoes in winter.'

'That's right,' said Steve, nodding his head vigorously. I was embarrassed. Didn't he realise the speaker was being ironic?

'Of course I did. Posh Tory bastard! He has no idea of the reality for many working-class people. "Our children will starve. Oh jolly hockey sticks".' He mimicked the speaker's accent and I was surprised to find that he could talk … well, proper English. His Manchester accent wasn't a speech impediment.

Steve invited me to go home with him before Christmas 'to see working-class life'. His parents made me very welcome and I slept in his sister's room in the three-bedroomed house. Breakfast was egg and bacon and a slice of white bread and butter.

'My mother puts the milk and sugar into the teapot.' Steve laughed gently as she poured it, smiling. He showed me around Stockport's streets of two-storeyed terraces, older than any of Rhodesia's houses, with tiny gardens, or none. There were small corner shops and a high street with a butcher, a baker and a greengrocer, but few open spaces. We went to a local pub in the evening and ate fish and chips on the way home. Everything seemed dark, but friendly and generous.

I spent a sombre Christmas in London with my brother Howard. We barely spoke about Rhodesia, but it was always in the back of our minds. He and a friend had rooms in a rather run-down terraced house in Ladbroke Grove, with gas fires and a shared kitchen. After celebrating New Year's Eve in a pub with several of his friends, I wondered how to get home to our cousins' flat. There were neither buses nor taxis. On an impulse, Howard tapped on the passenger window of a Bentley at traffic lights on Holland Park Avenue.

'Please could you take my sister to Piccadilly?' he asked the elegantly dressed, grey-haired owner.

I climbed in, astonished at Howard's audacity, proud of his initiative.

The debaters Steve and Peter were Labour Party members and ran the Left Club in the students' union. They were the only people I knew who followed the Rhodesian crisis and they were very interested in my copy of *The Newsletter*, which came by post from the London office of Fabrizio's organisation.

'We plan to run a bookstall once a week,' Steve told me one day. 'Order some extra *Newsletters*.'

I was roped into sitting on the bookstall taking money. One day a man in a suit appeared.

'I'm a member of the Socialist Labour League, who publish this paper.' He pointed to *The Newsletter*. 'I've come from Cardiff to discuss with you.'

So began a series of meetings in the university. One of the first speakers was Cliff Slaughter, whom I had seen in London with Fabrizio. Another was Sheila Torrance, national secretary of the Young Socialists. She was the same age as us and dressed smartly, not like a casual student.

'The Young Socialists was formerly the Labour Party's youth movement,' she told us. 'But we fought the Labour leaders' right-wing policies and won the majority on the National Committee and at the National Conference.'

This sounded dramatic.

'The leadership expelled the majority of National Committee members, but virtually their whole youth movement has come with us.'

Left Club changed its name to Young Socialists Student Society. I learned that the Labour government was betraying the working class. Speakers at our meetings talked about Karl Marx's Labour Theory of Value – difficult – or the fight against Stalinism – fascinating. I read Khrushchev's 1956 secret speech exposing Stalin's murderous crimes and the *Moscow Trials Anthology* which described the 1930s show trials that framed and executed most of the leaders of the Russian Revolution. On the other hand, Trotsky's thrilling, three-volume *History of the Russian Revolution,* which I read late into the night, conveyed the excitement and tumult of 1917.

But why did it all go wrong?

'Lenin and the Bolsheviks hoped the highly organised German working class would succeed in its own revolution,' explained Geoff Pilling, another visiting speaker. 'But it failed and Russian "white" generals, supported by troops from many European countries, waged a civil war to try and overturn the revolution.'

Most of the revolutionary cadres died in the civil war, I learned.

'After Lenin's death Stalin rose to control the Bolshevik Party. He developed a policy of peaceful coexistence with capitalism and used terror against political opponents.'

I was beginning to understand.

▼ Platform of the 1964 Young Socialists' Brighton conference, l to r: Sheila Torrance, Reg Underhill, John Robertson and the Labour Party youth officer. After mass expulsions from the Labour Party it became an independent youth movement

The Young Socialists' monthly paper, *Keep Left*, held its Annual General Meeting in January 1966. Peckham Rye Co-op hall in London was packed with working-class youth from all over the country. The 'rockers' wore leather jackets, others wore 'mod' clothes. Young women in the Young Socialists' leadership dressed smartly in a restrained mod fashion: mini-skirts and jumpers with shirt collars and cuffs peeking out. I was persuaded to represent the newly established Western Region in the speaking competition because everyone else refused. I was wearing purple stockings, a dark green corduroy mini-skirt, moss-green pullover, purple cardigan, purple-and-green pendant earrings and long, multiple strands of purple beads. My hair was piled on my head with a purple silk scarf tied in a large bow at the back.

When I reached the microphone there was uproar. The chair had to quell wolf-whistles and cat-calls.

'We must make the left MPs fight in parliament,' I parroted in my strong Rhodesian accent, followed by a few other jumbled phrases. The whistles started again and the chair called for order while I stuttered a few more ill-prepared words and exited to stormy applause. I didn't win.

The leader of the Socialist Labour League, Gerry Healy, was scheduled to speak at one of our university meetings. A good turnout was expected. I recognised his square, bespectacled face from pictures in *The Newsletter*, but I was surprised to see that he was quite a short man, nearly bald, in his 50s, older than our previous speakers. He wore a navy-blue suit and dark, spotted tie.

He began speaking so quietly that the people at the back of the room had to strain to hear him. Oh dear, I thought. Is he a poor speaker? But as he went on, he became more animated, emphasising his points with great energy, then dropping back into quiet explanations before returning to lively declamations and even making us laugh.

'And now, what about Rhodesia? The Labour leaders make noises about the racialist white government. They impose sanctions. But British imperialism has always been in favour of subjugating the black man in Africa. They don't want to change the status quo now if it's going to endanger their economic interests. They want to protect their profits from southern Africa's minerals and gold and diamonds.'

▲ Gerry Healy

He modulated his tone for emphasis. I leant forward to grasp every word.

'The blacks are fighting with their hands tied behind their backs. We say there is only one way to solve the Rhodesian crisis. Let them take their future into their *own* hands. Give them the means to fight for their rights. *Arm the African workers.*'

I felt a physical shock, as if I'd had a blow in the stomach. I covered my mouth, resting my elbow on the other arm, listening to the questions and discussion. *Arm the African workers.* I felt numb, I was almost shaking. Arm the Africans so they can take control of their future. Would this mean civil war? How would this affect the people I knew in Rhodesia? And those who treated Africans with contempt, considered them stupid, primitive, unable to govern themselves? I knew the Africans were at breaking point: we had seen riots before.

▲ The weekly *Newsletter* explained on 10th December 1966 that the Rhodesian affair would make Britain's present economic crisis more acute

Arm the African workers. No one else had offered a more convincing solution. This was a moment of epiphany. I must cast my lot firmly with Rhodesia's Africans, I thought. I must join Gerry Healy's organisation.

The Socialist Labour League

The Bristol branch of the Socialist Labour League was formally established, consisting of my friends Steve and Peter plus Andy, Alison and George. I was not invited. Presumably, as a white Rhodesian, I still had to prove myself. But I was included in systematic political activity directed towards Avonmouth docks.

'The dockers assemble each morning hoping to be chosen for work. If they're not chosen they earn only "fall-back" pay,' Peter explained.

I visualised the foreman on a raised platform, waving chits of paper, surrounded by clamouring men.

'The government plans to "decasualise" the docks, so the dockers will be properly employed, with a guaranteed wage.'

'That's good, isn't it?'

'Ah yes, but they'll change other working practices, to benefit the bosses. We say the docks should be run under workers' control.'

I went on *Newsletter* sales, taking a bus in darkness from the Hotwell Road, just below where I lived, reaching the windswept dock gates for half-past six. Steve and I stood on either side of the gate, holding up the paper.

'*Newsletter*, weekly socialist paper! No modernisation without workers' control,' he shouted in his Mancunian accent as hundreds of dockers streamed past.

'*Agenst modernisition witheowt wuhrkers' control*,' I repeated in Rhodesian on the other side.

If we sold six papers Steve was pleased. The dockers whistled at my miniskirts and coloured stockings: red, blue, turquoise, fishnet green, purple. Evening sales were in noisy, smoky pubs, thick with Bristol accents, packed with dockers, Wills cigarette workers and men from Bristol Siddeley aircraft factory. The government's unpopular Prices and Incomes policy created much discussion. Occasionally a docker would call out, 'What colour stockings tonight, darling?'

The National Union of Seamen went on strike for a pay increase and reduction of their 56-hour week to 40 hours. Strike-bound British ships clogged up ports worldwide and Prime Minster Harold Wilson declared a state of emergency. This was exciting stuff, the power of the working class in action.

I visited my family in Australia over the summer, but I wasn't sure I would want to join them there after my degree. Back in Bristol League members Alison and George met me in the students' union refectory.

'Welcome back. You're joining the League and you're coming to the international demonstration against the Vietnam war in Liège, in Belgium, on 15th October.'

I was startled, but pleased. Cyril Smith, a National Committee member who came from London to assist the new branch, had a formal discussion with me.

'We are a cadre organisation, which means members work under the direction of the branch, which in turn works under the direction of the National Committee. You will be a probationary member for six months.'

I felt very proud.

Hundreds of excited young people assembled at London's Victoria station on Friday evening for a special train. Contingents came from all over the country: smart working-class youth, rockers, students, a few hippies, unfamiliar regional accents. In a make-shift office at the beginning of the train the Young Socialists' national secretary Sheila and two other women checked our payments against their lists and we settled in our assigned compartments. The young woman I had seen at Clapham Common tube station with Fabrizio moved up and down the train talking to people about sales and articles for the Young Socialists' paper, *Keep Left*. I learned that she was the editor and her name was Aileen Jennings.

The long overnight journey began, train to ferry to train, with passport controls at Dover and Ostend. The local organising committee in Liège provided breakfast in a big hall with copious supplies of crusty white bread, cheese, ham and steaming drinks. At the meeting point of the main demonstration the assembled Belgian comrades greeted us with cheers and applause and we in turn cheered new contingents arriving from all over Europe – France, Holland, Germany, Scandinavia, Italy – all with placards and colourful banners. Everyone was addressed as *camarade*. I scanned the rows of the *Jeunesse Communiste Révolutionaire* from Paris, hoping Fabrizio was there, but I couldn't see him. Rhythmic chants resounded: *l'U-S – ass-ass-ins! Lib-ér-ez le – Viet-nam!*

We lined up six abreast, holding high the banners from Young Socialists' regions, factories and trade union branches, some very ornamental with pictures of past trade union leaders, Karl Marx or the Scottish workers' hero, Keir Hardie. The French contingent carried long, shallow banners in front of the rows of six people. Light-hearted attempts to communicate across the languages and translate the slogans added to our exuberance.

▲ International demonstration in Liège, Belgium, against the Vietnam war, 15th October 1966. We defended our Hungarian Revolution banner against the organisers' insistence that it should be taken down

At the front of the British contingent, National Committee member Mike Banda and another bulky League member unfurled a large banner commemorating the Hungarian Revolution of 1956. Other muscular trade unionists surrounded it and I soon understood why. A group of French and Belgian organisers appeared, insisting the banner be taken down. There was a heated exchange but Mike refused.

'The Stalinists sent tanks and planes into Hungary to suppress the revolution. We can't ignore that just because now they're supporting the Vietnamese.'

'This demonstration is for a united front against imperialism of the whole working class – including the Soviet Union and China – to stop the American escalation of the war.'

'Not if it means supporting Stalinist crimes.'

Voices became louder and angrier. We shifted protectively around the banner. It remained in place.

Thousands of marchers snaked through the streets of Liège, taking up the dramatic French chants. Slogans shouted in powerful unison echoed in the built-up areas. At the end we filed into a large hall for speeches and greetings, translated into both French and English from other languages, which took

▲ Aileen Jennings' speech on behalf of the British Young Socialists was translated into French and other languages

a long time. Aileen spoke on behalf of the Young Socialists, seriously and with conviction. Gerry Healy, speaking as National Secretary of the Socialist Labour League, referred to the Hungarian Revolution, but the antagonism in the meeting remained below the surface. The French speeches were particularly long. My attention drifted; we struggled to keep awake.

The rally ended on a high note with slogans of the march: 'Long live the Vietnamese Revolution!' and 'Long live the World Socialist Revolution! Destroy capitalism, cause of all wars!'

After tumultuous cheering we were given another meal before boarding our evening train. The day's organisation had been impressive; the march and rally were inspiring and we were in high spirits.

I was in a compartment with T* and his friend, who were part of our Bristol delegation, Young Communist League members who had doubts about its policies.

'Are you in the Socialist Labour League?' the friend asked me.

'Yes,' I said calmly, not mentioning that I'd been a member for only three weeks.

His face showed increased respect.

T was holding a book called *Hungarian Tragedy*, by Peter Fryer.

'I bought it on the bookstall at the front of the train. The Communist Party says Soviet tanks were sent into Hungary to crush a counter-revolution, but you Trots call the uprising a "revolution".'

'I know the *Daily Worker* sent Peter Fryer to Hungary, but they wouldn't print his reports and he was expelled from the Communist Party.'

'That's why I want to read this.'

T asked me about Rhodesia and South Africa as we continued chatting. He had brought his guitar and sang some republican songs from the Spanish

---

* Two people requested that I use their initial rather than name, to preserve their anonymity.

Civil War, which chimed with our hopes for far-away Vietnam. People crammed into the compartment to listen; the music was compelling and our emotions were heightened by the dramatic day.

As we approached Victoria T made a suggestion.

'I'll be driving back to Bristol on Monday morning because I have one or two things to collect in London. If you like, you could travel with me. We can stay at a friends' flat overnight.'

▲ Peter Fryer's eye-witness account of the Hungarian revolution

I didn't need much persuading. T was fun and interesting: tall with dark hair, receding even in his early 20s, and black-rimmed glasses. We had an early lunch snack at Victoria before embarking on the mundane tasks he needed to do in London. We talked and laughed, light-headed from lack of sleep. After an evening meal we went to the basement flat of his friend, who had left the key under a dustbin.

Within a month of returning from Australia I had joined the League and started a new relationship.

T left Bristol for a job in Sheffield and applied to join its well-established Socialist Labour League branch. I approached my final degree year diligently, focused on political struggle and my relationship with T.

We booked a place in the town for weekly Young Socialists meetings and talked to young people on working-class estates or in cramped areas of old Bristol with copies of *Keep Left*. We arranged a disco in a church hall near the Wills cigarette factory, with a local band playing. Trouble broke out as the stage curtains were ripped down and the band's drums were kicked in. We had a lot to learn.

At Easter we travelled overnight with a coach-load of working-class youth and students to the Young Socialists' national conference in Morecambe. At midday the Winter Gardens' conference facilities were abuzz with hundreds of excited working-class youth. A large banner on the platform proclaimed, 'Young Socialists National Committee – Left MPs must fight Wilson'. The conference was run entirely by people of my own age, or younger; delegates spoke at the microphone on a variety of political resolutions in a welter of regional

◄ *Keep Left* July-August 1967, the Young Socialists' lively monthly newspaper, which included spot colour in each edition. Circulation reached 10,000

accents. Votes were mostly unanimous. Stewards at the exit doors dissuaded bored delegates and visitors from leaving.

Towards the end of the afternoon Gerry Healy spoke. There was a rustle of curiosity as this unprepossessing man mounted the platform. He spoke quietly until everyone was straining to hear him and then worked up to a crescendo, thrusting his index finger upwards to emphasise his points.

'The ruling class wants to throw crumbs to working-class youth. They want to throw you on the scrapheap. We will *not* accept this. You young people hold the key to the *future*.'

Then he spoke quietly, a sort of aside, and everyone laughed. He had the attention of every single delegate. He ended with a rousing appeal to join the fight against the Labour government's betrayals and to struggle for world revolution. The applause was thunderous.

'Who was that little old fat man?' asked 16-year-old Linda as we walked back to the bed-and-breakfast accommodation to change for the evening.

'He's the leader of our movement.' I was rather shocked at her frank description.

'He really fights, doesn't he?'

The evening's dance was the highlight for most delegates. The decorative plaster moulding and red walls sparkled under brilliant chandeliers. I would have danced all night to the two bands but we had been told to discuss politically with our delegation, so I alternated between dancing and talking. T was on stewarding duties and I barely saw him all weekend. Accompanied by *Keep Left* editor Aileen, Comrade Healy wandered around with a thoughtful look on his face, talking to League members and any youth who wanted to speak to him. His presence gave political approval to the night's festivities.

At 11 o'clock we traipsed back to our hotel, exhausted. Next morning we made sure everyone was up for a full English breakfast and the continuing conference.

A telegram arrived from Fabrizio in Italy.

'Urgent. Need money for political work.' It gave details of where to telegraph it. I went straight to the bank and sent him £70, hoping it was enough. I was late meeting Steve, who was horrified when I explained why.

'Clare, this guy is just using you.'

'But it's not for him, it's for political work. He's a member of our fraternal organisation in France, the OCI.'

'You're being taken for a ride.'

Gerry Healy attended our next branch meeting, giving the political report to orientate our work in line with political developments.

'I want to raise something,' Steve said, looking at me accusingly. 'We're trying to collect money for the League's development fund and Clare has just sent £70 to her Italian contact.'

'It's for political work,' I explained hastily. 'He's the comrade in France who introduced me to the League.'

There was a brief silence. How would Comrade Healy react?

'The first thing to say is that it's astonishing that anyone should have so much money,' he said, in a calm voice.

Was it really so much? I had very little idea about the value of money because I always had enough. My father sent me an allowance. I led the same fairly economical life as my friends on grants from their local education authorities, and I never spent it all. The dockers were campaigning for a minimum wage of – how much? £15 pounds a week … so, yes, perhaps £70 was a lot.

Comrade Healy continued.

'The second thing is, if we are to support the work of our comrades in the French section it would be better done through formal channels, through the leadership.'

So he wasn't going to be cross and shout at me. He smiled, leaning towards me with a confidential air.

'I happen to know that the French section is not short of money.'

I applied to do an education diploma in Sheffield and join T after my degree course, but I agreed to stay in Bristol for the summer to help consolidate the League and Young Socialists work. In a branch meeting Alison looked me straight in the eye.

'What about finding a summer job, where you can exert political influence?' Others had already found jobs, but it hadn't occurred to me. I detected an underlying implication that I needed to experience working-class life.

I found a part-time job in the works canteen of Bristol Siddeley aircraft factory from eight in the morning until 3 o'clock, which didn't feel like part time to me. My day began with washing lettuce in the big stainless steel sinks, using lukewarm water in the chill mornings. Then we made up rolls to sell on the shop floor. They tried me out on a trolley round with a big brown teapot and a range of filled rolls and chocolate bars. I felt important pushing the heavy trolley down the walkway between giant machines that made components for aircraft. I poured tea, took the money and gave change. On my return the supervisor counted my supplies and measured how much tea was left with a calibrated measuring rod dipped into the teapot. Oh dear. I never had the right money. Clever Miss Chemistry-and-maths couldn't even sell tea and rolls and get the money right. They moved me to the canteen for office staff, where I sulked because I wanted to be among the *real* workers in overalls, with oily hands. In my first week a woman retired after 25 years working in the canteen, her legs swollen with varicose veins from a lifetime filling cheese-and-lettuce rolls, serving boiled potatoes and clearing tables.

Camaraderie and a sometimes filthy humour enlivened the day.

'I call this boiled foreskin,' said Julie, cackling with laughter as she portioned some unrecognisable meat on to plates.

Everything in the serving cabinets was ready. We relaxed for a moment. One of the canteen managers appeared on the far side and Julie suddenly started restacking plates.

'Quick, wipe the counter.'

'But I've already done it.' She dug her elbow into my ribs.

'Just – wipe – the – counter. When management appears you – look – busy.'

I went to the kitchen to collect an omelette. The tall young chef broke the egg into the pan with one hand, gave a stir with a fork, and moments later tipped a perfect, folded omelette on to the plate. He made a humorous crack at Edna, a tall, grey-haired woman. Calling out a foul, saucy reply she lifted her skirt, displaying knickers and suspenders as she passed him. He couldn't see, but we women in front of her burst into laughter as she strode on.

My time as a worker earning £7 a week ended when they found a permanent replacement.

Tensions mounted in ports across the country as implementation of the Devlin Plan to decasualise dock work approached. Karen, an experienced League member from Exeter, came to help us with *Newsletter* sales during the dockers' lunch break. She stood on a chair in the middle of a large café, brandishing papers above her head.

'Can I have your attention,' she called out. Everyone fell silent and turned to look at this attractive young woman.

'Devlin includes dangers that you need to know about. The end of casual labour and the £15 guaranteed minimum wage are good – but the bosses want to increase productivity.' There were murmurs of agreement. 'The *Labour* government's infamous Prices and Incomes policy has stopped the employers conceding a higher minimum wage.' She held up a small pamphlet. 'This pamphlet explains Devlin's implications and I hope you will buy one. Thank you.'

The hubbub of conversation started again and we moved around the tables selling pamphlets to almost everyone.

On the day that Devlin came into operation we arrived early at the dock gates with boxes of pamphlets. We couldn't sell them quickly enough – every single docker wanted one. I sensed how, in certain circumstances, thousands of men become a unified body.

I had learned the basic techniques of revolutionary propaganda and organisation in Bristol. Now it was time to move to a great northern industrial city.

1967
SHEFFIELD

Giant steel plants, strong trade unions. I was immediately swept into early morning *Newsletter* sales to campaign for an important London demonstration. Jean Kerrigan was Sheffield League branch secretary and full-time organiser for Yorkshire.

'The Communist Party dominates the shop stewards' committee at Shardlow's works,' she told me as we thrust flyers into the hands of thousands of men hurrying through the huge gates between prison-like, high walls.

'Factory-gate meeting at lunchtime,' we called out.

Jean parked her van so that the loudspeakers on the roof-rack faced into the factory gates as she spoke about our demonstration against the Labour government's attacks on trade unions. We sold papers and took addresses of anyone interested among about 100 men who came out to listen, milling around, smoking.

T had bought a semi-detached house with a mortgage of £30 a month in tree-lined Psalter Lane. We shared the house with his friends Tony and Vicky, now also League members, and two BBC friends, who each had a loft room. But after a National Committee meeting in London Jean raised the matter in a branch meeting.

'Your house is like a middle-class commune,' she said. 'Your BBC friends have nothing in common with us politically. And you and Tony, old school chums – this middle-class set-up isn't good politically.'

When they all moved out I enjoyed having the house to ourselves. At an education class on Marx's *Wage Labour and Capital* I learned what the derogatory attribute 'middle-class' really meant.

'Objectively, the working class has no choice but to oppose Capital, the worker *sells* his labour-power to the capitalist,' explained the lecturer from Leeds, pointing to a passage: *Labour-power, then, is a commodity, no more, no less so than is sugar. The first is measured by the clock, the other by the scales.*

'But the middle class, the "petty bourgeoisie", is the unstable grouping between the classes. Some sections will cast their lot with the working class and others will support the ruling class.'

Evenings and weekends were completely taken up with political work. Because I had a car I was directed to establish a Young Socialists branch in Barnsley, whose coal-mining bleakness awed me: village-like clumps of houses with barely a shop and only the occasional pub; desolate, scattered housing estates where nobody used the front door but went through the archway between houses to the kitchen door. Central Barnsley had a modest range of shops, pubs and cafés, and a busy bus station, the only place for a meal or cup of tea on Sundays.

▼ With my brother Howard and my second-hand Hillman Imp

I learned to understand the Yorkshire accent and its idiosyncratic phrases. I talked to teenagers hanging around near where they lived because they had no bus fare to reach the town centre, and certainly nothing to spend once there. Cathy and Maureen, who lived in outlying Cudworth, were keen to come on the London demonstration we were organising. Their fathers were miners so I was confident they would be against the government's wage freeze. I called at Cathy's house, where they were waiting anxiously, to discuss the arrangements with her parents.

'I will pick the girls up at seven in the morning to take them to Sheffield for the coach.'

Maureen nudged Cathy.

'We've never been to Sheffield,' she said, smiling.

Never been to Sheffield? But it was only 16 miles away.

'The demonstration starts at midday and then there'll be a meeting in Central Halls, at Westminster. The coach will bring us back and I'll bring them home by 11, or midnight at the latest.'

We waited in tense silence for Cathy's father.

'Well, lass, if Maureen's parents agree, you can go.' He smiled.

Bursting with excitement, the girls took me to Maureen's house. The whole scene was repeated but this time a huge dog – a whippet? a greyhound? – draped itself right across my lap as I sat on the sofa. I was appalled, I didn't want it there, but in the interests of persuading Maureen's parents I stroked its head until they had agreed and paid the ticket money.

Everyone in Barnsley worked in a pit or in a job associated with mining. My entire childhood, too, had been tied up with mines – diamonds, gold, copper – but in Barnsley I saw a different reality. The pits provided a meagre living with nothing for unessential expenditure. People led self-contained lives, perhaps keeping whippets or greyhounds, organising football leagues or managing their son's or daughter's bands. One father gave us jars of pickled red cabbage to sell at our Christmas bazaar in Leeds. Arthur's family consisted of his mother, three younger siblings, and a tall man, simple-minded, friendly but incapable of conversation. I guessed he must be the father, victim of some terrible head injury, a mining accident perhaps. How did the mother cope? Were the children teased about their father, or did children in this community understand tragedy?

My first teaching practice on the education diploma course was at a girls' grammar school outside Sheffield. The deputy headmistress called me into her study during the first break.

'We check that the pupils' skirts touch the floor when they kneel down in the hall,' she said. 'I'm afraid your skirt is too short.'

But it was modest compared with the fashions of the day.

'I'll wear something different tomorrow.'

'No, I'm afraid you need to go home and change, now.'

I drove home with tears welling in my eyes. I was furious and so was my tutor.

'Anachronistic grammar schools – the sooner they're all comprehensives, the better.'

My second teaching practice was at the further education college in Stocksbridge, which provided day-release classes for apprentices in the British Steel plant across the road. They were allowed to miss one shift to attend the classes, which was fine if they were on days. But apprentices on night shift came straight from work, struggling to keep awake, let alone concentrate. They chatted and swore as I tried to teach them geometry and algebra. My tutor came to observe me, but left the class.

'How can anyone teach in these conditions?' he said afterwards. In his final report he wrote that I had a gift for teaching apprentices.

I had a week off to get married. The class was inquisitive on my return.

'So how's married life then, Miss?'

'Not much different,' I said breezily.

'Oooh! I'd like to join your set, Miss.'

How I came to be marrying in the middle of my course is a complicated story.

Marriage

On my way to Australia to visit my parents for Christmas, I called to see Gerry at the Centre. The office at 186a Clapham High Street, above Dewhurst's butchers, was familiar because the previous summer I had spent a week painting Russian Revolution anniversary banners in premises at the back, above Plough Press at 180b, a cramped space where *The Newsletter* was printed, with printing press, guillotine, paper stacks and boxes of books piled high. A side passageway led up to a family flat, where I had slept on a sofa in a first-floor room above the noisy high street.

Gerry came out of his office at the top of the stairs, wearing a dark suit and tie.

▲ The Socialist Labour League's south London offices were at 186a Clapham High Street, above today's Caffe Nero

'Hello, comrade. Come and have a cup of tea in Lyons café.'

The café was two doors along.

'Do you want a bun, a cake?'

'I'd like beans on toast,' I said hesitantly.

'I'll check if they're still serving food.' Gerry was clearly a frequent customer and returned grinning broadly, surprisingly light on his feet for a rotund man. The woman brought two teas and my beans on toast.

'It's been paid for,' she said.

Gerry waved generously. We chatted inconsequentially about Australia and then returned to his office. Janet, the national organiser, had a desk facing the doorway. I was impressed by her modern electric typewriter. I sat facing Gerry's desk, his back was towards the rather grimy back window.

'Barnsley. An important coal-mining area.' He paused a moment. 'Your house – have the other people moved out?'

'They left last week.'

He was considering something.

'You know, this bohemian living together with T … it's a middle-class way of life, like the hippies. It has little to do with building a revolutionary leadership in the working class.' He was talking quietly, in a persuasive tone. 'You have decided to become a revolutionary cadre, you're a valued League member. Give it some thought while you're in Australia.'

I was very surprised. Was he suggesting we get married?

'Have a good trip and we'll see you in January.' He shook my hand; his grip was unexpectedly floppy.

I mulled over this conversation all the way to Heathrow. T and I had been together for 14 months. I shuddered at being likened to hippies with their 'laid back' rebellions, undisciplined protests, and drugs.

I wrote T a letter.

'Gerry described our living together as middle-class bohemianism. I suppose he was suggesting we should get married, but isn't marriage just a bourgeois institution, the foundation of the *class* society we're fighting to end? What do you think?'

I posted the letter and boarded the plane for the 30-hour flight.

Melbourne was pleasantly hot and my complete family was there: parents, sister and both brothers. I was on the veranda chatting to my younger brother Allan when the doorbell rang.

'It's a telegram, for you.'

I tore it open, guessing its contents.

'I'm going for a walk.'

The telegram read:

'I DO STOP DATE AT YOUR CONVENIENCE STOP LOVE T'.

I walked for more than an hour in suburban South Yarra's bland modern streets, enjoying the warm air on my bare arms and legs, my thoughts churning with excitement. T and I were going to be married. Until four days before I had never even considered the possibility. I was a fortnight short of turning 23 and marriage had been a distant, abstract idea. Suddenly, it was going to happen.

'Darling, what did the telegram say?' my mother asked. 'We're worried.'

I breathed deeply to calm my jitters.

'T has asked me to marry him.' Another deep breath. 'And I'm going to accept.'

It sounded very romantic and I kept reminding myself of my new status as an engaged woman. I wrote to T saying we should marry as soon as possible and by return airmail he replied that he would begin arrangements for a register office wedding from his father's home in Sussex. My parents were happy for me but must have had mixed feelings. They had met and liked T

▲ Christmas 1967, Melbourne, Australia: my parents, me, my brothers Allan and Howard and sister Norah

and my intellectual mother had also married at 23. But our revolutionary ideas troubled them and they probably realised I would stay in England.

My father wept when he saw me off at the airport. I was embarrassed, resentful; it felt like subtle blackmail and upset me. Once through the barriers I headed for the bar to order a bloody mary and had another on the plane.

The simple wedding was to be on 24th February 1968. The reception for family and close friends, fewer than 20 people, would be in T's father's farmhouse, with a buffet provided by a local caterer. My mother flew over but my father had work commitments. I pretended I was living with T's friends but showed her T's house. He had bought curtains for the main rooms while I was in Australia and fortunately they were quite nice. Mum looked around with an eye accustomed to South Africa's ridiculously high standards of household cleanliness and offered to pay a firm to do a thorough spring clean.

As wedding dress I bought a linen suit, with a lightly flared skirt and shaped jacket, quite psychedelic, with pink and orange flowers and green leaves on a paler orange background.

We saw Gerry on our way through London and outlined the wedding arrangements.

'I tell you what,' he said. 'Let Aileen and her husband Paul come too. Paul can take the photos.'

We knew Aileen as editor of *Keep Left* and as Gerry's co-driver when he came to Yorkshire; we barely knew Paul, a journalist on *The Newsletter*. But they would be a convincing pair of friends: young, attractive, intelligent.

▲ At Healy's suggestion, Paul and Aileen Jennings came to our wedding

My mother and I shared a room in the farmhouse while T slept in his childhood bedroom. My wedding-suit suddenly felt too work-a-day so I rushed off to Chichester to buy a similarly psychedelic, floral dress with an open neckline that felt more appropriate. I wore the suit for the Friday evening restaurant meal, when our respective families met each other.

The wedding Saturday dawned. An early morning hair appointment; painting my nails bright red; floral buttonholes for all the family members. Surprise that T was nervous as we drove to the Register Office. The woman Registrar's irritation at clattering typewriters intruding from across the corridor. Surprise when she handed me the marriage certificate, congratulating me in my married name, and inviting T to 'kiss the bride'. Effusive congratulations from everyone.

Was I any different from the person of ten minutes before?

'You two go and have a drink at the Angel Hotel,' suggested T's father. 'We'll go ahead.'

'That's quite normal,' encouraged my mother when she saw my surprise.

I had coffee and T had whisky in front of a roaring fire.

'We've done it!' he said, giving me a big hug. It felt unreal.

The All Trades Unions Alliance, the League's trade union arm, held a national conference in early summer. While the convenor of an engineering factory was speaking, Aileen tapped me on the shoulder.

'Gerry wants to see you and T.'

We followed her out into the rain. She was wearing a belted cream raincoat and high heels and her hair was done in an elaborate beehive. She led us to a back street where Gerry was waiting in a sheltered doorway. He held an umbrella over us.

After a brief exchange about the conference, he turned to T.

'We're setting up a new printshop in Clapham Old Town, in bigger premises. You have proved yourself in the League and we would like you to be the manager.'

T looked surprised, but pleased. I felt proud.

'When would this be?' He managed to sound calm.

'In the autumn. Work your notice and move down afterwards. Could you do that?'

T thought a moment, then nodded.

'Clare, you can find a teaching job in London. We've rented several flats across the road from the Centre so you can have one of them.'

My thoughts were racing. T would have to sell his house. What would happen to Barnsley Young Socialists? I'd be sorry to leave industrial Sheffield. But to be in London, at the Centre ... I looked at T and smiled. He too seemed excited at the prospect.

Gerry told Aileen to fetch another comrade. As we walked back to the hall I noticed that her heavily lacquered hair was unaffected by the rain.

May-June 1968

The year 1968 was memorable: marriage, moving to London, my first teaching job – and tumultuous, historic events.

On Monday 6th May Paris's Latin Quarter erupted when 20,000 students and teachers marched on the Sorbonne after CRS riot police invaded the central courtyard. Helmeted and shielded riot police charged demonstrators with teargas and considerable violence; the protesters responded with missiles and erected eight-foot-high barricades from overturned vehicles stacked below the elegant, seven-storey buildings. I read the reports assiduously.

'See that burning barricade?' I exclaimed to T. 'The café next to it is where I used to meet my friends.'

The Communist Party-controlled trade unions called a one-day general strike a week later and a million people demonstrated in Paris, in ranks 20 to 30 abreast, arms linked, singing the *Internationale,* carrying red flags. Newspaper reports were hostile to the demonstrators but an anarchist paper had a different viewpoint, describing a mass meeting at the Renault factory. Communist Party leaflets called for 'calm, vigilance and unity' and warned against 'provocateurs'. A speaker from the Communist Party-led Confédération Générale du Travail (CGT) addressed 10,000 workers with details of the wage structure without mentioning the violence against the students. But when he announced the march through central Paris the cheering crowd streamed out, halting remaining assembly lines. The response far exceeded expectations. At the end of the march CGT officials physically prevented demonstrators joining the student rally at the Champ de Mars with half a dozen solid rows of stewards, arms linked, on either side of the demonstrators, while loudspeakers instructed them to disperse in the opposite direction.

'The bastards,' I exclaimed. 'The report says they had 10,000 stewards.'

'The Communist Party has a mass base in the Paris suburbs,' said T. 'It remains from their resistance to German occupation.'

By 20th May 10 million workers were on strike. France was paralysed.

'Surely the Communist Party will be forced to take power?' I said to branch secretary Jean. 'This is a mass uprising.'

She shook her head.

'They'll compromise, they'll betray.' She was in her 20s and had grown up in the Communist Party, but had left it because of Stalinism's blood-stained crimes. 'They'll negotiate for reforms, to maintain control of the working class.'

I wanted to believe she was wrong.

'The Stalinists always act to protect the interests of the Soviet Union and their peaceful coexistence with imperialism,' said another experienced member. 'They certainly don't want to overthrow French capitalism.'

At the League's solidarity rally in London, National Committee member Mike Banda made a rousing speech.

'President de Gaulle is preparing military operations headquarters for civil war to smash the French workers and students. The Stalinists and social democrats are manoeuvring to emasculate the movement but the French working class will see through Stalinism's treachery. Their courageous uprising,' he thundered, 'marks the beginning of the European revolution.'

I shivered with excitement. We ended the rally singing the *Internationale,* arms raised, fists clenched, optimistic, elated.

The strikes continued, but the Communist and Socialist trade union leaders negotiated reforms and told the workers to return to work. In elections at the end of June right-wing parties won an overwhelming majority. I was bitterly disappointed. Overthrowing capitalism wasn't easy.

Special edition newspapers appeared with the headline 'Kennedy assassinated'. This time it was the assassinated President's brother, barely two months after the assassination of Civil Rights leader Martin Luther King. Political ferment was breaking out all over the world: Brazil, Mexico, even Stalinist-ruled Poland and fascist Spain. Palestinians hijacked an El Al plane and secured the release of political prisoners from Israeli jails.

'But the Israeli state remains intact and it's won support from people horrified by the hijack,' Jean told a branch meeting. 'We're opposed to individual terrorism. Only the working class can defeat Israeli oppression in the long term.'

A Vietnam Solidarity Campaign demonstration in London erupted in violence when 80,000 demonstrators encircled the American Embassy in Grosvenor Square and hurled stones, firecrackers and smoke bombs at mounted police. Their compelling slogan: 'London, Paris, Rome, Berlin – we shall fight and we shall win!' rang through the streets. But we didn't participate in the demonstration except to sell papers because we considered this loose grouping of left-wing organisations as simply a protest movement with no clear analysis and no programme to challenge capitalism.

Meanwhile women machinists at the Ford Motor Company, striking for equal pay for work of equal value, halted all car production. Ford was compelled to negotiate; Labour Minister Barbara Castle intervened, and the women won a thrilling victory.

The year's ferment continued. Thousands of students confronted Russian tanks in Wenceslas Square in Prague, where three years previously I had eaten sausages and bread from street stalls. Forty students in Mexico were massacred as they protested against police violence just before the Olympic Games started. When two black American medal-winners raised their fists in a Black Power salute during the United States anthem millions of us were inspired. On the other hand we saw terrible pictures of children starving in civil war after Biafra's secession from Nigeria.

The following April President de Gaulle was ousted in a referendum. It wasn't revolution, but I was jubilant.

1969
LONDON AND *WORKERS PRESS*

Across the road from the Centre, our studio flat was at 155a Clapham High Street, above a carpet shop at street level and accountants on the first floor. League members occupied five of the eight flats on the second and third floors. The bathroom opened off our flat's tiny entrance hall; the main room had three metal casement windows overlooking the high street with a small wall demarcating the kitchen. A modest walk-in cupboard provided limited storage. I moved ahead of T and told him to bring only the new wardrobe and my father's wedding present, a Chinese lacquer cabinet from Singapore.

▶ Party members lived in the eight flats at 155a Clapham High Street, above today's WH Smith. Mine was top left. The Centre was diagonally opposite behind the photographer

He sold the Sheffield house and remaining furniture. Meanwhile I learned to sleep through 24-hour traffic noise.

Gerry took me to Clapham Old Town, up an alleyway to a yard surrounded by industrial buildings with grey roofs, shabby walls and concrete flooring. I looked around, bemused by the bare complex.

'We'll have editorial offices upstairs.' He pointed to the left before turning into a cavernous warehouse. 'The printing presses will be here and the compositors in the building behind.' He surveyed the space. 'We'll be ready to produce a daily newspaper within a year. T will oversee the preparations and manage the printshop.'

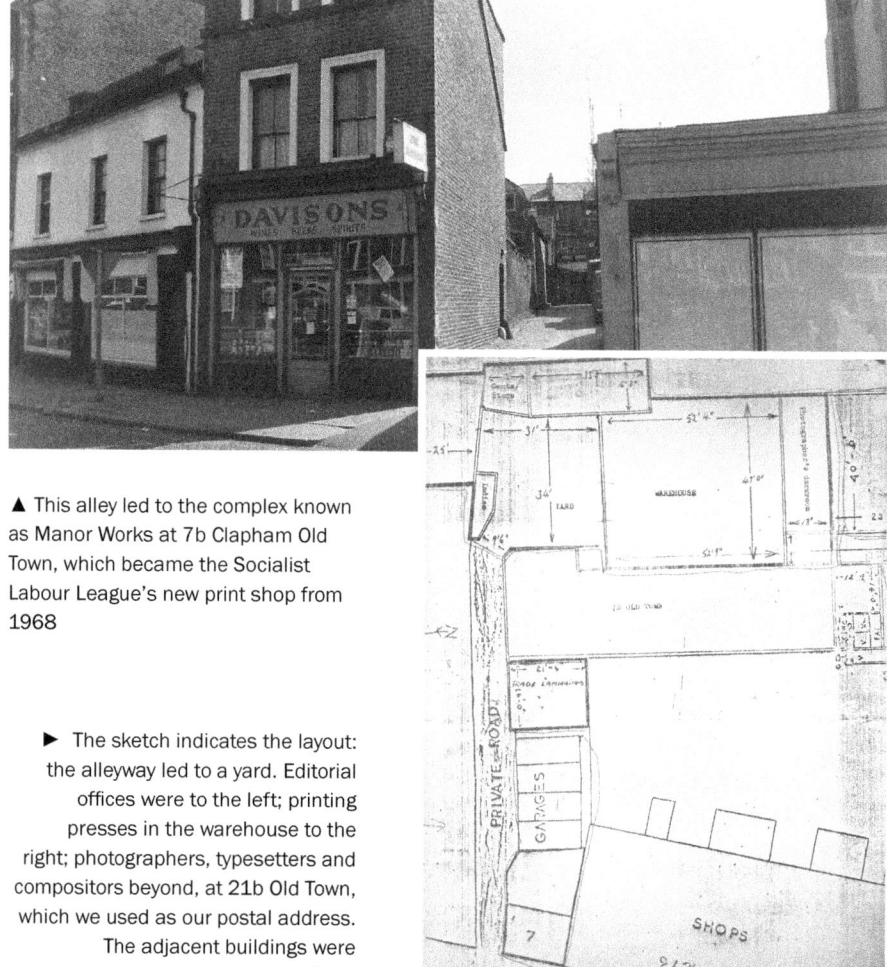

▲ This alley led to the complex known as Manor Works at 7b Clapham Old Town, which became the Socialist Labour League's new print shop from 1968

▶ The sketch indicates the layout: the alleyway led to a yard. Editorial offices were to the left; printing presses in the warehouse to the right; photographers, typesetters and compositors beyond, at 21b Old Town, which we used as our postal address. The adjacent buildings were used by other firms

At Clapham County Grammar School for Girls I taught general science to the lower years and chemistry to the sixth form for an annual salary of £1,000, which felt enormous. I was assigned to the sprawling south-east London League branch, which extended from the Thames at Vauxhall to Downham, in the depths of Lewisham. London's dense buildings intimidated me; the housing estates were claustrophobic clumps of identical five-storey, red-brick blocks of flats, interspersed with occasional tower blocks of neck-cricking height. Life was hurried, intense, loud, never free from traffic noise.

The Rhodesian referendum on becoming a republic and breaking ties with Britain was in the news. But the events felt far away; I was totally immersed in fighting capitalism in Britain, which I felt would assist the liberation struggles in Africa. Each evening we sold *Keep Left* to young people on the estates, teenage girls and boys hanging around, bored. I showed them the paper.

'Why don't you come to a Young Socialists' meeting on Wednesday?'

One boy started kicking a football around, but another was listening.

'What for?'

'Well, the Labour government is holding down wages and we think we should fight against it.'

'Yeah, my wages are rubbish.'

'I haven't even got a job.'

'Some of us are still at school.'

'You can't stop the government.'

'Yes, we can, if we build up a big movement. We have Young Socialists branches all over the country.'

I had their attention.

'You know Barbara Castle, in the government, she wants to attack the trade unions with new laws.'

'My dad says trade unions are rubbish.'

'No they're not, stupid. The unions fight for workers,' retorted one girl.

'I'm in the Post Office Engineering Union. I'm an apprentice,' said a skinny-looking boy.

'On May Day we're demonstrating against Barbara Castle's laws.'

'What, marching in the street, with banners, and shouting?'

They were intrigued, but sceptical.

'And we're planning a disco in the Royal Albert.'

'A disco? When?'

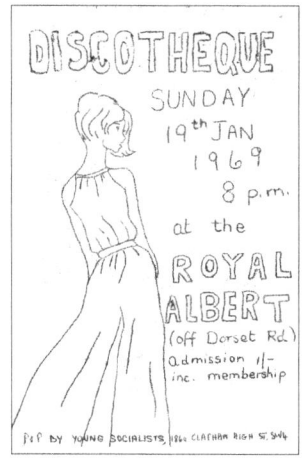

'Do you play football? There's a five-a-side tournament on Sunday week. Could you make up a team?'

'You and me can play, and Kevin will come, and Tony.'

'Come to the meeting on Wednesday and we'll tell you more.'

I always had good attendance at the rowdy meetings above a pub near the Oval station and my teaching skills helped to get the discussion going. Most of the young people spoke with a cockney accent, but we also had members with lilting West Indian accents and elegant names like Parbody, Winston, Kenyon, Delroy, Everton, Jevon. For the first time I was meeting black people on equal ground.

I called at Kevin's flat. His Irish parents invited me in.

'We oppose British troops being sent in to suppress the civil rights demonstrations,' I told them.

'Sure, they're there to support the hated Ulster police against the Catholics. Ireland was England's first colony, you know.'

'It's good that Bernadette Devlin has been elected as MP.' I tried to pretend I knew more than I did.

He shrugged.

'A young woman, your age. It's a victory, yes, but what can she do? Why should the British parliament rule Ireland?'

All the London Young Socialist branches were going on a coach trip to Margate. From our Oval branch alone we half filled the coach. Everyone turned up early, bubbling with excitement, dressed in holiday finery, eyeing up the opposite sex, West Indian boys in immaculate suits, girls in brilliant colours, sparkling and glamorous. Three late-comers arrived giggling and shrieking. During the journey League members worked down the coach, selling copies of *Keep Left*, discussing how to fight the Labour government, arranging meetings and football practices. At the half-way stop our exuberant coachload tumbled out as a west London coach prepared to leave.

'Hey, girls – where're you from?' Kevin called as they scrambled back on to their coach.

'Willesden,' they giggled.

▲ We opposed British troops being sent into Northern Ireland in 1969 to quell rioting in Belfast, Derry and elsewhere. Using force to maintain the status quo continued for years and the 'Troubles' lasted until 1998

'Got any friends?'
'Of course.'
'See you in Margate!'
There were shouts of delight when Dreamland's ferris wheel, scenic railway and helter skelter came into view, the sun-drenched beach beyond.
'Be back at five or we'll leave without you.'
We League members hovered to make sure no one was left on their own, then started to relax: a few rides in Dreamland, fish and chips, a dip in the sea and, most welcome of all, dozing on the beach in the sun.

The Lambeth dustmen went on strike. We sold papers to the pickets outside the depot where the dustcarts remained neatly parked in silent rows. One of the shop stewards called at the Centre.
'We've read your article in *The Newsletter* supporting our strike,' he said. 'We need a leaflet making our case. My committee asks if you could print it.'
'Of course. We'll print it free,' said Gerry.
They shook hands and he left, pleased.

'A dustman spends all day in dirty overalls, removing filthy rubbish,' commented Gerry as the downstairs front door slammed. 'Now he wears a suit, proud of his class, confident of its strength.'

Rubbish piled up uncollected while the newspapers railed against the dustmen 'endangering public health'. We planned to discuss the strike in the Young Socialists' meeting, with a visiting speaker, League member Geoff Pilling. About 20 boisterous young people milled round the room; some sat down when I called them to order, others continued talking.

Geoff waited, but the chatter continued. I knew how to attract their attention and get a dialogue underway – I was a teacher, after all – but Geoff wouldn't start.

'When you're quiet, I'll begin speaking,'

'Tony, please sit down,' I called out. 'Comrade Geoff is going to talk about the fight for better wages.'

'I don't get no wages. You know I ain't got no job.' He carried on larking about.

'This is hopeless,' said Geoff. 'These are just backward youth.'

We abandoned the meeting and asked everyone to leave. They grumbled as they went downstairs. At home I told T what had happened.

'Geoff was such an old fuddy-duddy. He wouldn't challenge them. He's used to lecturing well-behaved students, not rowdy, working-class youth.'

T was amused.

'But he's spoken at many Young Socialists meetings.'

Next day I told Sheila, the Young Socialists' national secretary, about the meeting's fiasco. I felt she agreed with me.

Piles of rubbish at every street corner became more noisome, press attacks more hysterical. Then strike-breaking drivers and scabs began collecting rubbish. I saw a dustcart on Clapham Road, next to a stinking pile. Three young men were hurling the bags into the back of the vehicle. Suddenly one of them shouted to his mates.

'There's Clare.'

'Hullo, Clare,' whistled Tony, with an insolent leer.

I was shocked. I didn't know what to do. My Young Socialist members – *scabbing on the strike*. I rushed back to the Centre to tell Sheila.

'They can't be members any more,' I blurted out.

A few days later, League members crammed into the Centre's two upper floors and both landings for a London aggregate meeting. A microphone system enabled everyone to hear Mike Banda's political report. His black hair

▲ Mike Banda

tumbled over his brown forehead, his Ceylonese accent gave a compelling flavour to his cultivated, richly illustrated speech.

'The employers are determined to break the Lambeth dustmen's strike; they have found scabs to do their dirty work. And who are the scabs?' He looked around. 'Youth who have been members of the Oval Young Socialists' branch for weeks.'

I shrank in shame, looking down at my notes.

'Comrade Clare, working in that branch, compromised politically with these backward youth and this is the result. We told the comrade. We warned her' – the collective 'we' of political authority – 'but she knew better.' My heart was thumping. 'She refused to challenge political backwardness among lumpen youth and the branch became fertile ground for recruiting strike-breakers.'

He sat down, glaring at me, with arms folded. The meeting was totally silent.

'Well, comrade?' Gerry leaned back in his chair.

I squeezed my way through the chairs to the microphone. Everyone was watching me. I looked at the window frame above their heads, grappling with how to correct my error.

'I should have challenged the youth … fought their backward ideas …'

'You delude yourself that all young workers are spontaneously class conscious,' interrupted Gerry. 'The middle class kow-tows to working-class backwardness.' He looked at me scornfully. 'Of course backwardness exists among workers. The ruling class has educated them from birth.'

Would any other members have made the same mistake? Probably not. Most were working class; I felt they had been inoculated against such basic mistakes.

'I idealised them because they were working-class youth …' I stuttered. 'I know we – the revolutionary organisation – must bring revolutionary consciousness into the working class …'

Gerry snorted.

'White South African shit,' he said with a dismissive wave of his hand. 'Go home, comrade.'

I retrieved my bag and made my way to the door. There was absolute silence on both floors. I tripped as I manoeuvred through the chairs.

'Oh, don't try and get sympathy,' said Gerry contemptuously.

I felt wretched, trying to understand why I had made such a mistake, smarting at the scathing criticisms. I knew Mike and Gerry were right.

The following afternoon I crept into the Centre after school, uncertain how I would be received. Gerry called me into his office.

'Sit down, comrade. You've thought about last night's meeting?'

'All day.'

'You made a mistake and now you must correct it.'

I nodded.

'You can do it, you know.'

I couldn't meet his eyes. I fiddled with my car keys.

'When you change your *practice* new forces begin to act on you. That's how you make a development, not by changing your *ideas*, as the idealists think. Changing your practice changes the material world and that changes you.'

His tone was gentle and encouraging. I looked up at him.

'You can do it, comrade. I'll help you.'

Launch of the daily paper

T was immersed in technical preparations for producing the daily paper in the Clapham Old Town premises. A huge web-offset printing press was installed in the warehouse alongside two smaller presses, a guillotine and a long workbench. Built-in desks were made in the editorial office, the kitchen was enlarged. Gerry called me over one afternoon.

'You've married a tile-layer.' He pointed to the perfect linoleum-tiled floor, expertly finished in the awkward corners at the foot of the narrow, winding staircase.

The League's national conference at Easter was part of the political preparation for launching the paper. We elected delegates and collected conference levies to cover costs of the hall, food and travel. Provincial comrades stayed with London members; each London branch brought six loaves of sandwiches for lunch on the first day.

The Hudson's Bay Company's wood-panelled Beaver Hall in the City of London was the unlikely venue for our Trotskyist conference. From the carved wooden rostrum a leading member introduced the document on International Perspectives. After discussion came the British Perspectives and more discussion. Gerry addressed the conference on the first day.

'Our daily paper will counter the lies of the capitalist gutter press. Among some Fleet Street journalists there is disillusion because they are tired of being compelled to write lies in their capitalist masters' newspapers. The entertainment industry is in crisis: actors face unemployment, writers and film directors feel strangled by the BBC and by capitalism's theatre and film companies, who censor them and prevent creative, meaningful work.'

He looked round the tiered hall.

'These people are attracted to the revolutionary movement because it offers the only alternative. Marxism shows that *only the working class* can take power, not the Black Panthers, the Women's Liberation movement, or any other oppressed section of the class *on its own*.'

▲ A new unit for the web offset press is manoeuvred into the warehouse

He paused and then began again in a matter-of-fact tone.

'For many months we have been holding weekly classes with people from the creative world. Some have applied to join the League and are present today as visitors.'

These were the unfamiliar comrades two rows behind me.

'We have a new branch whose members are journalists, writers, actors, theatre directors and designers. To protect them from unscrupulous misrepresentations we have called it the Outer London Branch.'

His voice rose:

'And if you want to know where the Outer London Branch is – well, it's in … *outer London*.'

Everyone laughed.

Early next morning D, my branch secretary who lived in the flat below me, knocked on my door with a £10 note in her hand.

'I need you to buy a duck.'

'A live duck?'

'Don't be silly. You know some of us eat in my flat at night before Gerry goes home. Well, I fell asleep last night and burned the duck he had bought for tonight to a cinder. I need you to buy another one.'

'Where on earth can I find a duck? Everywhere is closed.'

'East Street market is traditionally open on Easter Sunday morning. Drop the branch comrades, then go and buy a duck and bring it back for the guard to cook. Don't tell anyone else.'

T laughed when I closed the door. I knew not to gossip about Gerry's expensive duck.

Jack Gale from Leeds took the collection after a final, rallying speech from Gerry.

'Can I have the first £20 note or cheque? Yes, over there on the left … and two more up at the back.'

Gerry slipped off the platform to confer in the front row with Betty Hamilton, a mysterious French woman who was also a member of our fraternal organisation in France. She had black hair, elaborate make-up, heavy French elegance and lots of jewellery. I knew she had money, though how she came by it was unclear.

'We've reached £190. Any more £10 notes? This is magnificent, comrades, it will help to make the daily paper a reality. Let's go for the fivers.'

Gerry took the microphone.

'Comrade Hamilton has pledged to double it if we reach £300 in notes.'

'Can we make £300?' asked Jack. The stewards darted around the hall while Betty smiled, sphinx-like.

Of course we reached the target. Then the bowls were passed round for loose change.

As the launch date approached, we campaigned to sign up daily readers and establish delivery rounds.

'Will it be like the *Daily Worker*?' asked a Jamaican engineering union member.

'That's the Communist Party's paper, which follows Moscow's line and defends Stalin's atrocities and murders.'

'I thought you were communists?'

'Yes, but we're revolutionary communists. Trotsky said the revolution should be international. Stalin's theory was to build "Socialism in One Country".'

'Trotsky? Him who got an ice-pick in his head?'

'He was murdered because he opposed Stalin's betrayal of revolutions in every other country, which Moscow is still doing today.'

'They support the Cuban revolution, they trade with Cuba. They support workers in Jamaica …'

'They'll betray you in the end, like they did in Germany, when Hitler was campaigning for power.' I knew how to describe Stalinism's crimes but I foundered on more complex explanations about our 'conditional support' for Cuba, a country which inspired many West Indian workers.

'Jamaica is different from Germany,' he said. 'That was a long time ago … but you say you deliver me your paper? OK, I try it.'

Lez and Isla were teachers in my school.

'You and Isla are both Trotskyists,' Lez said. 'Can't you all join together and oppose the Stalinists more effectively?'

I didn't like being linked with Isla.

'She's in the Militant group which thinks we should join the Labour Party and campaign for revolutionary policies from within. But it doesn't work. We have to build an independent revolutionary leadership in the working class.'

'All you Trotskyist groups believe *you* are Trotsky's heirs,' he said. 'You, Militant, the International Socialists …'

'The International Socialists call the Soviet Union "state capitalism",' I said. 'But it's a "degenerated workers' state". We have to defend the gains of the Russian Revolution and at the same time fight the Stalinist bureaucracy's treachery.'

'Bloody complicated,' sighed Lez. 'I don't see much difference in your policies. But I'll buy your paper.'

The differences were so important that Gerry agreed to a public debate in Oxford against the International Socialists' leader, Tony Cliff, before an audience of workers from Oxford's giant car factories and a motley collection of students, trade unionists and members of both organisations. He took me, with Aileen and another comrade, to this rare event. Beside him on the speakers' table he displayed an erudite selection of books: Hegel, Marx, Plekhanov, Lenin, Trotsky.

In the back row a woman was marking a pile of school exercise books. She recognised me from a teachers' conference.

'Hullo,' she whispered. It was Tony Cliff's wife. 'I've come to support Tony, but I have all this marking to do.'

I was scandalised that she wasn't paying attention to this historic debate. I smiled weakly and tried to concentrate on the complex differences between Gerry and Tony Cliff.

The launch date for the daily paper was fixed for September 1969. Gerry began assembling the editorial board with *Newsletter* journalists at its core and asked me to attend a meeting of future staff. About 20 of us crammed awkwardly into the nearly completed editorial offices: my erstwhile Bristol comrades, Steve Hammond and Peter Read, both now journalists on provincial newspapers; League theoreticians Cliff Slaughter, Tom Kemp and Geoff Pilling; several unfamiliar comrades from Gerry's Friday evening entertainment-industry meetings and, to my surprise, Sheila, who was responsible for the Young Socialists. I felt tense excitement. Where did I fit in? Gerry began to speak.

'Conditions for the socialist revolution are developing. But the spontaneous consciousness of the working class is *bourgeois* consciousness. In *The German Ideology* Marx wrote: "The ideas of the ruling class are in every epoch the ruling ideas, i.e. the class which is the ruling material force of society is at the same time its ruling intellectual force." Marxists fight to develop the revolutionary theory that challenges capitalist ideology.'

He poured a glass of Perrier water.

'Lenin explained in his book *What is to be Done?* why an all-Russian newspaper was vital, to connect all the struggles of the class, to challenge "spontaneity" and to bring revolutionary consciousness into the working-class movement. Without revolutionary theory, he insisted, there can be no revolutionary movement. Our daily paper will be the vehicle' – he pronounced it 'vee-hickle', with emphasis on 'hick' – 'to take revolutionary theory into the working class.'

There was silent acquiescence. I felt everyone shared my excitement.

'The paper will cover international developments as well as the day-to-day struggles of workers in Britain. It will run theoretical and cultural articles. I can now tell you that the National Committee has decided to call the paper the *Workers Press*.'

The meeting stirred in approval. Practical arrangements had barely been mentioned. The meeting broke up and Gerry nodded to me as he and Aileen left: 'Sheila will talk to you.'

'I'm responsible for the paper's circulation,' she said a few days later. 'We need you to help with the postal dispatch every day after school, at half-past four.'

Gerry confirmed this.

'After the post you will work in the editorial office, filing the articles from each day's paper and doing the office cleaning, including the kitchen.'

'Every day?'

'You can do branch work at weekends. We don't want the overnight guards cleaning the editorial office.'

So my role would be doing the post, cleaning, and filing. Important work, yes, and I wouldn't have to give up my job, but …

'Have you ever actually used a broom?' asked T.

I laughed ruefully.

'Well, not much.'

'I'll show you how to use the liquid floor polish.'

Workers Press now dominated my life. Three early mornings a week I dropped bundles to other members on a 20-mile round trip in south-east London. The earlier I did it, the less traffic there was. I rushed into school through the back door, mercifully close to my form room. During morning break one or two colleagues in the staff room bought *Workers Press*. At lunchtime I dashed across the road to a café for a roast beef meal and headed to

▲ Brighton, 27th September 1969. Meeting to greet the daily *Workers Press*, l to r: Aileen Jennings, editor of the Young Socialists' paper *Keep Left*, Socialist Labour League secretary Gerry Healy, *Workers Press* editor Mike Banda and Cliff Slaughter, Central Committee

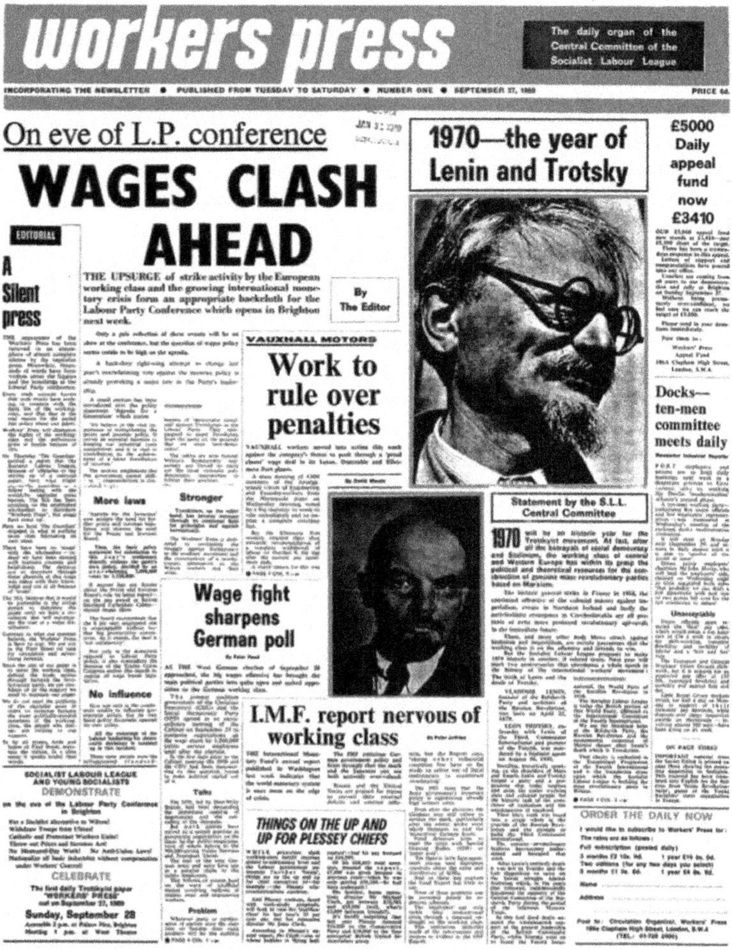

workers press

The daily organ of the Central Committee of the Socialist Labour League

INCORPORATING THE NEWSLETTER ● PUBLISHED FROM TUESDAY TO SATURDAY ● NUMBER ONE ● SEPTEMBER 27, 1969

PRICE 6d.

On eve of L.P. conference

WAGES CLASH AHEAD

By The Editor

EDITORIAL

A Silent press

More laws

Stronger

No influence

VAUXHALL MOTORS

Work to rule over penalties

Wage fight sharpens German poll

I.M.F. report nervous of working class

THINGS ON THE UP AND UP FOR PLESSEY CHIEFS

1970—the year of Lenin and Trotsky

Statement by the S.L.L. Central Committee

£5000 Daily appeal fund now £3410

Docks—ten-men committee meets daily

SOCIALIST LABOUR LEAGUE AND YOUNG SOCIALISTS

DEMONSTRATE

CELEBRATE

Sunday, September 28

ORDER THE DAILY NOW

▲ The first issue of *Workers Press*: 'The daily organ of the Central Committee of the Socialist Labour League', 27th September 1969

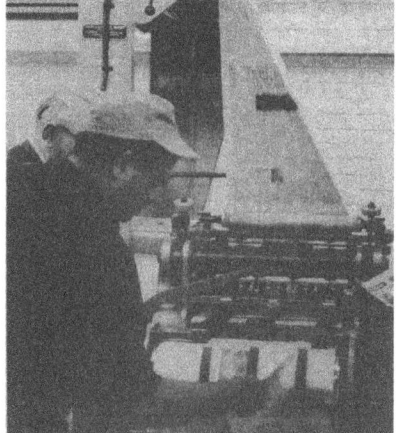

◄ The press rolls to print the very first issue of *Workers Press*

the huge building site next door for a quick sale. Straight after school, I bought a toasted cheese sandwich in the same café, did a quick sale outside Battersea Park station and drove to Clapham for the frenzied rush of the postal dispatch.

Our six-strong team fanned out the wrappers, poised for the sound of the web-offset press coming to life. I thrilled at the giant machine's power, tick-tick-ticking. Warehouse staff brought the folded papers across the yard to be wrapped at breakneck speed. We tossed the packets into big postal sacks and hurled them into the van waiting to rush to the sorting office by half-past five. After that the warehouse staff prepared branch bundles for drivers who collected their own parcels and dropped provincial consignments at the mainline stations.

Next I cleaned the kitchen: saucepans, plates, tidying, wiping the counters. I emptied the bins upstairs and swept and mopped the floors. Then I tore off the paper spewing noisily out of the Press Association and Reuters teleprinters and separated the items for the journalists to consider next morning. My final task was to snip the day's paper, paste the articles on to sheets of newsprint and file them in subject categories. A cup of tea and a Bounty bar helped.

On Saturday night D and I did a *Workers Press* sale in south-east London's crowded pubs.

'Socialist paper – fighting the Labour government's wage freeze. Only sixpence.' This was still the pre-decimalisation 'old money'.

The convenor of Deptford's United Glass factory wanted a daily delivery; a group of young workers in the Engineers' Club bought *Keep Left*. We bumped into uniformed Salvation Army members in Downham, eyed each other with polite hostility and worked out how to avoid meeting again as landlords wouldn't allow us in together. Alcohol fuelled the pub-goers' generosity, but we also had many political discussions and I enjoyed the repartee, a snapshot of working-class thinking.

Jamaican men in Catford were slamming dominoes noisily on to the table.

'Come on, have a drink,' one man pressed us.

'Thank you, we'll have Cokes,' said D, to my astonishment. The bubbles tickled as I sipped my drink quickly. They asked what work we did, interested in us rather than our politics.

'Maybe those men have never had a drink with a white woman. It's important to show that we're friendly,' she explained afterwards.

We had sold 80 papers by the end, boosted by keep-the-change donations, and were praised at the following week's London aggregate meeting. I enjoyed brief recognition as a star paper-seller.

Gerry took me beyond the warehouse, into the forbidden area where the typesetters and compositors worked.

'I want to show you something. I'm having big problems with T.'

The Linotype machines, like ungainly metallic organs with attached seats, were eerily silent. Gerry pointed contemptuously at a shallow white cupboard along the wall. He slid the slanting bar upwards and the doors concertinaed open to reveal the electricity mains switch and meter.

'I wanted everything in here to be nice, professional. Then T makes this ugly contraption. I have continual conflict with him. He resists being trained as a revolutionary.'

I didn't understand how this unglamorous cupboard was non-revolutionary, but I knew Gerry must be right.

My husband, T

My branch agreed I could have a week's holiday before school started. To my disappointment, Gerry couldn't spare T from the printshop. I went alone to his father's farm in Sussex, but it was boring without him.

After a few days I rang the Centre in case some important working-class struggle had broken out. Sheila was chilly.

'Why are you ringing?'

'Just to check in case you needed me.'

'I don't know why you're staying with those reactionary people.'

I felt affronted.

'I can come back immediately –'

'No, finish your holiday,' she said coldly. 'Be back for the Saturday sales.'

I felt angry and resentful. Where else could I have gone? To my own distant relatives, whom I hardly knew and who were possibly more 'reactionary' than T's father? She knew I had no money to go anywhere else as every spare penny went into League funds. I decided not to tell T but I never forgave Sheila for this icy conversation.

15th August 1971: President Nixon announced that the Federal Reserve Bank would no longer convert dollars to gold at the fixed rate of $35 an ounce. After an emergency meeting of the League's National Committee D reported back to our branch on this shock development.

'The gold exchange and the Bretton Woods Agreement have underpinned the world economy since the end of the second world war, providing an illusion of stability. Nixon's decision means the post-war boom is now over. Capitalism's economic crisis will create revolutionary upheavals all over the world.'

'In Britain as well?' asked one member.

'Yes. The conditions of our political work here have been transformed. We are now entering a pre-revolutionary period.'

'When will revolutionary conditions develop?' someone else asked.

'It could be years or it could be very rapid. We don't know, but we have to prepare. Clare, what do you think?'

Both my father and grandfather had been gold miners. I felt I knew about gold.

'Gold contains value, unlike paper money. The dollar is now just paper and cannot underpin the world economy. It's contradictory. They have to find another kind of stability.'

'No, Clare,' said D. 'It's not "contradictory". This is capitalism's final crisis. We can't think of "stability" any more. We have to prepare for the working class to take power.'

'Yes, yes, I know that.'

'But you said it was "contradictory".'

She reported my statement to Mike Banda.

'You're wrong to think it's "contradictory",' he told me. 'The foundation of the world economy has been destroyed.'

Oh dear. Then Gerry called me into his office.

'There is nothing "contradictory", comrade. This really is the beginning of a pre-revolutionary situation.'

A week later, a London aggregate meeting was called to explain the importance of Nixon's decision. The main speaker was Geoff Pilling, the League's economics expert.

'Lenin's characterisation of imperialism as the highest, or final, stage of capitalism is playing out in practice,' he said.

At the front was Robin, who was writing a book about Stalinism in Britain. Gerry took the microphone.

'These developments place responsibilities on the revolutionary cadre. Comrade Robin, you wrap everything in fancy words. Your brain has been damaged by the universities.'

Robin said something about the revolutionary role of the working class.

'Nice words, comrade. To you that's all it is: words, not the struggle, not the practice. You're just a hippy, comrade. You always carry half-a-dozen books around, they're your beads and baubles.'

I suppressed a smile. The image seemed appropriate.

'Where is Comrade T?' Gerry asked.

After some shuffling T reached the front.

'You, too. Your head has been filled with petty-bourgeois ideas from the universities.' Universities were always plural.

T stood at the microphone, tall and thin, in jeans and a navy jacket. Gerry poured a glass of Perrier water and looked up at him expectantly.

'The crisis of capitalism is becoming clearer every day –'

'Fucking words,' interrupted Gerry. 'Comrade, why do you resist revolutionary cadre training?'

T took a breath. He looked strained.

'I have to struggle against the idealist, petty-bourgeois theory I learned in the Communist Party … idealist philosophy will betray the revolution if it's not superseded …'

I looked at him anxiously, willing him to make the development required.

'We *try* to explain to you, we *show* you how to change your practice.' Gerry spoke quietly, tapping the table in emphasis. 'But you *insist* on continuing with these alien conceptions. Isn't it true that we have conflicts with you every single day in the printshop?'

T took another breath.

'I need to tackle these theoretical questions …'

'Sit down, comrade.' Gerry dismissed him with a wave of his hand.

I didn't know what to say when we reached home and T didn't want to talk. We drank tea in silence. I lay close to him in bed. What could he be doing wrong in the printshop? I didn't know.

Almost every time I saw Gerry he described a new row with T.

'He just can't do it right. Sometimes it seems hopeless.'

These criticisms were beginning to affect my relationship with T. I couldn't grasp how he was failing, but I accepted Gerry's assessment. Meanwhile I was becoming more and more immersed in political work; I felt I was progressing, but T was clearly not making the grade.

Late one evening he and I were in the Centre with Larry from the printshop. The overnight guard was sweeping the office. Gerry and Aileen arrived; their meeting must have gone badly because Gerry seemed irritated. He looked round at us.

'Did you get that quote from Linotype?' he asked T.

'The salesman didn't come back to me.'

Gerry looked exasperated. He breathed out heavily and turned to the guard, a comrade who stayed up all night and went sleepless to work next morning.

'Comrade, perhaps you could go and sweep upstairs.'

Larry turned to leave.

'Hold on, comrade,' Gerry said quietly. Aileen stood in the background, expressionless, waiting to drive Gerry home. I stood near the phone. Gerry was in front of me, facing T on the other side of the counter, near the door.

'I've been asking you for three days to work on this quote. How can we plan for the project when you can't even assemble the information?'

'I have most of it worked out –'

'Most isn't good enough. Why do you give me so much trouble with every little detail? I can't rely on you to do a single thing properly.' Gerry was talking quietly in an aggrieved tone. 'Why?'

T didn't say anything.

'I've suggested reading to help you. I've tried to explain, but you just can't make the development. We've created a revolutionary printshop and now you're endangering it.'

The high-street traffic rumbled ceaselessly outside; in the office there was a taut silence. T looked very tense. Larry stood behind him, neutral but alert; Aileen looked weary. I watched, in utter confusion. I sensed that Gerry wanted us as an audience.

'You're just a petty-bourgeois.' His voice was louder and his tone sneering. He walked round to the other side of the counter and looked up into T's face. 'You just can't make it, can you?' he taunted, and punched T lightly on his left cheek. 'You can't, can you?' He punched the right cheek, then his left, again.

I was horrified. Gerry had stopped Larry leaving to ensure he was safe to provoke T to the utmost. But T held his nerve and remained still. After a long minute Gerry stepped away.

'Aileen, take me home. I'm tired of all this shit.'

▲ Healy's family home at 77 Sternhold Avenue, Streatham, until he moved to Clapham

T and I crossed the road without a word. I was in utter turmoil and I supposed he was too. It had really upset me to see Gerry provoke him. He was so much more politically capable than I was, but what was he doing so wrong that it drove Gerry to treat him like that? What was he 'resisting'?

My loyalties were being tested to breaking point. Gerry embodied all the League's achievements. His incisive political analysis convinced comrades; he had marshalled resources; his brilliant initiatives inspired a whole movement. Now he said that T was *endangering* the printshop ...

I faced a bitter dilemma, but my perpetual exhaustion enabled me to fall asleep immediately. T may not have been so lucky.

Two days later Gerry called me into his glass-partitioned space in the *Workers Press* office.

'Sit down, comrade. I've sacked T.' He waited for my reaction.

'When ...'

'This morning. I suggested he go straight to the Labour Exchange. He won't have difficulty finding another job.'

I was shocked and upset that it had come to this. Gerry spoke gently.

'I had to do it. In this political situation we can't endanger our work with comrades who are unable to make the change.'

The word 'endanger' again. I nodded, but I wanted to cry. I went downstairs in a confused jumble of emotions.

I was in the bathroom putting spiky rollers in my wet hair when T arrived home. I turned to look at him and was surprised to see that he was smiling.

'I've got a job as a driver.'

'Where?'

'At Sainsbury's Stamford Street depot, near Blackfriars Bridge. I start tomorrow, driving a three-ton truck, delivering to the different branches.'

I stared at him.

'I don't know how you manage to sleep with those painful spikes in your hair.' I heard him whistling as he put the kettle on. 'I suppose Gerry told you,' he called out from the kitchen.

'Yes, he did.' I put in the last roller, covered everything with a big hairnet and came out of the bathroom. I watched him, trying to assess how he felt. 'Gerry also told me to find someone else to cover my work in the *Workers Press* office on three evenings a week so I can campaign for the Right to Work marches.'

'I'll bet you're pleased.'

A strange new equilibrium developed between T and me. He told me about his working day.

'You know about the pepper shortage?'

'Of course. Every single shop's run out.'

'Well, Sainsbury's still has supplies. The drivers were nicking pepper, trying to fill small paper bags from the big hemp bags, sneezing all over the place. The supervisor was becoming suspicious.'

We laughed, but I felt uncertain. We were drifting apart. I was losing T. The joy had gone out of our marriage and I felt we were in different places politically.

One night, I summoned the courage to make the break. I waited until we were in bed, with the light off, because I couldn't look him in the eye.

'I think we should separate.'

He let out a long, slow breath.

'OK. I was expecting this. I'll move out as soon as I can find somewhere else.'

I lay listening to the all-night, non-stop traffic. *He knows our relationship is over. He's accepted without argument.* I felt determined, but also very sad.

'I've told T to go,' I said to Gerry at the first opportunity. He seemed pleased.

'You're working very hard to become a revolutionary. I'll help you, comrade.'

A few days later T told me he had found a room nearby.

'I don't want to take much. You keep the stuff in the flat, and the car.'

'That's very generous,' I said, but I didn't dare look at him in case I cried. I helped him take his clothes and books to the dreary, furnished room – old fashioned, grubby, constrained. *This is necessary, inevitable. I have to accept it.*

Late that night, after my branch work, I joined the team of League members who worked into the early hours to wrap 200,000 copies of a quarterly trade union journal after the printers had gone home. Sheila came over to me.

'How are you?' she asked kindly.

'I just feel like crying all the time.' I looked down at the wrappers, tears welling up in my eyes.

'Look, just go home. I'll tell Larry you're not staying.'

About a year later T asked me to meet him for breakfast at the café in Stonhouse Street, very close to our – *my* – flat. I was a bit surprised, but went as arranged.

'What's this about?'

'It's sort of to say goodbye. I'm moving to another flat in north London.'

I felt sad, guilty, awkward, regretful. What could I say? I ate my beans on toast, drank my tea, made small talk. I asked him to greet his father. I kissed him on the cheek and left, feeling terrible.

1972 the Right to Work Marches

Youth unemployment was soaring and the League decided the Young Socialists should organise 'Right to Work' marches. I worked with fellow League member Tony O'Brien, an energetic young carpenter and shop steward on his building site, to recruit young people through *Keep Left* sales around the estates and high streets.

We organised football and cricket, which the West Indian boys were particularly enthusiastic about. I borrowed a magnificent set of cricket gear from my school: bats, wickets, knee pads, gloves and ball. Thirty excited players turned up at Ruskin Park, selected a suitable, grassy area and arranged everything. Afterwards, they packed up the equipment with astonishing reverence, begging to play every week.

'Sorry, I can't borrow the kit very often,' I laughed.

Two unemployed Young Socialists, Darren and Mick, came with me to Deptford Engineer's Club. I enquired about the union branch meeting.

'It starts at eight. You'll find the committee members upstairs.'

Three men sitting at a table with files, a money box and pints of beer agreed we could speak for five minutes. We waited outside to be invited in.

'Come to the front, Sister,' said the chairman. About 20 men were looking at us, smoking, sipping beer. Darren and Mick handed them leaflets. I must do this right, I thought.

'Youth unemployment has reached an all-time high. In January unemployed youth will walk to London on our Right to Work Marches from areas of high unemployment, like Glasgow, Swansea, Liverpool, Newcastle and Deal. Not sorrowful, like the Jarrow marches of the 1930s. They will be *demanding* the right to work. We're asking your branch to make a donation to the campaign.'

'It's a scandal that school leavers can't get a job,' said the chairman. 'Any questions?'

'Will they walk all they way?'

'Yes. A support team will transport their equipment and clothes. Trade union branches along the route are already offering food and accommodation.'

'Brother Thompson, is the branch in a position to make a donation?' The chairman turned to the man beside the money box.

'Yes, Brother. We have funds.'

'I propose we donate £30,' said the man sitting on his right.

'Seconded,' said a voice from the floor.

'All those in favour?' Every hand went up.

'Thank you Sister and Brothers. Wait outside and Brother Thompson will bring you a cheque in a few minutes.'

We thanked the meeting and left.

'So much money!' whispered Darren. Mick did a silent dance of delight.

Later that night League members met at Robert's house to centralise the week's branch money, which I would to take to the Centre.

'Deptford Engineers gave £30 for the march,' I said proudly.

'I have £50 from my draughtsmen's branch,' said Robert, who was a new member. 'And here is what my wife, Jenny, collected.' He pointed to a cardboard box holding four enormous cloth bags, each heavy with coins. Everyone fell silent. Jenny wasn't even a member. She suddenly appeared with a tray of teacups.

'Jenny, this is amazing. Where does it come from?' asked D.

'There's a big building site in the City, next to my work. I gave leaflets to the shop steward.' She smiled. 'He agreed to do a collection round the site on payday.'

I stared at the shy young woman whom I had scarcely noticed before.

▲ Just before the Glasgow Right to Work March set off, an official miners' strike began and continued to the end of February

'I had to bring the money home over four nights because it was so heavy. It's several hundred pounds.'

'Look at how much we've raised in one week,' I said to D as we drove home.

'Working-class anger about youth unemployment runs very deep. Our campaign is at exactly the right time.'

As the start of the Glasgow march approached, 280,000 miners began a national strike for a wage increase. Their pay was barely higher than mine as a new teacher, for a very dangerous job. Our Right to Work campaign suddenly seemed central to the fight for working-class power.

I called into the Centre early on Thursday morning. Gerry had told me to see Sheila, the march's central organiser.

'We need you to drive one of the support minibuses on the Glasgow march, for the full six weeks,' she said. 'I'm afraid you'll have to lose your job. You'll leave on Saturday.'

I was thrilled. The march was much more important to me than my job. I would have to get a doctor's sick note. My head was spinning and I arrived at school late to find a supply teacher taking my class. Puzzled, I sent him away. Two minutes later he was back, with the head of science.

'Clare,' she said quietly, between clenched teeth. 'You're taking my class to the Natural History Museum.' It had completely slipped my mind.

I had to borrow the bus fare from one of the girls and spent the morning thinking how to leave my job. I had sixth-form chemistry exam papers to mark, which I couldn't dump on my colleagues. I finished marking them in a free period just before Friday lunch. I gobbled roast beef in my usual café, worrying how to repay the bus fare. When I saw one of the girl's friends passing I thrust the money into her hand before jumping on a bus. I rang the school from Battersea Park station.

'I'm not coming back this afternoon. I can't take any more.' I slammed down the receiver and ran for the train to the minibus hire depot. I was shaking.

Later that afternoon I told the doctor I was very depressed. He gave me a sick note and told me to come back in two weeks. I didn't go back, because by then I was somewhere south of the Scottish border.

Rowdy, excited marchers kitted up in weather-proof army-surplus coats, hats, capes and boots were gathered in a Glasgow hall when Sheila and I arrived in a minibus packed with kitchen equipment, sleeping bags and other paraphernalia. She suddenly realised we had left the camp beds behind. I had already driven for seven hours, but now had to go back to the half-way point to meet another driver bringing the beds from London. I arrived back in Glasgow shortly before midnight, exhausted and resentful. Sheila looked at me.

'Oh, stop feeling sorry for yourself. Go to sleep if you're tired.'

Huh, I thought. *You* shouldn't have forgotten the beds.

▼ The Glasgow Right to Work March reaches the English border

▲ A welcome meal from Ayrshire miners

▲ Hatless and with banner dipped, the Swansea to London marchers pay their respects as they pass Pantglas School, site of Aberfan's 1966 disaster

▲ The trial of Charles I, a scene from the play, *The English Revolution*, performed during each leg of the march and at the Empire Pool

▼ Nearly 2,000 Bristol Rolls Royce workers in their lunch break greet the Welsh marchers

The march started on Sunday. For six weeks I drove ahead each day to confirm the overnight accommodation and to campaign for the evening public meeting. My team consisted of John Simmance, the Young Socialists' national committee member, and two marchers in thick winter gear. I wore thick jumpers, a brown suede-effect coat whose underarm seams were coming apart, mock-velvet trousers and a long orange scarf. We all had Right to Work stickers plastered on our sleeves.

Carlisle, south of the Scottish border, was totally hostile to the march and three days before arrival we still hadn't identified accommodation. We visited every single hall.

'Oh, you're Vanessa Redgrave's communists, are you?' said a church warden. 'No, you can't stay here.'

Along with other actors, Vanessa had recently joined the League, attracting press attention. We were shown the witch-hunting lead article in the local paper about 'Red Vanessa' coming to Carlisle with a group of rabble-rousing actors and hooligans from Glasgow's roughest estates. An article alongside vilified the striking miners.

We met hostility everywhere. It was bitterly cold. We ate our sandwiches huddled in the minibus, furious, wondering what to do.

'Let's try the council trade unions,' said John.

'Tenants' halls? We don't have any,' said the shop steward at the Town Hall, a rotund man who seemed irritated at being disturbed. 'Best thing is not to come to Carlisle.'

'Management arse-licker,' muttered John on the way out.

Disconsolate, we went on the high street with *Workers Press* and *Keep Left* but sold hardly any papers, let alone tickets for Sunday's rally and play. One worker stopped to talk.

'Carlisle's Labour Party is very right wing, totally corrupt. You won't get anywhere.'

We rejoined the marchers at that night's accommodation in the trade union club attached to a factory that made the local speciality, Scotch pies, which we devoured with mashed potatoes and baked beans. The public meeting was already underway, addressed by march leader John Barrie, a local trade unionist and Mike Banda, from the League's National Committee. At the end the marchers sang the rousing song that actor-singer Ram John Holder had specially written and recorded for the march. It had a compelling beat and they sang with conviction:

> We demand the right to work, we demand it!
> We demand the right to live, which this system cannot give,
> So we'll fight the system now, take the power, we know how,
> And we want it!

Next day we continued searching for accommodation in Carlisle, meeting refusal everywhere. We decided to visit miners picketing a power station. Our minibus was covered with posters saying 'YOUNG SOCIALISTS RIGHT TO WORK MARCH' and 'WE DEMAND THE RIGHT TO WORK!' I parked opposite the gates where a group of men were huddled round a brazier. As we approached they walked towards us, holding out their hands.

'We know who you are.'

We stood round the brazier, talking. We're in the front line of revolutionary struggle, I thought. Bloody Carlisle isn't going to stop us.

We eventually found a hall, ten miles outside the city. As we drove back to rejoin the marchers the earlier snow had stopped, but the road was dark. The two marchers dozed off in the warmth while John and I mulled things over. Suddenly he nudged me.

'Wake up. Do you want to kill us?'

'Oh God,' I said, wetting my eyelids with spit. 'Have we any sweets left?'

A problem had arisen. Two of the younger girls were misbehaving at every opportunity, teasing the boys, shrieking, swearing, singing football songs and giggling incessantly. The other marchers, boys and girls from the same desolate estates surrounding Glasgow, were exasperated. After the girls got drunk and disrupted the public meeting, the marchers voted unanimously to exclude them. That night the cook and Mike Banda drove them home to Glasgow in the kitchen van.

The march arrived in Carlisle next day, escorted front and back by police cars with flashing blue lights. To the marchers' horror, the two girls were waiting at a junction after hitch-hiking all the way from Glasgow.

Sheila had arrived from London and spoke to the police.

'These girls are not part of the march. They were driven back to Glasgow last night and are no longer our responsibility.'

'You'll have to come with us while we check. They're under-age.'

After ferrying the 50 marchers to the distant hall, I joined Sheila at the police station. At one in the morning, it was confirmed that a Glasgow police car had seen the girls being dropped home the night before.

'OK. We'll drive them back to Glasgow in relay with other police stations,' the officer told us. There was violent swearing from the adjacent room when the girls heard the news.

Sunday was a rest day before the evening's political rally in the town hall, which had been pre-booked and paid for, so the authorities couldn't back out. Coachloads were coming from Glasgow and we campaigned on council estates to sell tickets locally. A cast of actors had travelled overnight from London to perform a play, *The English Revolution*, written specially for the march by playwrights John Arden, Tom Kempinski and Roger Smith. The marchers watched with rapt attention till it ended with the actors marching on the spot in army-surplus capes and hats, singing the Right to Work song. The marchers leapt to their feet and joined in as the audience applauded enthusiastically.

Next morning I handed the minibus keys to a replacement driver, bade farewell to the marchers and took a train to Swansea for the start of the Welsh march. I taught the song to the lads from Welsh coalmining communities, among them a boy with a suitcase of frilled shirts and a rich voice straight out of a Welsh chapel, two scruffy-haired 'greasers' in leather jackets, chains and jewellery, and resilient Megan from Pontypridd whose quick wit matched the boys'.

The poverty of the pit villages shocked me and the inferior quality of the roads brought home Wales's underdevelopment. Our route wound into the valleys through Merthyr Tydfil and Aberfan, site of the disaster four years previously when over 100 children had died. A marcher who had volunteered at the time wept at the memory.

Coal was running out because of the miners' strike. The government had declared a State of Emergency and there were rolling power cuts. I drove back with my campaign team to our overnight stop in Maerdy, along perilously winding roads over the mountains. Not a single light was visible anywhere, the sky was overcast and we faced total, impenetrable blackness beyond our headlights. Then a glimmer of light appeared from Maerdy's magnificent Miners' Welfare. The bar had battery-powered lights and a portable gas heater. We heard that the boys had enjoyed hot water luxury in the pit showers owned by the miners' union; they were to sleep in the cosy bar.

'You two girls will sleep in a dressing room,' said the miner who led Megan and me ceremoniously upstairs. The gilded decoration of the cavernous opera house glinted in his torchlight. We washed as best we could with a bowl of hot water and the light of a torch in the freezing room.

The Bristol Siddeley aircraft factory, now owned by Rolls Royce, ran along the left side of the road. Hundreds, no, thousands of men and women were standing outside, wearing the protective brown coats of factory workers, some with overcoats on top.

I stopped my poster-festooned minibus.

Two agitated shop stewards rushed over.

'Where are the marchers?'

'About 20 minutes away,' I looked beyond them at the endless stretch of people stamping their feet and chatting in the winter sun.

'Quick – ferry them in, or everyone will go back inside.'

I drove back to the marchers striding purposefully behind the banner.

'The whole factory is waiting outside for you. Get in, I'll take you in groups.'

'We can't do that!'

'We're marching all the way to London.' The Welsh voices were emphatic.

'They've come out in their lunch hour. Just fucking get in!'

I dropped the first group near the factory where they huddled shamefaced until I brought the rest and then marched past the applauding crowd with arms raised in clenched fists.

'Well done, lads!'

'Show the Tory bastards!'

'We're right behind you!'

This was our best day yet. I drove ahead to wait for my campaign team, glancing at the canteen building of my student holiday job, marvelling at how much had happened in the intervening five years.

When a 17-year-old marcher collapsed, the hospital diagnosed long-term malnutrition. I couldn't believe this was possible in 1970s Britain. From then on he became a capable member of my campaign team.

I was with the marchers 24 hours a day and developed a close relationship with them despite being 27, middle-class, Rhodesian.

'There's a war in Rhodesia,' said Rhys. 'Why's that?'

'Well, some whites want to keep it white-ruled, but most of the people are black.'

▲ London demonstration in early 1972. The white minority Rhodesian government's declaration of independence from Britain led to a long civil war.

'Are you worried about your family?'
'Actually, they're now back in South Africa, where I was born.'
'Ah, so that's better.'
'It's worse in some ways. The apartheid regime keeps white and black people completely apart.' I described the black ghetto townships, perpetual arrests, the 90-day detention law, 'suicides' from the eighth floor of police headquarters. 'It's much worse than the Tories here…'
'Why don't they fight back?'
'But they do.'
'So are you going back to fight?'
I was startled.
'Uhm … you see, apartheid is part of the capitalist system. The Tories, the capitalists in Britain, they support South Africa. The best way I can fight apartheid is by fighting to overthrow capitalism here.'

I suddenly felt very insecure. Rhys had found my weakness. I was still a privileged white South African. Two of my cousins were fighting apartheid in dangerous situations and one had been arrested. But I was safely here in England. South Africa was my political Achilles heel. I had tried to soften my accent, to learn working-class turns of phrase, I 'effed and blinded' when appropriate. But I could never forget Gerry's epithet: 'White South African shit'.

'Well, have you got a boyfriend then, Clare?' Rhys persevered.

'No, I'm going through a divorce.'

'You're not! You're too warm to get divorced.'

'No, it's true.' I tried to sound dismissive but I felt heartache. For the second time Rhys had struck a vulnerable point in the facade I presented to the world. My marriage had ended; southern African politics had ripped me away from the two countries I loved; I felt deracinated, I still didn't belong here.

Yet the marchers had taken me as they found me; we had developed mutual respect. Maybe I didn't need to be ashamed of my South African origins.

The march continued along a pre-planned route, facing hostility in Chippenham akin to Carlisle but a warm welcome in Swindon. All my efforts were directed at overcoming problems and keeping the march on the road and I couldn't absorb the importance of *Workers Press* reports on the miners' flying picket at Saltley Coke depot or Northern Ireland's Derry massacre by the British Army that became known as 'Bloody Sunday'.

We assembled in the performers' area of Wembley's Empire Pool stadium. Each contingent called out greetings to the others, excited and nervous at the same time. The wait was unbearable. Sheila stood nearby, pale and tense. Gerry strolled over.

'You think they're not coming?' he teased, with a big grin on his face.

I peeped into the arena and saw a few scattered figures in the vast expanse of tiered seats. Oh God, I thought. This time we've blown it. I rejoined the Welsh contingent, saying nothing.

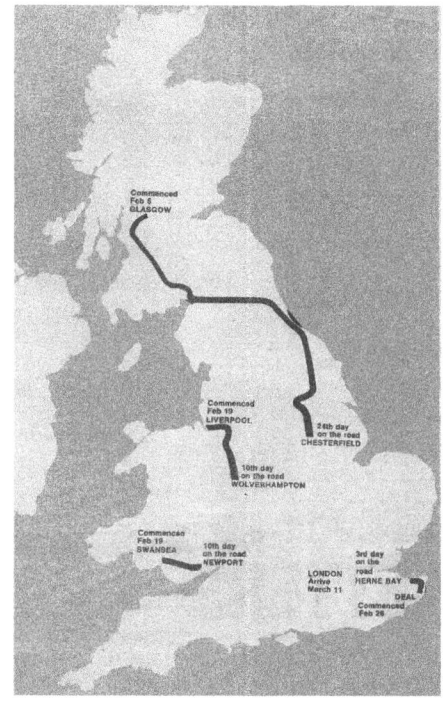

▶ By the end of February all five Right to Work marches were on their way to London

▲ Joyous arrival at the Empire Pool, Wembley

But when we marched in, to the accompaniment of Ram John Holder, over 8,000 were standing in their seats applauding.

Gerry addressed the marchers.

'By your marches you have roused decisive sections of the working class to action. You have dealt a mighty blow to the bans and proscriptions of the Tory government. You will occupy a place of honour for all time in our great movement.'

I came of age politically during the Right to Work marches.

Dagenham and the docks

A waiting letter terminated my employment with the Wandsworth Division of the Inner London Education Authority because of my unexplained absence. I could no longer work in inner London but I found a temporary-terminal job in a school in South Norwood.

My new League branch, Dagenham, was miles away to the east and included the Royal Docks, the huge Ford factories and vast housing estates with almost entirely white working-class families steeped in East End tradition. I set about establishing a Young Socialists' branch through meetings, sales on the high street and the estates, football and a coach trip to Southend. A disco was scheduled in Hornchurch. When I called to collect the amateur sound system the teenage owner was out.

▲ Scarborough 1972: John Simmance opens the lively Young Socialists' annual conference.

▼ The large attendance and the youth on London's May Day march reflected the success of the Right to Work campaign in mobilising young people

'Try his friend across the road,' said his apologetic mother.

The friend was easily persuaded by the promise of payment. Halfway through the reasonably successful disco, I spoke from the stage about the Tory government's attacks on the working class, inviting everyone to join the Young Socialists. Later, the young disc jockey spoke into his microphone.

'The way to solve your problems lies in Jesus Christ. Believe in him and you will be saved.'

I was furious.

'I'm afraid we can't pay you anything,' I said at the end. 'We've only taken £40, which we need to pay for the hall.'

Incredulous, he looked at my two stewards, a karate-black-belt Ford worker and a six-foot body-builder. He decided not to argue.

The Young Socialists' annual Summer Camp was in Essex in late July, attended by nearly a thousand Young Socialists, League members and trade unionists. I loved this fortnight under canvas. Conical tents were laid out in tidy rows in a large field bordered with hedgerows. On one side were two large marquees for lectures and meals and several smaller ones for the kitchen, stores and office. Beyond was a large recreation area. On the outskirts were portable toilets and the wash tent, created by dividing a marquee in two for male and female ablutions. I was responsible for the women's section, rising early to light the boiler, keep it topped up and ensure everything flowed smoothly. A woman comrade went round the campsite giving three mallet blows to the tent pegs with her unwelcome cry: 'Time to get up in here'.

Families had their own tents. There was no hanky-panky in the other tents – the day's tight timetable and vigilance of League members ensured that – and there were certainly no drugs because, as we emphasised to new recruits, that would open the movement to police provocation.

I found the days pleasurably long, filled with a variety of activities: lectures, duty rotas, games or relaxation and evening entertainments. In a talent show T sang Spanish Civil War songs, a Judo black-belt comrade from Durham broke bricks with his head, and Jamaican Ron gave a mournful rendition of 'The Green, Green Grass of Home'.

We were a young movement. Gerry, at 58, was probably the oldest on site and had his own two-roomed tent, set aside from the main camp. A hush fell in the main marquee as he lectured on dialectical materialism. Others lectured on capitalism's economic crisis, Trotsky's bitter struggle against Stalin and the betrayal in Germany by the Communist and Social Democrat Parties, whose leaders refused to unite against Hitler.

Just after the camp started five London dockers were suddenly arrested for 'secondary picketing', recently made illegal. Ports around the country immediately went on strike, widespread rolling strikes began in other industries and the Trades Union Congress called a one-day general strike. The campsite was agog with excitement. Surely this was the beginning of the revolution? We should close the camp and march on Pentonville Prison.

No, said our political leaders. The spontaneous movement of the working class will not achieve revolution. Without revolutionary theory, which cannot develop in workers' day-to-day struggle for survival, the mass movement is doomed to fail. A Marxist understanding of how capitalism works needs to be brought into the working class from outside and this is what the camp is trying to do.

I accepted the decision but I was disappointed – and envious of the three comrades who were sent to London to cover the mass demonstrations.

Next evening the actors at the camp performed a play in which a miner came home from the pit, covered in black coal dust. We watched in silence as his wife washed him clean. A policeman character waited outside the marquee, ready to burst on stage.

Next morning the *Daily Telegraph* published an aerial photo of the camp 'laid out in military formation' with a picture of a 'uniformed guard' in our camp of 'Trotskyists planning to overthrow the government'. In the hysteria surrounding the dock strike we had become a target for a press witch-hunt. We tightened security round the site's perimeter to keep out prowling journalists. We laughed at the picture of the actor 'guards' but everyone suddenly understood the camp's importance.

'The state is watching our every move,' Gerry told the morning lecture.

The five jailed dockers were released but the dock strike continued over redundancies and casual labour in container firms; the government again declared a State of Emergency. Another teacher and I were directed to cover the London picket lines with *Workers Press* during the remaining summer holiday. Early each morning we started at the West India Docks and went on to Chobham Farm container depot and then the Royal Docks, discussing with the strikers. After the lunchtime picket change we went round again, carrying

▲ July 1972: Jailed docker Con Clancy carried shoulder-high after his release from Pentonville Prison. I saw him regularly at the Chobham Farm picket afterwards

our papers in proper shoulder bags, *never* in plastic bags. We dressed smartly, unlike the scruffy 'revisionists' from other self-styled Trotskyists organisations.

After the strike ended we heard that the National Front planned a march against immigration, invoking Enoch Powell's infamous 'rivers of blood' speech. Traditional East End militancy also had a reactionary side and we worried that dockers would support the march. At lunchtime in a canteen inside the West India Docks, six burly dockers came over to me and started shouting, attracting everyone's attention.

'Why are you communists here? You should be thrown out.'

'Take your n****r-loving filth somewhere else.'

'Who let you in? This is docks property.'

'Throw them out.'

I stood still, frightened, hoping for protection from other dockers who knew *Workers Press* had supported the strike. After a few minutes the watching dockers turned away or shrugged. The thugs left the canteen and the tense moment was over.

A few days later *Workers Press* printed a hard-hitting, double-page interview with a West India Docks shop steward about the National Front, its political ancestry and its links with fascism. We sold lots of copies. Dockers' participation on the National Front march was negligible.

In late summer I found another temporary-terminal job at a Croydon grammar school, even further from my branch in Dagenham.

'The incoming Head of Science won't arrive until January,' said the Principal. 'You will teach A-level physics and his lower classes.'

'But I have no physics in my degree. I only studied it to A-level.'

'At this stage I want *any* science teacher.'

This was an efficient school, pleasant to work in. At lunchtime and in every free period I studied the physics for my two A-level classes.

On an October afternoon Gerry called me into his office.

'Well, comrade, we want you to work with Comrade Dot Gibson in the finance office.'

I held my breath. I really wanted this.

'Start as soon as possible.'

I gave one month's notice and abandoned my sixth-formers in the middle of November.

Work at the Centre

In December 1973 I began work at the Centre in the third-floor finance office with Dot and Linda, long-standing League members in their 30s, both with families. Sheila and D worked downstairs in the front office with the Young Socialists' national secretary.

One morning there was an enormous row. D had taken Gerry's suit to the dry cleaners without emptying the pockets.

'All my papers! Everything!' He was waving his arms, yelling. 'My papers!'

He went on and on. I was puzzled. D was also the London area secretary, she led international delegations to France and Germany, she was a key member of the leadership. Why should she take Gerry's suit to the dry cleaners? Why hadn't he emptied the pockets himself? Eventually he flounced out of the building.

'See if you can get the suit back,' suggested Sheila.

D went out, and didn't come back. By lunchtime it was clear that she had 'taken off', as we called it when comrades disappeared because of political difficulties. Gerry reacted contemptuously.

'She doesn't want to be trained.'

Sheila phoned D's brother who suggested she would head to her sister's in France. Dot rushed to Victoria Station and persuaded her to come back.

I continued my branch work in Dagenham, driving home exhausted each night.

During a Saturday lunch-time *Workers Press* sale on Heathway, near the Ford factory, branch member Keith and I went into a pub where the National Front was rumoured to meet. Five lads in their late teens followed us out and started punching Keith, knocking his papers to the ground. He fought back, warding off blows from all sides.

'You fucking bastards', I cried, whacking the youths ineffectually with my shoulder bag. Keith gave them more trouble than they had anticipated and they headed back inside.

'Cowards! Five of you against one!'

'Two!' shouted a loud voice. A man, who looked like a boxer, had run across Heathway. We thanked him, Keith dusted himself off and we went on our way.

We reported the incident to Mike Banda.

'I've heard that a campaign in west London successfully drove out fascists by picketing the pub where they met. Should we do the same in Dagenham?' I asked.

Mike saw things differently.

'That would only draw attention to their existence. It's best to build the League and Young Socialists steadily in the area. That's how we'll defeat them.'

I was bitterly disappointed. Mike's approach felt cowardly and shameful. Half a mile away was the huge Ford factory, the biggest in the country, with 23,000 workers, all in trade unions. Other factories nearby were also all unionised; this was a strong working-class area. Surely we could mount a campaign through the trades council and door-to-door canvassing?

But we had to accept Mike's ruling. We never went in the pub again.

Our leadership analysed capitalism's worldwide crisis and the revolutionary situation developing in Britain. A *league* was no longer considered an adequate form of political organisation. We needed a *party* with broader membership. A massive recruitment drive now dominated all our work. I wasn't clear how a 'party' would function. Wouldn't it dilute revolutionary commitment? The League was a cadre organisation which responded in a disciplined way to the demands of the political situation. How would it function with a mass membership?

▲ 1978: Young workers from Ford's Dagenham plant

Widespread hatred of the Tory government helped us recruit large numbers: an extended East Ham family; Sikh ticket collector Mr Singh, who was later nearly beaten to death at Plaistow station; Anwar Karim, who had led airport workers during the 1971 Bengali uprising. Ford worker Richard from Bristol, tall, blonde, always tidy in his double-breasted black raincoat, brought welcome energy into our branch.

'All I want is to work in a big factory. And there's room in my bed for you,' he told me. 'I'm ready any time.'

I hesitated. He shared my political commitment, but he was still new in the League; his Bristol accent was engaging, he was good looking, but I wasn't really attracted to him. He later became a foreman at Ford's – the ultimate betrayal in our thinking.

The campaign for the soon-to-be launched Workers Revolutionary Party included a *Pageant of Working Class History* at Wembley's Empire Pool, packed with 10,000 people. Actors, writers, and directors had worked in five working-class areas with amateurs to create plays about their own history. In Wales it was the 1901 Taff Vale judgement which made striking unions liable for employers' loss of profits; in Jarrow, the 'gibbeting' of miner Jobling's hanged body.

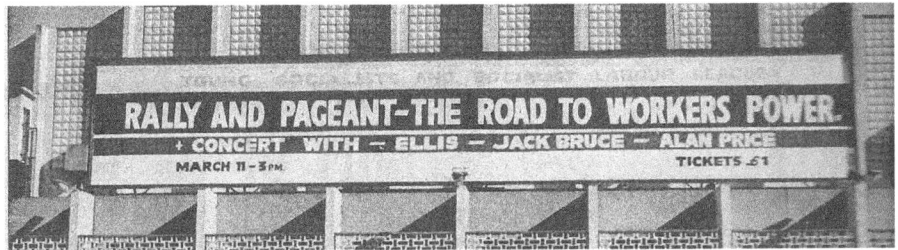

▲ Several large events were organised in 1973 as part of the campaign to transform the Socialist Labour League into the revolutionary party

Working-class struggles were portrayed in regional accents by descendants of the people involved, making spectacular use of the arena's technical facilities. The finance office set up in a back room also acted as League headquarters where Sheila discussed recruitment figures and issued area secretaries with leaflets and tickets for our next campaign, the All Trades Unions Alliance conference in Manchester. Gerry came in and nodded approvingly.

'When you have a success, go *straight in* with the next campaign. Never let the enthusiasm die down,' he said.

We were in perpetual campaigning mode.

I now joined USDAW, the shopworkers' union of 400,000 members. Dot, Vivian and I were elected as delegates from our respective branches for the Annual Delegate Meeting.

'Clare, 'USDAW is a conservative union and they think we're mad left-wingers. You can't wear your fur coat. Wear something plainer.'

I felt resentful. I loved the warm luxury of my jumble-sale coat, despite its worn armpits.

The union paid for travel and accommodation for four days. By selecting an economical bed-and-breakfast hotel we had money over for the League's development fund. My beige corduroy coat was barely warm enough, but I enjoyed Blackpool's holiday atmosphere. We sold *Workers Press* to the delegates jostling in the conference registration queues: all ages, diverse accents. As we settled in the splendid Empress Ballroom, a middle-aged union officer, smiling triumphantly, conducted three glamorous young women to their seats. They wore highly patterned coats, long flowing skirts, whirling earrings and scarves that seemed to float behind them as they walked. The full-length, leopard-patterned coat of the third one glistened and swirled in its fullness as she walked down the aisle.

'And you stopped me wearing my fur coat.'

▲▼ March 1973: Pageant of Working Class History in the Empire Pool, Wembley, organised by the Young Socialists and Socialist Labour League

'They're delegates from the Biba fashion store in Kensington. Recruiting them is a major coup for the union officer.'

The conference was far more interesting than I had anticipated. Unilever delegates from evocatively named Port Sunlight No.2 branch spoke about working conditions. Butchers lamented frozen meat from the European Common Market hitting British suppliers. Women workers described the impossibility of family shopping because everywhere closed before they finished work. Wages Councils, made up of unions, employers and independent members, negotiated a legally enforceable minimum wage for each branch of retailing and hairdressing, but wages were notoriously low. I felt humbled to hear the mundane details of the day-by-day, step-by-step fight to improve pay and working conditions.

My branch resolution was political. Vivian helped me prepare my speech, making sure I understood every point. She and Dot were some ten years older than me and worked systematically, well grounded in working-class organisational traditions.

I faced the 2,000 delegates.

'Brothers and sisters …' A man in the second row wiggled his index finger at me throughout my speech, trying to sabotage my concentration. Bloody right-winger, I thought, looking beyond him at those who were listening. I had a well-prepared speech and teaching experience, so he didn't succeed in derailing me.

Although our resolutions were defeated, hundreds voted with us and stopped to discuss as we sold papers on the way out: Labour or Communist Party members, International Socialists. Many appeared to know Dot and Vivian from previous years.

For the conference ball I dressed up as much as I could, with an attractive blouse. The band was more suited to the middle-aged delegates, but I danced a few times. Some delegates had brought their wives; I noticed other informal pairings. The Biba delegates were constantly in demand for dances and never paid for a drink.

An International Socialist member from Tyneside Co-op approached me as the conference drew to a close. He had a lively sense of humour and a seductive Geordie accent.

'Nothing important is happening tomorrow. How about you and me just free-wheeling for a day?'

I was flattered. He was attractive, we could explore Blackpool – and who knew where it could end?

'I'd have loved to, but I have to leave tonight, to work in my League branch tomorrow.' I smiled to let him know I was disappointed. Clearly the International Socialists didn't make the same demands on their cadres.

All eight studio flats opposite the Centre were now being rented by the League. Gerry moved into a flat downstairs, opposite D's, furnished with a sofa, armchair, two bookcases, a table and some folding chairs. The bed was in an alcove in the unused kitchen. During the afternoons Gerry used the flat to prepare meeting notes or to discuss with individual comrades.

One evening he called me down for a late-night discussion. I told him about my recruitment successes in Dagenham and East Ham, where we were developing a big branch. He wiped his chin with his hand, as if checking his stubble, and made some comments, recommending one of Trotsky's pamphlets. I was standing, ready to leave, when he suddenly came closer and kissed me on the mouth, slowly, tentatively pushing his tongue into mine. I was very surprised, but reciprocated.

'Take off your dress,' he said, kicking off his leather slippers as he started undoing his tie and belt.

It was as simple as that. On his sofa I had my first sexual encounter in 18 months. The contact of flesh on flesh was pleasurable but inconclusive.

I went back upstairs in turmoil after the least romantic seduction I had ever experienced – by the leader of the world party of socialist revolution. As always, I fell asleep exhausted.

Next day was Saturday. We sold papers on Upton Park High Street, stopping for lunch in a pie-and-mash shop. I pushed the previous night's encounter out of my mind until we split up at 4 o'clock to call on readers before the evening pub sales. I needed to be alone, so I went to Plashet Park and sat on the grass.

Is Gerry ill? I wondered. Should I see Mike Banda to tell him Gerry is losing it?

No, Gerry is fully in control of his faculties. And can you be sure how Mike will respond?

But why would a leader with huge historical responsibilities want a sexual relationship with me, a middle-class member with manifest political weaknesses?

Perhaps he thinks you can make a political development.

But I'm still 'white South African shit'. He *must* be ill.

It's lonely being a leader, isolated from everyone else. He needs love and tenderness like the rest of us.

Would I become known as his mistress? Surely not?

It's a big honour that he chose you.

But it's very strange. And he's not at all sexually attractive.

He's charismatic. He has the power to make things happen. He's built this big organisation.

Is this the only relationship I am destined to have?

Maybe this is something you have to do for the revolution.

I couldn't resolve the question. I had to wait and see what happened. When I saw Gerry on the ensuing days, there was not a flicker of recall.

A train had been chartered for the All Trades Unions Alliance conference in Manchester and we had booked a coach to transport delegates from Essex and Dagenham to Euston Station. Late the night before, I had a puncture. With no spare tyre, I couldn't drive home. Sheila was scathing when I phoned with our final ticket numbers.

'You'll have to find another car to pick your people up.'

I stayed overnight with branch members. Because of the blistering heat I was wearing a floral sun-dress that exposed far more flesh than was seemly for a trade union conference, but I could do nothing about it. At 6 o'clock next morning I rang a supporter who had a huge white American Ford. He agreed to drive me round collecting our delegates.

I saw little of the conference as I was in the finance office. But I heard Gerry, the final speaker. He worked up to a crescendo for the climax.

'The preconditions for the social revolution are maturing rapidly. There is no middle road. Either we defeat this government and smash its state apparatus or they will destroy us. Join us in launching our new party in November.'

The 4,000 delegates were enthralled. So was I. Had his sexual approach to me been an aberration? Would it ever happen again?

The conference ended with a cabaret performed by actor members. Corin Redgrave sang in Noel Coward style, parodying ruling-class arrogance, accompanied on the piano by Lisa Fredericks in a long, shimmering dress, split right up to the hip and much more suggestive than my sun-dress. As I watched from a side entrance, Gerry ambled over to me.

▶ Gerry Healy speaking at Belle Vue: 'The preconditions for the social revolution are maturing rapidly'

▼ July 1973: The All Trades Unions Alliance conference in Belle Vue, Manchester

'I'll see you again soon,' he said in a low voice and moved off. He had certainly noticed my bare shoulders.

1974 Three-day week

Dot began shrieking, waving her arms, knocking papers to the floor. I stood still, astonished that my innocent question had caused such uproar. Her screams brought Sheila up from two floors below, followed by Gerry.

'What's going on?'
'I asked for my wages.'
'Wait outside.'

It was Friday afternoon. Our wages should have been paid on Thursday. I leaned against the bannisters, wondering what I had done.

'She doesn't understand a thing,' Dot wailed as she blew her nose.

Gerry and Sheila calmed her down. Linda brought me my wage packet with the neutral expression we all adopted when a political row was taking place.

'You'll have to go,' Gerry said as he came out. 'You bring something foreign into this office. Finish your work for today and find another job on Monday.'

He called me down to his flat that night. His expression was grave. He's unlikely to be intimate tonight, I thought. I'm in disgrace.

'The OPEC oil producers' embargo has created a worldwide crisis. The miners' work-to-rule is directly challenging the government and they've declared a State of Emergency. We were right to launch the Workers Revolutionary Party last month. Big revolutionary struggles are ahead.'

He looked directly at me.

'That's why we can't have you working at the Centre.'

So I really had been sacked, after barely a year. The reasons were unclear to me.

'I'll help you. It's possible to do the right thing for the wrong reasons, and then different forces act on you and enable you to change, to make a leap in development.'

I was bitterly disappointed.

'Take off your dress,' he said, undoing his tie.

I had to complete a few tasks at the Centre on Monday morning. Gerry was irritated.

'Hurry up. I want you out of here.'

'Will you look for another teaching job?' Sheila asked as I left.

'No, I'll try temping agencies.'

In the spacious ladies' toilets near the Oval I piled my hair on my head and pinned thick locks in arcs. I adjusted my make-up and pendant earrings, put on my fur coat, slung my bag over my shoulder and painted my nails scarlet. I looked in the large mirror while I waved my hands dry, feeling more confident.

'I'm trying to find a job,' I told the toilet attendant. 'Will this do?'

'You look lovely, dear. Good luck!'

Without difficulty I got a series of temporary jobs from agencies in Fleet Street. The government brought in the Three-Day Work Order on 1 January 1974 to conserve fuel stocks, limiting commercial electricity consumption to three days a week. The atmosphere along Fleet Street was surreal with only candles and torches in the pale winter light. In the *Daily Mail*'s glass entrance hall the security guards' gold buttons glinted in flickering candlelight. Wrapped in a blanket, the employment agency woman consulted her lists by torchlight and sent me to an engineering company where they ran powerful lights on batteries, recharged on days when electricity was allowed. In due course, I found a permanent secretarial job using exciting new technology, a computerised IBM typewriter, on the seventh floor of a Fleet Street building. Because computers were exempt from the controls, I obtained clearance to keep the light on above my desk, which lit the whole office and pleased my new boss.

It was a time of political turmoil. In February Prime Minister Heath suddenly called a General Election, which resulted in a hung parliament. The resulting minority Labour government settled the miners' demands. Meanwhile extensive Provisional Irish Republican Army bombing of the mainland continued. There was upheaval in the Party as well. A group on the Central Committee, led by Alan Thornett, an important trade unionist in Oxford's British Leyland car factories, disagreed with founding the Party, among other things. He presented a major political challenge and the whole Party machinery was mobilised to counter his views. I trusted the leadership and voted for his expulsion, but I was sorry that we lost about 100 good comrades.

Re-elected Prime Minister Harold Wilson called another election for October to try and achieve a working majority. The Workers Revolutionary Party was not yet a year old but we decided to stand candidates. At an interview for a better job as secretary to a Senior Vice President in Chase Manhattan Bank I had to ask for two weeks' holiday for the election, of still unknown date.

'Who are you campaigning for?'

I hesitated.

'Vanessa Redgrave.'

'A fine actress.'

So my American boss, who represented finance capital, knew about my politics from the start. The work was very interesting. I typed notes from his visits to obscure places like the United Arab Emirates, Bahrain, Oman, Qatar.

Meantime I found an empty shop on East Ham High Street for Vanessa's election headquarters. We knew we were unlikely to unseat the Labour candidate, but this was an opportunity to put the Party on the political map. A large team of members, readers and new contacts addressed election flyers

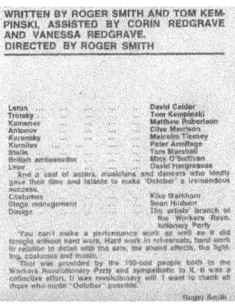 

◀ Roger Smith, WRP member and playwright

◀◀ February 1974: A rally at Alexandra Palace in north London included a play, *October*, written by Roger Smith and Tom Kempinski, with an impressive cast list

▲ The Party stood 10 candidates in the second 1974 General Election. These young workers participated in the campaign team for Vanessa Redgrave in Newham North-East constituency

▼ Young Socialist Sylvester Smart was the WRP candidate in Lambeth Central

◀ Posters and thousands of election addresses were needed for each election candidate. Dave Bruce was involved in production and distribution

for every voter in the constituency and helped knock on doors. An Italian photographer asked to accompany Vanessa campaigning, snapping from every view, hurrying ahead, changing angles. He was very deferential and when she finally asked him, in Italian, if he had enough pictures, he replied, 'Si Signora. Grazie mille, Signora,' and left.

▲ Like thousands of commuters, I enjoyed the *Evening Standard*'s Bristow cartoons on the train journey to my east London Party branch

Curiosity about Vanessa boosted attendance at election meetings. The Young Socialists' speaker alongside her was the *Keep Left* editor, a compelling speaker, with a skilful turn of phrase, but her quick answers to questions rather upstaged Vanessa, and Gerry later instructed her firmly to take a back seat.

From the balcony in East Ham Town Hall we watched the votes being counted. The result was announced at two in the morning: a few hundred for Vanessa. She made a dignified speech, to jeers from victorious Labour supporters.

We had recruited dozens of members. I felt confident that our Party could speak to hundreds of thousands of people, even millions.

▲ 'When was the last time a man said you had a great pair of jeans?'
This was my favourite tube station advert

◄ For several years I was given responsibility for organising fund-raising Christmas bazaars and summer fairs where, apparently, my political weaknesses would not cause problems. I was even sent around the country to help run local bazaars

▲ January 1975: The Keep Left Annual General Meeting attracted a huge audience of young people

▲ February 1975: Free the 'Shrewsbury Two' march. Des Warren and Ricky Tomlinson had been imprisoned in 1972 for 'conspiracy to intimidate' while picketing in Shropshire

◄ May 1975: March against the hated 1971 Immigration Act and other racist laws

▼ October 1975: World Conference of Revolutionary Youth in London

Cowley

They were putting something on my arm … a pumping feeling … something cold shoved in my mouth. I drifted in and out of sleep. Big windows, glass … daylight … white beds to left and right. Two men in white coats. A light shining straight into my eyes. The younger man spoke.

'Hello Clare. How are you feeling?'

'Uh … Umm … all right …'

The taller, Asian man touched my head. Something was round it.

'It's healing.'

I squinted at them.

'Where am I?'

'In hospital,' said the younger man.

'Why?'

'You were in an accident. You were thrown out of the back window when the car overturned. You were wandering on the motorway.'

'The motorway? I don't remember …'

'You have post-traumatic amnesia. You'll never remember.'

'What … what's on my head?'

'A bandage. We had to operate. You cracked your skull and had a blood clot on the brain, a subdural haematoma. We drilled into your skull to suck it out.'

I slipped back into sleep.

'What hospital is this?' I asked the nurse taking my blood pressure.

'The Radcliffe Infirmary, in Oxford. 'It's not often a patient's in intensive care twice.'

I was puzzled.

'They put you here when they thought you were all right. But you started gabbling foreign words, so we called Mr Mohan, the tall doctor. He decided to operate and you went back to intensive care.'

A vague recollection formed of lying on a table in the middle of a large room, wires and tubes, a telephone on the nearby counter, trying to get up.

'No, no, Clare. You must lie down.' A nurse. How did she know my name?

'I must phone to check on ticket sales for the Trotsky Anniversary.'

'Later. Not now. Just lie down.'

I remembered earlier events perfectly, arriving home just after midnight. After Marmite toast and a cup of tea I had uncovered my sewing machine to make a summery top, ruched with elastic thread, from a piece of pink and turquoise fabric with subtle wavy stripes. The broad straps would be attached front and back, perfect for the sweltering August weather. I had just pressed the seam on the straps when the door buzzer sounded. It was D.

'I'm really sorry, but I'm afraid you'll have to go to Oxford for the Cowley sale.'

'Oh dear. Will I be driving?'

'You can all share the driving. Meet Bob and Alison at five. I'm really sorry.'

Bugger it. I still had to conduct a nightly routine – scrubbing my legs and feet to remove yesterday's darkening colour and reapplying fake tanning lotion for tomorrow. Keeping my bare legs looking good was very important to me. I slept for two-and-a-half hours, put on my cream skirt with two flounces above its hem, and safety-pinned the straps to my new blouse. A lace-edged bolero provided the necessary modesty for a factory gate sale and my job at Chase Manhattan Bank. Turquoise high-heeled sandals and turquoise pendant earrings completed the outfit.

I snuggled down on the car's back seat to sleep. That's where my memory ended.

Pam pretended to be my sister, as instructed by Sheila, and was allowed to see me.

'What happened?' I asked.

'Bob fell asleep and the car overturned. He and Alison are both OK, but the car is a write-off. The doctor asked me if it was normal to talk about the Trotsky Anniversary.'

We laughed.

My brother Howard arrived next, with my former husband T. They seemed upset.

'No one knew how to contact your family,' said T. 'I phoned Cape Town, but was told your parents had moved, so I contacted the police.'

'Mum rang me, very distressed,' said Howard.

Sheila arranged that at least one Party member visited me every day, many all the way from London. And others came: my ex-father-in-law, my two Rhodesian cousins, my close colleague from Chase and both my bosses. I was feeling better every day, elated, in a sort of euphoric haze. The ward doctor shone his torch into my eyes.

'Remarkable.'

An Oxford member had washed my blood-stained clothes. On top of the neatly folded pile were the pink-and-turquoise straps and eight tiny gold safety pins. I chuckled, recalling the Edwardian story-book nanny who forbade safety pins 'in case you have an accident and the nurses see them'.

I fell asleep when I tried to listen to classical music. I couldn't concentrate on *Workers Press*. I chatted to the three other young women in the glassed-in veranda, all in traction. I had a bath and washed what was left of my hair – the front of my skull had been shaved for the operation. I looked at the glossy photos of the Trotsky Anniversary rally: a huge audience, Gerry emphasising a point, hands raised, small eyes screwed up in his podgy face. It all seemed far away.

I wanted to phone my parents.

'We can't reverse international charges from a call box,' said the operator.

'Look, I'm in hospital after a major accident. I was nearly killed. I need to speak to my parents.' She consulted her supervisor and put me through. It was wonderful to hear their voices.

'The police called at four in the morning,' said my mother.

'I was ready to take the next plane,' said my father, 'but the ward sister dissuaded me.'

'What about your face?' My mother's voice trembled.

'Just blood-shot eyes and bruises. Cuts all over my body, a cracked skull. But my face is OK.'

'Come and convalesce in South Africa. I'll fly over and fetch you.'

Enticing, but did I want to recover in the privileges of the apartheid police state?

'I don't think I could handle the long flight. Could we perhaps go to the south of France?'

After three weeks I was discharged.

'You can go back to work in December,' Mr Mohan told me.

'In four months' time?'

'One day a week at first and then build it up.'

Fern from Essex collected me in her Mini. She shepherded me gently out into the sunshine and drove calmly back to London. I had a scarf wound round my head, my skin was pale and I still had bruises under my eyes. She took me to D's flat, opposite Gerry's, so that I wouldn't be on my own. As we reached the second floor Gerry was just leaving, plump in his grey suit. He glared at Fern. He thoroughly disliked her, because she was too independent and wasn't afraid of him.

'Come in a moment.' He ushered me in and slammed the door. He seemed uncharacteristically pleased to see me.

'There was a huge swell in the Party when they heard about your accident. People all over the country have been phoning Sheila. You have a lot of support.'

He led me straight to his bed in the alcove and pushed me down, unzipping his fly, quite excited. I wasn't unwilling, but sex was really not foremost in my mind right then. He pressed the top of my head until I pushed his hand away.

'I have a broken skull. Didn't they tell you?'

We heard Fern outside with my luggage. He zipped up and opened the door, furious.

'Hurry up,' he said contemptuously and slammed the door again.

He returned with his eager little prick, but when we heard Fern again he decided to go down to his waiting car.

'You can convalesce at the College of Marxist Education in Derbyshire, but wait a bit. It's still a building site,' Sheila told me. Two weeks later Fern drove me there.

Skilled volunteer labour had just finished converting the big house into a College, to replace the annual summer camps, which were no longer feasible. The nominal owner was Corin Redgrave and locals were told it was a drama centre. About 30 Party members were attending a one-week course. I stayed in the spare bedroom of the director's flat and tried to

▲ College of Marxist Education in Derbyshire

attend some of the sessions but couldn't concentrate. I slept most of the time. Ten days later my mother and I flew to Nice and spent the first week in a hotel in Antibes, high on a cliff overlooking the bay and its azure sea. I slept and swam in the hotel pool or tried talking to the deferential staff. One morning, I saw a tiny item in the local paper: 'Police raid actor Corin Redgrave's *maison secondaire*'.

The article said that an arms cache had been found. I was startled. I had been there less than a week before. Of course there was no arms cache – that just wasn't our politics. My mother hurried into town to buy an English paper, which confirmed that there had been a massive raid but no one had been arrested. Corin Redgrave had protested at this unjustified invasion of the house.

'If the police found arms, they must have put them there,' the college director was quoted as saying.

Our second and third weeks were in a hotel on the Nice seafront. I swam at the public beach, pleased to be among ordinary working-class people rather than the exclusive guests at the Antibes hotel. I had long discussions with one of the hotel porters about the general strike of May-June 1968. My mother arranged little explorations, found hidden restaurants, and left me on my own when appropriate. It was a long time since we had spent so much time together. When she rearranged her sheets in the dark I noticed how graceful her arms still were and hoped that mine would be too when I reached 57.

Our last day was in early October. During my morning swim I felt a cold change in the current. It was time to go home, nine weeks after the accident.

Norman, a long-standing Party member, collected us from Heathrow. His Yorkshire charm completely won over my mother.

'We read about the police raid on the College,' I said.

'I'll tell you something very surprising,' said Norman. 'On the Saturday evening I collected all the Sunday papers from Fleet Street.'

'For the *Workers Press* editorial office.'

'Yes. Then I read in *The Observer* that the police had raided our College and an arms cache had been found. Well, I immediately phoned the College.'

'And?'

'Gerry and several Central Committee members were there for the international school –'

'Had it been raided?'

'No, not yet. While I was reading the article to them over the phone, a large number of police cars with searchlights suddenly swooped in.'

'The article about the raid was printed *before* it had happened?'

'Yes, that's the point.'

'You mean it was pre-arranged between *The Observer* and the police, or the government?'

'Exactly.'

'It's a frame-up, a conspiracy against us.'

My mother didn't quite know what to make of this, but I was really glad to be back in the fight.

▲ Nurses campaigning for a pay rise

Workers Press ends

'The Fleet Street newspapers are produced with old technology,' Gerry told me.

'I've seen it, inside the machine rooms of *The Sun* and *The Telegraph* when the union allows us in to sell *Workers Press*.'

'The unions won't even discuss modernisation because it would put most of their members out of work but we plan to grasp the opportunities presented by the new technology. We're preparing to produce the daily paper with our own Party staff.'

He looked at me intently.

'While you're still convalescing, you can train in computer typesetting. This is totally confidential, of course.'

Aileen's mother, Mickie Shaw, who had been a Pitman's secretarial teacher, trained me in a secret two-roomed office in Stonhouse Street, off Clapham High Street. The windows of the small shop had been frosted for privacy. On three desks in the front room were strange typewriter-like terminals displaying a line of electronic text which disappeared when the machine punched holes into paper tape.

'The six holes on the TTS tape represent all the letters and numbers plus control codes to determine other characteristics,' Mickie explained.

She rolled up the tape, took it to the back room and fed it through the mechanism on the front of a metal box the size of a tall washing machine.

'This is the typesetting computer.'

'Most people have never seen a computer,' I said.

'It exposes images on to photographic bromide paper which feeds into this light-sealed box.' She dislodged a metal canister on the outside and took it into the passage connecting the front and back rooms. A squat gadget, like a toaster on its side, rested on a shelf with a metal basket below.

'This is the processor. When the doors are closed this becomes a dark room.' She fed the bromide's leading edge into the rollers and hurried out, closing the door.

Another comrade worked in the back room under festoons of text-covered, drying bromides. He fed a dry one through another machine to wax its underside, trimmed it and positioned it on a sheet of paper pre-printed with pale blue guidelines. 'Pages of a book,' he explained.

I found the new terms fascinating: font, picas and points, leading, justified type, hanging indents. Gerry and Aileen called in one day.

'How is Clare doing?'

'Like a duck to water,' said Mickie, smiling.

In mid-December Gerry made me a cup of tea in a china cup and saucer. He sat in his armchair, comfortable in his slippers, his braces and tie emphasising his rotund belly. He dropped an artificial sweetener into his cup.

'We are secretly establishing a printshop in Runcorn with new equipment,' he said, stirring his cup. 'Our comrades are being trained by the suppliers but a socialist party can't print with non-union labour so we can't start until the NGA union accepts our staff as members.'

'Will they?'

'Oh, these print unions are dinosaurs, but we have a plan.' Gerry chuckled. 'Comrade Ray is the manager. He has invited the NGA official to meet staff before the Christmas party to discuss joining the union.'

'Does he know the Party connection?'

'No, he thinks it's just a new commercial press. If we present a brand new printshop whose staff want to join the union, we hope they'll agree it's better to have them in the union than outside.'

'Might they refuse?'

'The new trade union legislation states that workers have the right to join a union. Both anti-union management and Neanderthal unions have to accept it.' Gerry rubbed his hands together gleefully. I laughed.

'So, comrade, you will go to Runcorn for the Christmas party. You'll be part of the staff for the day.'

A carload of trusted Party members left London early to drive 200 miles to Runcorn. The printshop, Astmoor Litho, was in a wide, metallic building, windowless and featureless, like all the others on the industrial estate. The short entrance passage opened into a vast warehouse lit by sloping rooflights. Ray came to greet us.

'The engineers are still setting up the web-offset press.' He pointed to the towering metal columns and associated rollers, platforms and machine-pieces on the right. 'They've already broken for Christmas. Over here are the Heidelberg and Roland presses for smaller print jobs.'

The partitioned left-hand side of the factory was decorated with Christmas streamers ready for the afternoon event. A separate glass-partitioned room housed two typesetting computers and four keyboards. In the adjacent 'composing' area long, slanting frames held the mounting sheets. We greeted comrades working in different areas.

'Next we have the cameras and plate-making,' said Ray.

'And all this advanced technology belongs to *our* Party,' marvelled one comrade.

We assembled in the canteen in the adjacent warehouse to plan the union's visit. Tony Banda, Mike's brother, was the Central Committee member in charge, an experienced printer, wiry and energetic.

'You must all have a convincing story ready about how you came to be working here. Clare and Liz, you could say you used to work with Ray's wife, and she contacted you when Ray came to open the factory. I'll keep out of sight, of course.'

'It must look as if day-to-day work has been proceeding for some time,' said Ray. 'Keep working while I show the official around.'

We talked quietly over lunch, tense, ready for the afternoon's charade.

Right on time, Mr Cotton arrived, a man in his late 40s, with light brown hair and prominent teeth, wearing a grey suit, slightly portly. Ray, now also wearing a suit, brought him into the computer room where Liz and I sat typing. The lenses inside the VIP typesetter clunked alarmingly as they moved to change the point size.

'We change the photographic film strip inside the computer to vary the font,' Mickie explained to Mr Cotton as the tape spilled out in a loose tangle next to the computer. He looked bemused. We continued typing as he moved to other production areas.

Manager Ray left when we assembled in the composing area for the meeting. Mr Cotton explained union membership and the subscription rates. We asked a few prepared questions.

'If you wish to apply to join the NGA, I have application forms here.' He handed them out and we completed them straight away.

'Most of us have been in trade unions in other industries,' said one printer. 'We know how important they are for working conditions.'

'These will go to the district committee for ratification.' Mr Cotton was very pleased. 'I feel confident we will welcome you into NGA membership as the Astmoor Litho Chapel in the New Year.'

Ray was called back in. A table covered with fresh newsprint had been laid with glasses and bottles of beer and wine. Trays of food were brought in, someone turned on the music and the Christmas party began. We pulled crackers and put on silly paper hats. Mr Cotton grinned broadly as he moved around. He seemed to enjoy talking to us young women and we were gently coquettish as we related our stories.

'I'll leave you to enjoy your party. Merry Christmas and Happy New Year.' We didn't relax until Ray reported that he had driven off. We cheered and turned the music up loud.

'Remember, we still have to drive back to London,' said our driver.

February 1976: a 10pm emergency sub-district committee meeting in East Ham, about a dozen comrades in the house of one member. Mike Banda sat waiting, brooding over a cup of tea until everyone had arrived.

'The Party faces a very serious situation. The printers who produce the *Workers Press* receive cripplingly high wages and we can no longer afford them.'

Anxious silence.

'I have to tell you we can no longer produce *Workers Press*. Tomorrow's issue, already printed and on its way to the branches, will be the last.'

A comrade gasped. Others shifted in their seats, looking at Mike in disbelief.

'Central Committee members are explaining this tonight to District Committee meetings all over the country. Each parcel of papers has a letter inside informing members that this is the last issue.'

In tense silence we considered this. For over five years the daily paper had been central to our branch work. We delivered it to regular readers, we sold it at workplaces and on housing estates, through it we had created the network of supporters around our branches. Now Mike had just announced its end.

Finally someone spoke.

'Will we have something else instead? A weekly paper?'

'We'll issue news-sheets, or circulars. We have yet to decide.'

Mike seemed remarkably untroubled.

'So, we should tell the members tomorrow?'

'Yes, and arrange branch meetings, inform the readers, collect in any money they owe.'

We discussed practicalities. It was like making arrangements after a death. We dispersed in gloom. Even though I had had secret knowledge, the sudden announcement had caught me unaware and I too was shocked.

1976
NEWS LINE

'Tony Banda will talk to you about plans for the new daily paper.' Gerry smiled with satisfaction.

I waited for two anxious weeks until Tony arranged a meeting. He invited me to sit down and switched off the music from his vast classical collection. He seemed nervous.

'The paper will be printed in Runcorn, but the editorial offices and typesetting will be here in London. We want you to leave your job and work as a typesetter.'

I immediately accepted.

'Whew. That's a relief.'

I looked at him, astonished. Didn't he realise that I wanted to work on the paper more than anything else?

Gerry called a meeting of Party members who would produce the paper: printers, comrades on layout and design, typesetters, proof-readers, photographers, former *Workers Press* journalists and new ones.

'The paper will have a tabloid format and will include television programmes, sport and horse racing, to appeal to a broader mass of workers. We want it to have a light, spacious appearance, rather like the *Daily Mail*.'

So, not filled with political and cultural articles, as *Workers Press* had been. I was surprised.

'We have chosen a neutral name, *News Line,* that doesn't limit it to workers with a political interest.'

'Will it have advertising?'

'No. This is a Party paper. We will finance it through sales and the Fighting Fund.'

The former composing room at the back of the Centre's complex became the light and spacious editorial office. Metal casement windows ran alongside the warehouse roof on the long, north-facing wall and the approach passage on the west side. The rear walls adjoined the yard of the fire station next door. Partitions surmounted with Perspex windows separated the typesetters, journalists, telex machine, news tapes, and the editor's office. The journalists had manual typewriters but ours were IBM electric typewriters with special 'Bardata' golfballs. We typed on shiny paper, fed the sheets into a scanner, read the text on the screen and then punched TTS tapes which we transmitted to Runcorn through a telephone modem, systematically recording the tape's number, time and three-letter identifier. Six desks and two scanner terminals in the typesetting area. Everything was plain, efficient and workaday, but this was cutting-edge technology.

▲ Our new daily paper *News Line* was launched on 1st May 1976. It covered industrial disputes, international events, Party activities, cultural and theoretical articles, sports and horse racing

Friday 30th April, 1976: production of the first issue. The journalists had worked on newspapers before, but we typesetters and the Runcorn printshop were the new, unproven component. Gerry huffed in and out all day. I was tense with excitement.

Feature articles and the television programmes had been sent ahead. Now the sub-editors passed us the breaking news to typeset. In the afternoon the Press Association terminal clattered out the horse racing. Each racecourse had six races of up to 28 horses. We typeset the complex tabulation of information about each horse, incomprehensible to us but vital to the punters, using a system of mnemonics: MONKEY for one kind of race. We typed: ΔM ΔO ΔN ΔK ΔE ΔY and inserted the relevant information in between. But the codes didn't work.

'There are columns on some lines and different ones on others,' Runcorn reported.

Our technical expert Dave Bruce, who had set up the complex, ultra-modern typesetting system and who had written the formats and codes for the races, tried to work out why. We checked and rechecked that we had typed everything correctly. Dave redefined the MONKEY formats but the tabulated columns still came out haphazardly. At 6 o'clock we were still struggling; by eight we realised we weren't going to succeed. We sat at our desks, tense, ready to do anything, but only Dave had the knowledge to solve the problem. Everything else was complete and half a page had been set aside for the races.

Gerry was furious.

'We will NOT print the paper if we can't include the race cards,' he shouted.

Mickie came on the phone from Runcorn, calm as always.

'Couldn't we just set the horses' forms in run-on text? All the information will be there, just not tabulated.'

I handed the phone to Gerry and he accepted Mickie's suggestion. Her authority as a long-standing member had given him a way out of the impasse. We removed the MONKEY codes, repunched the tapes and waited for Runcorn to report. Gerry kept reappearing.

'I will not let you fuck-up the horse-racing in this paper,' he shouted at Dave, hunched over the scanner, attempting to work out what had gone wrong. 'You'll have to sort this out before the next issue.' He stormed out with short, angry strides, forcefully swinging the door into the entrance passage.

A few minutes later Aileen came in, her long coat swinging behind her, bag slung over her shoulder. She looked completely unflustered and went calmly over to Dave, who expected another summons to see Gerry.

'I can't even think when there's all this shouting, all this pressure,' he said between his teeth.

'Oh Dave, for goodness' sake,' she said quietly. 'It's going to be like this for the next three weeks.'

Dave seemed to relax. Aileen had defused the overheated atmosphere.

The modem phone rang.

'We're ready to print.' Tony Banda's voice was weary.

▲ Enthusiastic crowds cheer Libyan leader Colonel Gaddafi (centre), May Day 1976

▲ 'Hands off Lebanon' picket at the Syrian Embassy, July 1976

▲ Trico strike for equal pay, August 1976

▲ Our Christmas Bazaars were popular for their bargains. This is the only *Workers Press* or *News Line* picture of me ever – with my back to the camera

▲ July 1976: Anti-racist march. Slogans included 'Hands off Blacks – Hands off the Irish'

▲ The bitter Grunwick dispute for trade union recognition lasted from 1976 till 1978

'Good,' said Aileen. 'Now we can all go home. I'll tell Gerry.'

It was midnight. We left Dave to work in the quiet of the night to resolve the tabulation problems.

The summer of 1976 was exceptionally hot. Despite open windows, open doors, fans and canvas postbags draped outside the west-facing windows to block the afternoon sun, the editorial office was unbearable. Typesetting advance television programmes eased us into the day's hectic timetable. After the 10 o'clock editorial meeting production got underway, punctuated by frequent pots of tea and a quick lunch in the canteen at the far side. In the afternoon the dispatch van left for Runcorn, taking early pictures; page-layouts and later pictures were transmitted on the Muirhead K470B machine. The van returned late at night with the London papers, distributing bundles at motorway meeting points on the way.

An uprising broke out in Soweto, near Johannesburg, in July 1976. Tens of thousands of school students exploded in the huge black township, and the actions spread to other areas. I read the Reuters tapes with excitement – this was the biggest international event since *News Line* had started. Was it the beginning of revolution in South Africa? I went to work enthusiastically each day, proud to be working on the first daily newspaper in Britain to use computer-typesetting and web-offset printing, far more advanced than Fleet Street's dying technology. Our paper challenged the Stalinists' daily *Morning Star*, outshone the miserable publications of other left-wing groups and countered the lies of the capitalist press.

Camaraderie and determination dominated the editorial office, but there were also tensions.

'Good morning, girls,' said one journalist.

'We're *comrades*,' I muttered.

By 7 o'clock in the evening only we typesetters were left. Even sub-editor Paul Jennings was gone by 8pm. We answered Runcorn's queries, typeset the next day's television, emptied ashtrays, scrubbed nicotine stains off the Perspex windows on the journalists' side, swept and mopped. The overnight guards, like other staff, were not allowed in because our production processes were a closely guarded secret. We had no refreshments during the long evenings and left only when the paper went to press at nine, ten, or later.

Word reached Sheila that we were resentful. She summonsed us to a meeting in her office up the narrow, winding stairs above the kitchen.

'I understand there are complaints.'

Silence. Then we made our points.

'We're the only ones who make tea.'

'Everyone goes home and we're left in charge.'

'We work the latest but we have to do the cleaning.'

'We're hungry in the evening.'

'This is nonsense,' said Sheila. 'This is just capitulation to bourgeois feminism.' Horror of horrors … 'We are communists. Some of the journalists are new to the Party but they bring essential expertise to the paper.'

'We know that.'

'Look, you couldn't produce the paper without them. You just couldn't do it. If you want changes you must raise it with us, not grumble in the background. Of course you can have food if you're hungry.'

Our dedication as Party comrades had been invoked and we accepted Sheila's reprimand. I felt rather ashamed. That afternoon one of the typesetters made a pot of tea and took the cups round on a tray. The journalists were embarrassed.

'It's OK, we'll help ourselves.'

Next evening our proof-reader produced a tin of tuna and a plain yoghurt. She chopped up a small onion and mixed it all together to eat with Ryvita biscuits in two shifts in the silent canteen. We could have food if we wanted it, but we had to organise it ourselves.

Sub-editor Paul agreed that each evening around 7 o'clock one of us could leave for branch work. Nothing else changed.

We worked six days a week, Sunday to Friday, from nine in the morning. I now reached my distant Dagenham branch only on Saturdays and my one early night, which did not go unnoticed by Sheila. The Southbank sub-district secretary spoke to me.

'Sheila says you're to move into the Vauxhall branch.'

'It can't happen just like that.'

'She says it's to be straight away.'

'I can't leave Dagenham without preparation.'

I mentioned this to Janet, who had been national organiser in Socialist Labour League days. She was adamant.

'No, both branches have to agree first, and plan it.'

Sheila phoned me on the internal system.

'You'll move to Vauxhall immediately.'

'I'll have to finish things off in Dagenham first.'

'This is ridiculous. I'm instructing you to move today.'

'I want to appeal to the Political Committee.'

'You go ahead and do that.' She slammed the phone down.

I typed a memo. Gerry had it in his hand when he spoke to me.

'Sheila is just trying to strengthen the Southbank sub-district. How much time do you need to leave the Dagenham branch?'

'About two weeks.'

'OK. I'll let Sheila know.'

I thought the principles of revolutionary organisation had triumphed. I hadn't yet grasped that I was under Gerry's protection.

News Line editor was Alex Mitchell, a charismatic Australian extrovert in his 30s who had an impressive track record as an investigative journalist. Gerry had sent him to Portugal and Japan to report on working-class struggles. He also made links with anti-imperialist groups in the Middle East and Africa and went to Lebanon and Libya, sometimes with Gerry. He enjoyed having an audience and regaled us typesetters with an account of his trip to Lebanon's civil war areas.

'This taxi-driver has an artificial leg, driving on terrible roads, dodging holes and bits of bombed buildings, avoiding snipers, telling us to keep our heads down. When he brakes he has to use his hand to move his artificial leg on to the pedal. We were shit-scared.'

Another time he described a conference in Libya.

'This *Jamahiriya*, it's a kind of government of all the people over themselves,

▲ Damour: children who survived the siege of the Palestinian Tel al-Zaatar camp in East Beirut in 1976

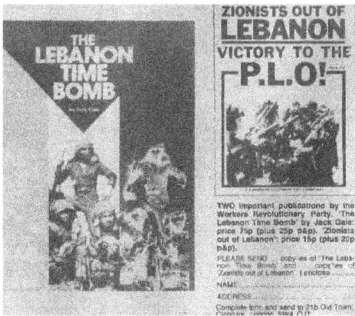

▲ Two WRP publications on the war in Lebanon

with continuous assemblies. And the international delegations – they flew in these guys straight from the bush, freedom fighters from the wars in Angola and Rhodesia.' He shook his head. 'We sat on carpets in these huge tents, eating dates and nuts. Gaddafi uses the oil wealth to support movements all over the world struggling against imperialism. That's why the ruling class hates him.'

Occasionally Alex conducted foreign visitors round the office. We never knew who they were. Libyans? Palestinians? He introduced them to the sports editor or another journalist, but never to us typesetters. I didn't understand why Gerry let these contacts see the editorial office when everyone else was banned.

'Everybody go to lunch now,' Paul said to the typesetters. 'We've a heavy afternoon ahead.'

I rang Runcorn.

'The race cards haven't arrived yet. There'll be no one here for 20 minutes.'

Alex strode in.

'Yes, there will be. *You* will stay.'

'But Paul said –'

Alex slapped me hard across my left cheek. He picked up the phone.

'There *will* be someone here,' he said to the bemused Runcorn comrade before stomping off to lunch.

I was furious; my face was smarting. I tossed a sheaf of papers on to the scanner and sat down, wondering what to do. This Johnny-come-lately, this self-important journalist, how dare he. I've been in the Party ten years. And him? Three years, catapulted into a leadership position, which he doesn't even understand. Shall I complain to Gerry?

I decided to do nothing, but I felt contempt for this man who believed authority was achieved by force.

One of our hard-working typesetters told us rather formally that she was pregnant. Next day Alex summoned the other five women typesetters to a meeting in the small, dingy room across the path. We were surprised, because he didn't oversee our work.

'Comrades, capitalism's crisis places big responsibilities on the Party.' He was temporising, he seemed nervous. He took a deep breath.

'You may know that your comrade is pregnant.'

No one said anything and he couldn't meet our eyes.

▲▼ **Battle of Lewisham, south-east London, 13th August 1977:** 500 National Front demonstrators, escorted by 2,500 police, were pelted with missiles as they attempted to hold a national march through an area with a large black population. Police used riot shields for the first time outside Northern Ireland and rode horses against a section of the 4,000 anti-fascist protestors. The National Front's hopes to be considered a respectable political force never recovered

'This is unthinkable,' he continued. 'In this revolutionary situation ... I mean ... our revolutionary responsibilities ...' He sucked his breath in through his teeth, shaking his head, gesticulating with his left hand, looking down at the floor. He was thrashing around, very uncomfortable.

I guessed Gerry had told him to call this ludicrous meeting. Alex, who made secret sexual advances to every woman he could, was trying to tell us: *do not get pregnant*. The wolf warning of the forest's perils.

We went back to our keyboards but didn't discuss the meeting. We had no time to gossip and we were aware that anything we said could go back to Gerry.

Firemen's strike

Thirty thousand firemen occupied fire stations in a national strike that began before Christmas 1977 and battled on into the new year. Many were ex-military and they had never been on strike before, but felt their demand was just, for a pay increase. Because it was against the Labour government's public-sector pay freeze it was political. Fleet Street attacked them viciously but public sympathy was widespread. *News Line* was eagerly read at every fire station for its news, information about the strike, and interviews with firemen from all over the country.

After work, two of us typesetters began regular late-night visits to Lambeth fire station on the Albert Embankment. The pickets huddled round braziers in front of the high doors that normally disgorged fire engines but were now festooned with strike banners and posters. Passing cars hooted support. We were welcomed warmly and had long discussions with the men, who felt betrayed by the Labour government. A 'Green Goddess' army fire engine passed, desperately clanging its old-fashioned bells. The pickets acknowledged the crew with a small wave.

'Those squaddies don't have any choice and they'll be tackling dangerous fires with minimal training and antiquated equipment.'

The Party planned a big rally and hoped a fireman would speak. The union's B Division operations headquarters were opposite the fire station adjoining the editorial office. I called to see the division secretary, redhead Mick Redman from Lambeth, tall, fit and athletic.

'Could you speak at our rally?' I asked in the hubbub of phone calls from striking fire stations. He checked the date with the union head office.

▶ The Blue Watch pickets at Lee Green fire station, south-east London, wave to the dozens of drivers hooting in support of their seven-week strike, Christmas 1977

'Yes, that's fine.'
'Great, we'll put you down as speaking "in unofficial capacity".' Trade unions always took care not to appear to support a Trotskyist party.
'No, I'll speak officially.'
'Are you sure?'
Mick rang union head office again.
'That's confirmed.'
I hurried up to Sheila's office.
'What is it?' she said, with the bad-smell-in-the-room look on her face. I wasn't intimidated. I had important news.
'A fireman has agreed to speak at the rally: B Division secretary, in official capacity.'
'He can't be speaking officially.' She was exasperated.
'He confirmed with head office.'
'Leave the details on my desk.' She hurried out, irritated, and met someone on the stairs.
'We have a fireman to speak at the rally.' Her voice sounded excited.

For seven weeks of the strike I talked to firemen early every morning and late at night. They were in the vanguard of the working class, in a political battle against the Labour government. I was pleased when they described *News Line* as their 'lifeline'. I became familiar with the intricate details of their struggle, the machinations of the employers and government, the tactics of the union leadership and the determination of the rank and file. I shared their bitterness at the final compromise. After the strike ended I continued selling papers at Lambeth's 8am watch change, where I knew everyone, including the crew on the fireboat moored across the road on the Thames. An alarm call sounded for St Thomas' Hospital, half a mile down river.

DIARY OF A FIREMAN

▲ Throughout the strike a *News Line* journalist recorded the daily experiences of a particular fireman

'Stay on the boat, Clare. It's almost certainly a false alarm.'

I was excited, but what if it was a real fire? After 20 minutes bobbing alongside the hospital the all-clear sounded and we returned to the Lambeth moorings.

I had never worked so closely with a group of workers. Firemen Mick, Roger and Ray became almost my friends. I recruited them into the Party along with Tony S, a long-time *News Line* reader, and three others. Gerry held a meeting with them and a long-standing fireman Party member from Kent. Eight big, muscular men squeezed into Gerry's small office, facing his short-legged, squat frame behind a desk. I heard afterwards that he had talked about philosophy and Lenin's *Volume 38*. They were never integrated into the Party and drifted off in due course.

Why couldn't we keep these men who had been in the forefront of working-class struggle?

The camaraderie-of-struggle I shared with firemen was different from the comradeship of Party members. And spending so much time with firemen raised other questions. I was pressed to go out for a drink by a fireman who liked long discussions but didn't really agree with us politically. I was flattered, but didn't go. I wasn't interested in dalliances, and I certainly didn't have time to socialise. In the back of my mind, in an unformulated way, I hoped that one day I would be able to form a relationship with … perhaps a fireman, or some other politically advanced worker. But he would need to share my revolutionary awareness, or be part of the Party. Someone, somewhere, some time.

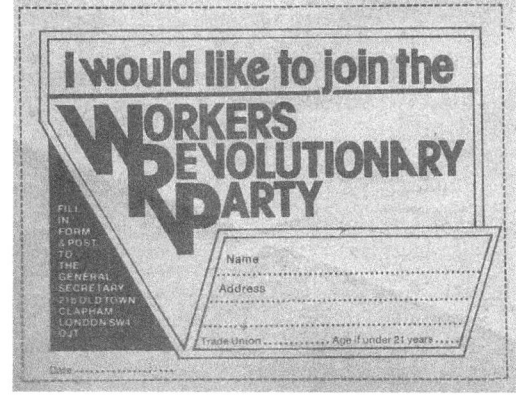

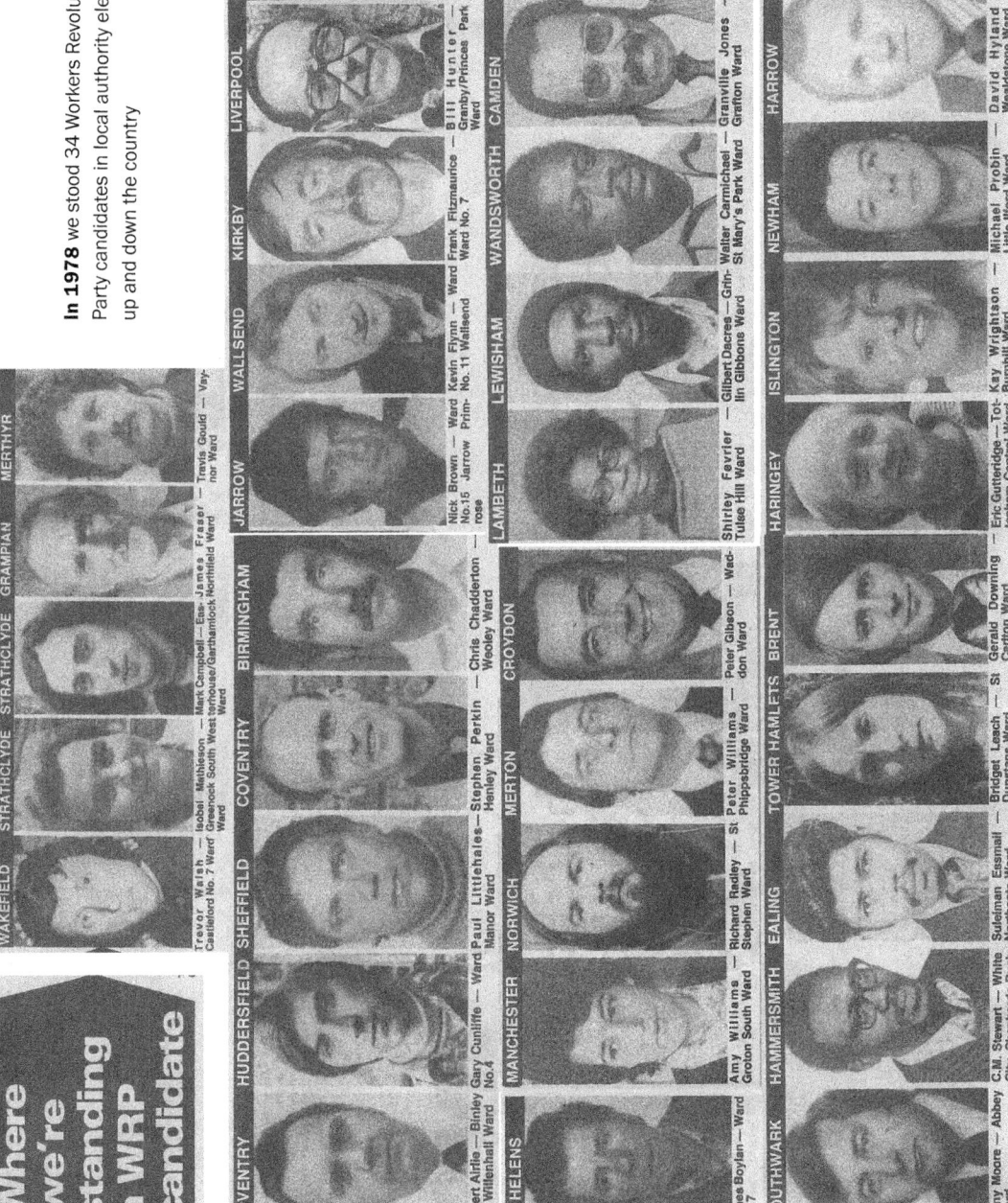

Runcorn printshop

'What's your opinion of the other comrades in the typesetting department?'

Gerry listened carefully to my cautious assessments.

'Please type me a report, confidential, of course.'

I felt rather important; perhaps I was going to be given more responsibility. I typed carefully in odd moments when no one could see: 'Corinna's mind is only half on the *News Line* because of her canteen supervising responsibilities … this comrade has lots of experience.' Another worked diligently. I handed it to Aileen in a sealed envelope and waited for a response, but nothing happened. Perhaps my report wasn't good enough.

By autumn 1978 Runcorn production was running later and later, sometimes going to press as late as 11. We tried to bring our end of production forward, but nothing seemed to help. Sheila complained to Paul.

'Comrades wait at motorway service stations in the middle of the night but the van is always late. And London branches can't finish deliveries in time to get to work. Something has to be done.'

Gerry called me in.

'I'm sending you to Runcorn to deal with the late production. Collect your things and arrange for someone to drop you at Euston station.'

'How long will I go for?' I was both thrilled and apprehensive.

'As long as it takes. See me before you leave.'

Paul was pleased, but worried about the typesetting. My sub-district secretary was exasperated. I went home to pack a few clothes, collected my train fare from the finance office, gobbled an early lunch and saw Gerry.

'I give you full authority to make any changes you think necessary,' he told me.

I was awed. I had never had such responsibility.

The printers were cleaning the web-offset press in the main warehouse when I arrived. Giant reels of paper were stacked three-high nearby.

'We've printed the final section of a book. The sections will be stitched on that machine.' Piles of wrapped paper were on a trolley next to two smaller sheet-fed presses. Nearby were the guillotine and dispatch bench. Three vans were parked beside a forklift truck in front of the huge doors at the far end. Everything looked systematic and well organised.

Tony Banda arrived in a rather thin coat and scarf, with a rucksack slung over one shoulder. He looked tired but greeted me warmly. He was politically responsible for the north-west area but Gerry had instructed him to spend more time in the factory to overcome the late production, so far without success. He gathered staff in the composing area.

'Comrade Clare has been sent by the Central Committee department to look at the late production, which is creating havoc in the branches.' He sounded frustrated. 'Comrades, we must deal with this.' After a brief discussion about early morning factory sales, which rather surprised me, production continued.

I helped in the typesetting area until just after 10pm, when we had supper left in the oven. The London drivers and the machine-minders had already eaten. Comrades from outside arrived with branch money to go on the London van and had brief discussions about sales and meetings. When the last printing plate was on the web-offset press a strident warning bell rang. The machine slowly came to life, building up to breathtaking speed, tipping out papers four per second, folded, trimmed, a colour news picture on every front page, one tossed out of line every 50 copies as the stream moved along rollers to the dispatch area. The printers moved around *inside* the units checking ink and water as the web of paper streamed up, down, above them. Speed, power, endless flow. My excitement amused them.

Next day I wore my orange-red shirt with black polka dots. Over it I wore a sleeveless, well-worn, blue denim dress. It seemed to me a perfect quasi-uniform, akin to printers' traditional blue denim.

I was shown how to wax the bromides and trim them on the comping frame, but aligning the columns on the layout sheet was more difficult than I had expected.

'Where are the cameramen and printers this morning?' I asked.

'In their branches. They work later unless we're printing books or the *Young Socialist* paper.'

'Why did it take an hour to go to press after the typesetting cleared last night?'

'A backlog of plates, perhaps. Maybe a cameraman was back late.'

I asked a cameraman what had happened.

'Late pictures from London delay things. Maybe we didn't anticipate how much we needed to do. Colour separation takes time, multiple pictures. London doesn't always realise this. And if page one is late …'

Tony held a lunchtime meeting in the canteen.

'Would it help if the plate-making and pre-press started earlier?' I asked.

There was general acquiescence, but I felt this wasn't the root of the problem. Everyone looked tired.

'Comrades, we *must* tackle this late production,' nagged Tony. 'Jim, you need to go to your branch meeting tonight but you'll be back to drive the papers.'

'So there'll be one cameraman short?' I asked.

'I'll make the plates that are ready before I go.'

As I learned how to do single-line corrections – meticulous, fiddly work – I asked each comrade about the late production but they gave me inconclusive answers.

'Doesn't the time spent in your branches affect production?'

'If we didn't go to our branches the north-west area would collapse,' said one comrade. 'And being stuck in here all day would kill us.' He inserted another correction. 'After all, we're doing this because we want to build the Party.'

'Branch work gives our printing work meaning,' said the proof-reader. 'Late copy and late pictures from London are the main cause of delay.'

'Well, it seems sort of chaotic, haphazard.'

I spoke to Paul Jennings on the phone.

'I can't pinpoint the problem. Everyone works very hard, but work in the branches takes a lot of time. The "biscuit club" and chat round the teapot sometimes seems more important than cracking the day's production.'

'Biscuit club?'

'Jim collects money from those who want a biscuit at the tea break,' I laughed. 'And we have fabulous lunch and supper.'

'Keep trying. We're doing our best to send things earlier.'

The paper finished half an hour earlier that night.

Next morning I asked for a meeting during the tea-break. I had begun to realise that Tony was contributing to the late production. After years stuck in the London print shop he revelled in doing political work in an important industrial area and rushed around visiting branches, seeing contacts in the big factories, bringing his enormous experience to bear. But he had lost sight of the tight organisation and discipline needed to produce a daily newspaper and I had to challenge this.

'Comrades here work longer hours than we do in London,' I said. 'But the work seems to whirl around in an uncoordinated way. Branch work intrudes, with comrades sometimes here, sometimes not, and always tired.'

One comrade fidgeted. Another took a sip of tea. I looked towards the canteen windows, frosted for security reasons.

'There needs to be a much more focused, concentrated approach to each day's production. If it's brought forward everyone will be less tired. It may mean *less* branch work, or planning it in a way that gives precedence to *production*.'

They were all looking at their cups, or at the wall, not at me, and certainly not at Tony.

Mickie Shaw spoke.

'We need enough comrades here to complete the early pages. Sometimes the television pages are still being comped in the afternoon when the foreign and sports pages are already waiting.'

'We must support Comrade Clare's suggestions,' said Tony.

Printing was two hours earlier that night.

'You've done it,' said Paul next morning, 'After three days you've managed what Tony's been unable to resolve for six months.'

'It's only happened once. Don't be too optimistic.'

Gerry spoke to me later. He always used the private wire to avoid wasting money on phone calls.

'How do you assess the problem?'

'Too much rushing around to branches to the detriment of the printshop work, a rather decentralised production team, everyone exhausted.'

'Ah yes, I recognise Tony's leadership.'

'He's the main one pushing them out to their branches. I believe he sleeps here sometimes, and doesn't bother going home.'

'That has to stop. I'll tell him. Consolidate, and check other issues.'

Meanwhile, in the High Court, the long-awaited trial began in our defamation case against the *Observer* newspaper for its 1975 article suggesting that the Party kept an 'arms cache' in the College of Marxist Education.

'You must stay in Runcorn until the trial is over,' Gerry told me. 'We're challenging the state and they'll be watching our every move.'

The plaintiffs were Gerry, Corin and Vanessa Redgrave, and three other Party members. Gerry dropped out later. They argued that the *Observer* article was a tissue of lies which had inflicted enormous damage on their characters and reputations and they asked for substantial damages.

After three weeks the judge entered a shock judgement in favour of the *Observer* and awarded full costs of £70,000 against the plaintiffs. The jury had decided that yes, the article was defamatory, but no damages were awarded because the plaintiffs' reputations were 'not materially damaged'.

We were outraged and began an immediate campaign to raise £70,000. Each day's front page had an appeal for our *Observer* Libel Fund. Donations poured in from our own supporters and from others who were incensed at the judgement despite disagreeing with our political views.

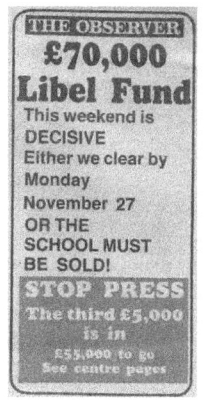

▲ Front page 'earhole' in each day's *News Line* campaigned to raise the court costs for the *Observer* libel trial

I wrote to my parents reminding my mother that we had read about the police raid three years before in the south of France, when the *Observer* printed its allegations. I asked if they could donate something. My father rang me.

'How much do you want? £1,000? £5,000?'

This was way beyond my hopes.

'Five thousand would be great.'

'I'll send you a cheque.'

I sent a note to Gerry via the London van. He spoke to me the next day.

'You can't stay in Runcorn forever, you know.'

I felt aggrieved. I wasn't there by choice.

'Come back tonight on the overnight train. Get Norman to collect you from the station.'

The train arrived just before six. I emerged wearily into Euston's dark morning to meet Norman.

'Gerry's waiting for you. I'm to take you straight to the flats.'

I knocked on the door. He was in his dressing gown.

'Come in, comrade.'

I started to report on what I had done, but he waved dismissively.

'Take your clothes off.'

I felt sticky and sweaty in the clothes I had worn for a day and a night, but he seemed unconcerned. I was exhausted and felt rather repulsed. Had he really brought me back from Runcorn for sex? I gave in to a joyless writhe on his sofa before he hastened to get ready for the office.

I went home for a bath before the day's production.

A revolutionary daily paper

The weekly *Newsletter* and daily *Workers Press*, followed by the daily News Line, were an integral part of my political life. I sold them and worked on production, finance and distribution for 20 years. They were important tools of organisation for the Party. We were the only Marxist organisation in Britain to sustain a daily paper through the turbulent 1970s and early 1980s. *News Line* was a lively and interesting publication and covered stories the capitalist press would not; it supported the voiceless; it was read by workers, trade unionists, youth and intellectuals who sought an alternative to the Fleet Street newspapers. The Marxist analysis of world and national events, articles on cultural and other subjects, sports reports and accounts of Party events were appreciated by many readers. The weekly youth paper, *Young Socialist*, was vital in organising our large youth movement.

The pictures on the following pages are a sample of how, during a time of turmoil, *News Line* recorded not simply what politicians were doing but what was happening in the working class

Winter of Discontent: The winter of 1978-9 was the coldest for 16 years. The ongoing pay freeze of James Callaghan's Labour government resulted in strikes in wide sections of the working class

◀ Liverpool social workers demand the council begin negotiations on their claim. They had been on strike for nearly three months

◀ Striking bakery workers

▼ Ancillary workers at St Stephen's Hospital in the Westminster Hospital group strike in support of victimised colleagues

▼▼ A 14-hour strike at London's Great Ormond Street hospital for sick children

► **Home Helps**: 'We are worth £100 a week, never mind £60'

▼ Home Helps making their point in Cheshire

▼ Civil Service staff picket outside the High Court

▼ The fight to save the Corby steel plant

Racist violence: Over many years, *News Line* carried reports of communities fighting shockingly frequent racist attacks, police violence and the effects of the racist immigration laws

◀ 1979: London demonstrators called for the repeal of the 1971 Immigration Act and the SUS (stop-and-search) laws, for the limitation of the powers of immigration and police officers, and to disband the Special Patrol Group

▶ WRP banner on the 20,000-strong march against the racist immigration laws, November 1979

▼ Marking the anniversary of the death in April 1979 of teacher Blair Peach, killed during a march against the National Front in Southall, west London

◀ 1980: March in East Ham against local racist murders

▼ 1983: Asian women who spoke out against their mistreatment at the hands of the police

▲ Cartoon Campbell died in police custody in 1980. His family attended the inquest

▶ Parents of 21-year-old Colin Roach, who died of shotgun wounds while in police custody in January 1983

▼ Fighting the National Front

PAMPHLET STILL AVAILABLE
The National Front and how to fight it
PRICE 10p

Available (7p postage) from Workers Revolutionary Party, 21b, Old Town, Clapham, London SW4 OJT

1979 General Election: The Workers Revolutionary Party (WRP) stood 60 candidates in the 1979 election. This qualified us to make a party political broadcast on television, like other parties

THURROCK
MICHAEL DALY

CITY OF WESTMINSTER, PADDINGTON
OLA TUNJI BANJO

EDINBURGH EAST
TERENCE BROTHERSTONE

LEWISHAM EAST
HERBERT HAREWOOD

COVENTRY, SOUTH-EAST
ALAN WILKINS

DERBY SOUTH
WILLIAM BIGGS

SALFORD WEST
STUART CARTER

HOUGHTON-LE-SPRING
DAVID TEMPLE

▲ Peter Gibson campaigns in Croydon Central

▲ Calvin Stuart campaigns in White City, west London

The Young Socialists movement was the bedrock of Party organisation. The Annual General Meeting of their weekly paper, Young Socialist, took place early each year, usually in London. The national conferences in the spring were exciting weekend events held in banqueting halls at seaside resorts, where off-season accommodation was affordable. Thousands of young people were involved in political discussion and activities

▲ Young Socialists' National Secretary Simon Pirani discusses political issues with young women at the Notting Hill Carnival in London

▼ 1980: We mark the 40th anniversary of Leon Trotsky's 1940 assassination in Mexico by an agent of Stalin. Alongside trade unionists and workers from all over the country, Young Socialists were a large component of our national political rallies

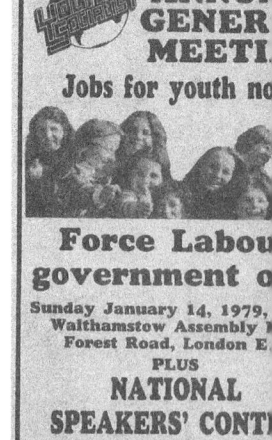

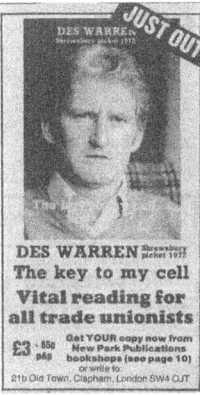

Party publications: The Spring 1972 issue of our theoretical journal, Fourth International and the 1982 account by building worker Des Warren of his jailing for conspiracy, The Key to my Cell, published by New Park Publications. The Paperbacks Centre in London's Charlotte Street was our first bookshop; we eventually had six in different parts of the country

Tribute to a Party member: I had known George Myers, a Party organiser who died in a motorbike accident in 1980, since our student days. Here, his brother Bob speaks at his funeral in Hull, a shameful event on several counts. Following three deaths, the Central Committee had banned motorbikes; and driving-when-tired rules had supposedly tightened after I was nearly killed when the driver fell asleep. But George had still been directed by the Centre to use a motorbike to travel between widespread branches in his area. Like all us cadres, he would have been permanently tired. Healy refused to accept that the Party may have had some responsibility for George's death, ignored his family's wishes, and insisted on organising George's funeral as a Party event

International reports: As well as developments within Britain, *News Line* covered international events in the Middle East, southern Africa, Poland, Latin America and elsewhere

▲ *News Line* sent reporters to the Middle East: Stephen Johns to Tel Aviv, John Spencer to Cairo and Jack Gale to Beirut

▲ *News Line* marked the anniversary of the 1977 brutal murder in prison of South African anti-apartheid activist Steve Biko, and followed events in Chile and Iran

▲ We published an eye-witness series from Poland when the independent union Solidarity formed in the Gdansk shipyards in opposition to Communist Party control

▲ *News Line's* first colour issue, published Saturday 7th July 1979, led on events in Nicaragua. Ours was the only colour newspaper in Britain until Eddie Shah began *Today* in 1986, followed by Fleet Street three years later

▼ When Israel occupied southern Lebanon in 1982, we campaigned in defence of the Palestine Liberation Organisation (PLO), with interviews and reports, including from photographer Don McCullin

▲ **The Rhodesia ceasefire agreement** signed on 21st December 1979 ended the country's 15-year war, introduced majority rule and granted Zimbabwe independence. Patriotic Front leaders Robert Mugabe and Joshua Nkomo are in the foreground. Prime Minister Margaret Thatcher watches in the background

◀ Patriotic Front supporters demonstrated against Rhodesian Prime Minister Ian Smith as he arrived for the Rhodesia conference

▶ Covering the 1980 Moscow Olympics was a high point of our sports reporting and included colour pictures. Reporting from the heart of the Soviet Union was an unprecedented experience for Trotskyist journalists

Under Margaret Thatcher's hated Conservative government in the 1980s, the battle to defend wages and for union recognition continued in wide sections of industry. At the same time, local councils faced massive cuts while opposition to nuclear weapons increased

▶ Beefeater Gin distillery workers strike in Vauxhall

◀ Chix bubble gum strikers win union recognition

▶ At YKK Fasteners, workers strike for union recognition

▶ Lambeth council workers demonstrate against government cuts to funding for local councils

▲ In 1981 the long-running women's Greenham Common Peace Camp set up outside the US Air Force base in Buckinghamshire

▶ 1983: A weekend of anti-nuclear demonstrations

The 'Troubles' in Northern Ireland continued through the 1970s to the 1990s, with tragic consequences

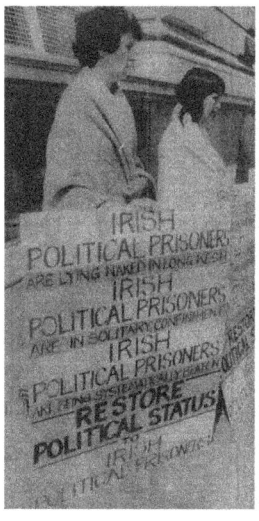

◀ Women's picket outside 10 Downing Street protesting against internment and torture in Irish jails and demanding political prisoner status for Republicans

◀ Protest at Downing Street by Belfast women whose sons had been killed by the British Army

▶ Bobby Sands' family at his funeral, 7th May 1981, attended by 100,000 people. A member of the Provisional Irish Republican Army (IRA), Sands died on hunger strike while imprisoned at HM Prison Maze (Long Kesh) for firearms possession. He had been elected as an MP to the British Parliament during the hunger strike, attracting media interest around the world

▼ 'British troops out of Ireland'. A banner on our 1982 Mayday march in London restated the position we had held since the British Army was first sent into Northern Ireland in 1969

The New Cross Fire: '13 dead and nothing said': Thirteen young people died during or after a fire that raged through Yvonne Ruddock's 16th birthday party in New Cross Road, south-east London, on 18th January 1981. Several racially motivated arson attacks had previously taken place in the local area and lack of serious police investigation into the fire led the New Cross Massacre Action Committee to demand an independent inquiry. Slow reaction and indifference by Prime Minister Thatcher and some authorities added to the families' pain

▲ Scene of the birthday party fire

▲ Mrs Amzra Ruddock (foreground) with friends and relatives at the graveside of her two children, Yvonne, 16 and Paul, 22, who were among the 13 dead

▲ **Black People's Day of Action:** On Monday 2nd March 1981, six weeks after the New Cross fire, more than 10,000 people, angered by alleged police brutality and incompetence, marched from Deptford, south-east London, to Hyde Park, in central London. Fleet Street newspapers were extremely hostile or, at best, dismissive

▲ Anger after the New Cross fire

▲ **Brixton and other inner city areas explode:** Later in the year, a wave of riots took place in cities across Britain, most famously in Brixton. The Scarman Report was commissioned by the government 'to inquire urgently into the serious disorder in Brixton on 10–12 April 1981 and to report, with the power to make recommendations'. Lord Scarman described the relationship between the police and the black community as a 'tale of failure'

Youth unemployment: Our campaign against youth unemployment began with the 1972 Right to Work Marches and continued with setting up seven Youth Training Centres in different parts of the country. As joblessness continued to rise across Europe, we organised a series of Euro-Marches in collaboration with our sections in other countries to highlight the problem

▲ Spirited Euro-Marchers in Italy

► The 1978 Euro-Long March took place in two legs

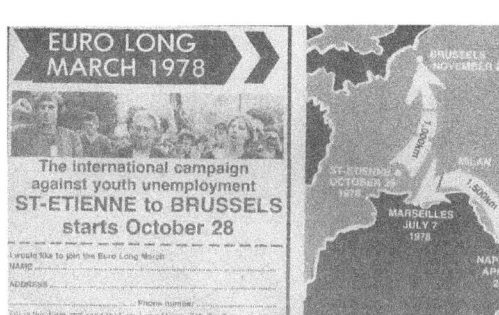

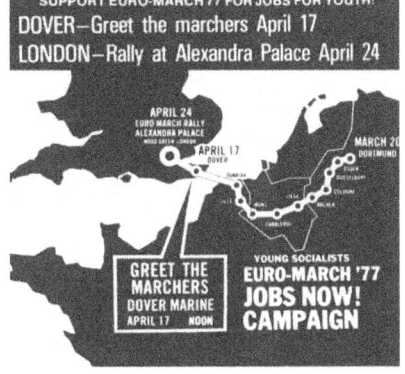

148   MY SEARCH FOR REVOLUTION

Unemployment figures rose steadily to a peak in September 1982. Youth were severely hit and were forced on to the government's cheap labour schemes. At the same time funding for traditional apprenticeships was being cut

2,168,874

◀ **From top:**
December 1980
July 1981
October 1981
June 1982
August 1982

XMAS DOLE FOR 2,244,299

2,851,623

2,998,644

Deliberate Tory jobs misery
3,292,702...

▼ September 1981: Wendy Griffiths, 17, became the millionth teenager to join the cheap-labour Youth Opportunities Programme (YOP). She joined Ford for six months and was paid £23.50 a week

▲ These YOP trainees from Liverpool joined the building workers' union, UCATT. They were warmly welcomed to the All Trades Union Alliance Conference in Sheffield by Peter Gibson, a member of the Central London bus committee of the T&GWU transport union

My parents

My father was taken ill during a visit to London and ended up in hospital.

'The emergency doctor we called is a "Coloured" South African, who left in 1960 after the Sharpeville massacre. He was driven from his country because of the politics and now he helps us here in London.' Mum was very emotional.

Dad recovered but remained weak so my mother arranged wheelchair assistance for the return flight. I asked Gerry if I could drive them to the airport.

'Why not take them to visit Vanessa on the way? It will help them understand your connection with the Party.'

I collected them three hours earlier than necessary.

'I have a surprise stop on the way. You'll be very pleased.'

I pulled up outside an elegant terraced house in Hammersmith.

'We're going to have tea with Vanessa Redgrave.'

'Oh *Mazel tov*!' Out burst the congratulatory expression from Mum's Johannesburg Jewish friends. She was delighted beyond my expectations.

Vanessa, statuesque, charming, greeted us graciously.

'I tried to think of something very English so I've made cucumber sandwiches. Would you like Earl Grey tea?'

She talked about the television film she was making and about her daughters and son. She and Mum discussed Shakespeare, Shaw and Coward. Dad quietly enjoyed the afternoon.

'Please call me Elizabeth,' Mum said as we left. Across the continents began a sort of friendship, which Gerry had told Vanessa to cultivate, but I was happy because my mother really valued it.

In May 1981 Gerry summonsed me to his office. Architect's drawings were laid out on the table.

'The owner of the upholstery business next door is selling the property.' He pointed across the yard to the large industrial building which ran alongside the warehouse for the full length of our premises. A large double door to our yard was permanently closed and a fire escape to the south descended to the passage alongside the editorial offices.

'The Party's publishing company, New Park Publications, owns the buildings we're in now. If we had this other building we could expand and develop our work.' He indicated the architect's drawings. 'We could have meeting spaces, a bigger canteen, offices, a proper film department. The Young Socialists could leave 186a Clapham High Street.'

The architect's drawings looked impressive. The property also included ramshackle outbuildings along the alley and the small building at the bottom on the main road, a former shop. But why was Gerry showing me?

'Land always increases in value. I believe this is an excellent opportunity for your parents to invest.'

I looked at him in astonishment.

'They could buy it for you, the Party could rent the buildings from you and you could live in this townhouse.' The drawings showed a proposed, two-storey building at the bottom of the alley, simulating Clapham's 19th-century architecture. 'I think you should go to South Africa to put the proposal to them.'

I felt overwhelmed at the enormity of Gerry's plan.

'How much would the building be?'

'He wants £70,000. We need to act soon. You should go quickly.'

My parents were surprised when I rang, but happy for me to visit. I felt anxious about how to present the proposal: £70,000! Did they have that much money? I didn't care about spending my inheritance because capitalism's private property would be swept away by the coming revolution. But would I be able to convince them?

Mum collected me from Johannesburg's airport.

'Dad is becoming weaker.'

'Oh dear.'

'He insists I maintain my other interests because he says I'll need them after he has gone.'

'He shouldn't think like that. Seventy-four isn't very old.' I was shocked.

'I can't bear to think of it, but I had to face it last year when he was ill.'

I loved my parent's welcoming, relaxed flat. My mother had added blue hydrangeas to her exuberant bunch of dried flowers in a copper jug in the far corner of the lounge. The yellow curtains from our house in Salisbury framed the windows. On the floor was the magnificent Persian carpet from my maternal grandparents' house, on the left their solid Dutch cupboard with blue Delftware displayed on top. Near the centre of the room stood my paternal grandfather's wavy-edged walnut table, repaired and covered with glass because his loyal servant had used it unsuccessfully as a barricade against British soldiers requisitioning his house during the Anglo-Boer War. Watercolours of mine headgears and the Drakensberg mountains hung above the long bookcase.

Dad and I chatted as we laid the table. After lunch I laid out the architect's drawings while they listened carefully.

'This alleyway leads into the complex. I would let the main building to the Party as offices. The staircase here would link it to the *News Line* offices. I could live in the townhouse there.'

They were aware that my life was inextricably linked to the Party, but what they did they think of the proposal?

'We'll think about it and let you know, darling.' My father was the mining executive again. Mum looked thoughtful.

I asked if we could visit Soweto, which had been so important in the school students' uprising five years before.

'You need a police permit, but Quakers are a recognised religious group so I'm eligible.'

Mum drove my father's beloved Jaguar, which she disliked for its ostentation, while he sat in the passenger seat. Soweto was a vast, grid-like city. Long rows of small, single-storey houses with corrugated-iron roofs snaked over the rolling hills as far as we could see. Main roads were tarred; wide, unmade streets separated the rows of houses, some colourfully painted, some with gardens, the occasional tree, a washing line. Pride was juxtaposed with desolation. As the dormitory town for Johannesburg's workers it had an air of absence. We passed schools, municipal beerhalls, the bustling Putco bus station, the massive Baragwanath Hospital. As I took photos a young woman looked at me as if to say: So we're a tourist attraction now, are we? I felt uncomfortable, and returned to the car.

▲ I wrote three feature articles on South Africa for News Line

'Darling, we've decided to support you on this one,' my father said.

Only a handful of comrades on the Political Committee knew that I owned the new property, which virtually doubled our previous space. Party carpenters converted the upper floor into a canteen with ample space for 40 staff, a big office for Sheila and a library. The partition walls were removable to create a large meeting room. A small printing press, *News Line* dispatch and a fully equipped film department were on the ground floor. Access to the yard was reinstated. Above the new building a towering telescopic aerial was erected to listen – to what? We weren't sure, but it was to do with the work of Comrade Charlie, who had been seconded from our German section. His tiny security office next to the canteen, overlooking the alleyway, was full of mysterious technical equipment and was never left unlocked.

In September 1981 my brother Allan rang the *News Line* office at nine in the evening. I took the call in Alex's empty office.

'I'm afraid Dad died this afternoon.'

Although I had known it was coming, I felt devastated and sat still in the dark for a few minutes. My pulse was racing and my hands were shaking. I didn't feel like telling the other comrades so I continued typing the next day's television programmes, grateful for a mindless task, until Runcorn gave the all-clear to leave.

Four of us women assembled at the gate to leave.

'You must wait for Sheila,' said Charlie, who was on the gate.

I was frustrated.

'This is ridiculous. I walk around my branch much later than this.'

'You know women comrades must be escorted.' Charlie was a stickler for rules.

Aileen was puzzled at my impatience.

'Clare, you can wait a minute or two.'

I felt ready to burst. I wanted the privacy of my own flat. I stepped up to the gate, swung the metal arm open and pushed through. I walked as fast as I could down the alley, ignoring Charlie's voice calling me back.

I passed the fire station and the bus stands. I heard running footsteps behind me.

'Clare, you know you shouldn't walk home alone.' It was Everton, a Jamaican member who was on overnight guard duty, a normal human being who would understand how I felt.

'Oh Everton, I've just heard that my father has died.'

Ten minutes later Aileen knocked on my door.

'Everton told us. Now sit down and have a good cry.' She pushed me into a chair. 'I'll go and tell Gerry. Sheila will make you a cup of tea.'

I felt Aileen understood my distress because she had lost her own father. Sheila tried to be sympathetic. Aileen returned to say Gerry wanted to see me but his condolences barely registered.

At work next day, my colleagues tried to express sympathy but everyone was young and most hadn't experienced death. Norman came from the dispatch department.

'Sorry about your father.' He laid his hand gently on my arm. The brief, physical contact was very comforting.

Then Vanessa came.

'Gerry told me about your father. I'm very sorry. I know I would be very sad if my father died.'

She sounded sincere and I appreciated her words.

Christmas Eve offered a lucrative opportunity to clear our branch debts with extensive sales boosted by generous seasonal donations. We began the early morning with a carefully planned route. First, the milk depot in Vauxhall with its moving lines of newly washed bottles; then the huge, bustling Borough Sorting Office at 6am – 'Here, girls, have a tot of whisky'; on to the train drivers' canteen in Waterloo Station and a quick round of the ticket collectors; into the bowels of St Thomas' hospital among the laundry and catering staff, boilermen and cleaners. To Lambeth dustmen's depot next, then the fire-engine maintenance workshop, the telephone exchange on South Lambeth Road, the fire station watch-change at 8am, the Beefeater bonded gin factory at the Oval and, finally, the Greater London Council's headquarters at County Hall. After breakfast and a bit of Christmas shopping we did a lively lunchtime pub sale.

I took the coin-heavy sales money into the Centre. Sheila had checked that everyone had somewhere to go on Christmas day and comrades with family up country had already left. There were no decorations – we were revolutionaries, after all – but Gerry enjoyed being benevolent at Christmas and distributed turkeys to staff families and groups of comrades. The birds had been delivered that morning, and were laid out in the canteen for the security guards to match

▲ Beefeater gin strikers near the Oval cricket ground, in my branch area

names and sizes on the list.

'I hate turkeys,' Charlie muttered as the 18th one was taken away. 'We even have to cook them.'

'Who for?'

'For Gerry, for Mike and Janet, the guards over the holiday, and your flats.'

'But we can cook our own,' I protested.

'We've been told to do it.'

Aileen stopped me on my way out.

'Have you bought the extra food for the flats?'

'Not yet.'

'Come on, let's get it now.' She was irritated.

In a small supermarket she tossed everything imaginable into the trolley: ham, nuts, cheese and crackers, biscuits, mince pies, salad dressing, mayonnaise, lettuce, pickles, chocolates, sprouts, Christmas puddings. I was shocked at the extravagance.

'Wouldn't Fine Fare be cheaper?'

'No time. There'll be a huge row when Gerry asks if enough food's been bought.'

I dumped the feast in my kitchenette, and made ready to go back to my branch. As I clattered down the stairs in my high heels, I met Gerry coming up. He stopped on the landing, startled.

'Oh.' He was looking up at me. 'Oh ... you're wearing a new pair of tights.'

They were just ordinary tights. The maroon pleats of my short tartan skirt swirled round my thighs below its loose-cut, matching jacket. My legs had clearly thrilled him and he was struggling to recompose himself. I giggled inwardly.

'I'm just off on a pub sale.'

He rearranged his expression as the revolutionary leader.

'The paper has a good headline.' He shuffled upstairs.

We finished the sale well before closing time because the customers were rowdy and drunk. Back home at 11 o'clock I started relaxing. Christmas fell on a Friday so we would be off work until Monday – three whole days with no paper to produce and none to sell.

We congregated on Christmas day in the top flat, furthest from Gerry's: six young women plus other staff at the Centre without families to go to. We had wine and beer left over from the Christmas bazaar and other alcohol we had brought ourselves. Potatoes were roasting in the oven, vegetables were ready to boil, someone was carving the turkey cooked overnight by the guards, music was playing. We ate Christmas dinner with all the trimmings, chatting and laughing, genuinely enjoying ourselves. Sheila came in with plates for her and her husband.

'I just want food, no wine. All right, I'll take a beer for Paddy.'

She returned to her flat across the corridor. After organising Gerry's solitary Christmas dinner, Aileen appeared.

'I'm driving to Nottingham to join Paul and his family.' She turned to one of the young women. 'Gerry wants you to cover for me. Go and see how he wants to arrange it.'

I rang my mother reverse-charges from Sheila's phone. This was the first mournful Christmas since my father had died. I told her I was seeing my brother Howard, Sarah and their son in north London on Sunday.

We watched non-stop television, including the Morecambe and Wise show and at least three feature films, a rare treat. We ate some more, drank wine. From time to time the comrade who was covering for Aileen directed one of us to go and see Gerry. When it was my turn he looked disapprovingly at my red sparkly tights.

'Why are you wearing those?'

'A bit of fun for Christmas.'

'It's rather silly.'

Strange. He had appreciated my legs the day before.

We were joined by an outgoing guard from the Centre because there was no public transport home. I went downstairs to let him in.

'My god,' he said. 'Four locked doors before you reach your own front door. That's a lot of keys.'

'Don't I know. In August my handbag was stolen at 6.30am while I was delivering papers. My car front window was smashed in 90 seconds. I lost lots of branch money and my house keys so I was hauled into the Political Committee.'

'Why?'

'Well, who had the keys – thieves or The State? Charlie changed all the locks, four new keys for everyone in eight flats, two for the accountants on the first floor.'

'That must have cost a fortune.'

'I paid, of course. A week and a half's wages – and the lost branch money. I was in disgrace. I felt like the perpetrator, not the victim.'

This comrade, an actor, stood by the kitchen counter, drinking doggedly until it was time to stagger across the road to where the men were accommodated.

On Boxing Day Gerry invited three of us to watch the rousing film, *God's Englishman*, about Oliver Cromwell in the tumult of the English bourgeois revolution.

'Cromwell told his troops: "Trust in God and keep your powder dry",' Gerry pointed out. 'He knew that revolutionary theory was essential, although his "theory" was religion. But revolutionaries also had to be *practical*.'

Would Gerry be the Cromwell figure in our revolution?

As the year ended I looked back, assessing my life. I felt the sorrow of my father's death. My commitment to the socialist revolution was undimmed but my personal life was not so clear. When Gerry had first seduced me I had thought he needed some kind of human warmth, I had felt an obligation to him and to the revolutionary struggle. But our 'relationship' consisted merely of an occasional sexual encounter, unromantic, perfunctory. I disliked the stale smell of his lower standards of cleanliness. I wanted more than just a greasy, naked rub-around; I dreaded him calling me downstairs: 'Take off your dress.' But how would he react if I started a relationship with anyone else? How could I manage it anyway? I couldn't bring anyone home to the flats and if I stayed out it would be noticed.

I didn't know what to do. This had been a troubled Christmas.

1982
FINANCE OFFICE

Gerry suddenly disrupted every routine in my life. He pulled me out of the *News Line* office and sent me driving all over London collecting money from contacts identified by branch secretaries, reporting back to him at 5 o'clock every evening. I was an instrument in some unfathomable conflict with Sheila. After several weeks he sent me to work in the finance office.

I was bitterly disappointed. The finance office lacked the excitement of breaking news and advanced technology. Paul Jennings fought back, and Gerry agreed that each afternoon I would help typeset the race cards. Gerry also told me to assist in the *News Line* cuttings library after we had counted money in the morning. My self-belief fell to a low point. I had considered I was essential to the paper's production but now I was just Dot's finance assistant, a fill-in typesetter, an odd-job comrade.

Gerry next instructed me to take a team every day for early-morning factory-gate sales at the giant British Leyland car plants in Cowley, Oxford. Sheila considered this a waste of resources and ruled that I couldn't use leading branch members so I developed a wider pool of comrades and explained the purpose of the sales to each new team member.

'Alan Thornett, a leading shop steward at Cowley, was on the Party Central Committee but he challenged our political line in 1974.'

'He was expelled, wasn't he?'

'Yes, and we lost a major group of industrial shop stewards. That's why Comrade Healy believes it's vital to strengthen our influence in the Cowley factories now.'

▲ Malvinas: Prime Minister Thatcher launched a naval task force against Argentina to regain control of the Falkland Islands

I felt unsure of the political value of this daily marathon, but Comrade Healy had asked me to do it and I intended to do it properly. We sold few papers but I became well-known at the Cowley gates and many workers greeted me. There were startled looks during the Falklands invasion when our headline said: 'This is not our war'. But we changed to condemning the war after Mike Banda insisted we couldn't be neutral.

'We have to *oppose* British imperialism's predatory actions, even against a reactionary South American dictatorship.' He cited Trotsky's 'revolutionary defeatist' analysis of a similar situation in relation to 1930s Brazil.

One shop steward who had supported the Party against Thornett stopped to talk and sometimes gave me messages for Gerry. Another worker made a regular comment:

'Good morning, my dear. Monday morning – washing day. You should be at home getting your washing machine out.'

My life settled into a new routine of rising at half past four every day. I couldn't attend evening meetings; I was out of sync with everyone else in the Party. I negotiated a pattern of life with the latest comrade who had been allocated to share my flat. We turned the large wardrobe at right angles to the wall to demarcate our personal space and agreed that, if she happened to be home early, we wouldn't talk as I prepared to sleep at 9 o'clock.

The finance office's responsibilities had expanded enormously since I had worked there in 1973. The office was directly across the yard from the main gate. Energetic Dot Gibson, now in her mid-forties, managed Party finances and all its companies: Astmoor Litho, the smaller Grafton Litho, our

▲ We had three Youth Training Centres in 1981 with four more later

publishing company New Park Publications, six bookshops and seven Youth Training Centres. She worked closely with Gerry, who oversaw every detail. Our computerised accounting system was the responsibility of Robert Harris, a relaxed and friendly boffin whose clothes could have come from Oxfam and who had an unnerving habit of fearlessly saying what he really thought. Mike Banda's wife Janet worked with us in the mornings when she wasn't rushing around for her three children.

I arrived back from Cowley at about nine each morning and helped count the incoming money using a noisy coin-counting machine and a whirring note-counter. Comrades communicated with us from the warehouse through a small, bolted hatch with a letterbox below for branch payments. Banking was a daily drama: Robert loaded everything into the car waiting in the yard to rush to the bank by 3 o'clock. I went too if Dot needed to talk to the manager. We parked directly outside the bank on double yellow lines, by agreement with Clapham Junction traffic police. The driver carried in the heavy leather briefcases, bulging with bagged-up coins, while I passed the paying-in books, cheques and notes over the counter to the teller.

'We'll weigh the coins after you've gone,' she said. 'We never order coins from head office because you bring us all we need.'

Near the end of July Dot was particularly tense. She shivered when she heard Gerry's key in the finance office door. He sauntered in, a portly figure, waving dismissively at Robert and me.

'Shut the hatch. Go upstairs for a cup of tea. I want to talk to Mrs Gibson.'

When we returned Dot was typing a sheet of figures. She took it into Gerry's office and we heard him shouting. She hurried back, put a new sheet of paper into her typewriter and started typing again. Gerry burst in, stood over her desk and yelled.

'You have to pay attention to what I say, comrade. You have to listen.' He wiped his hand across his face in a gesture of frustration. 'I can't lead this Party when comrades won't listen.'

He turned towards the door and then looked back at Dot with a mock-pathetic leer.

'Please, Mrs Gibson, please just try and get it right.' He slammed the door and we heard the adjacent gents' toilet door swing open.

Gerry screaming was something of a revelation to me. I had once heard him shout in the *News Line* office when he had interrupted the fine-tuned production and sent everyone home over some Political Committee row. But shouting in the finance office seemed to be common. If the figures weren't correct, or they weren't presented as Gerry wanted, there was a big row. I found it hard to understand.

Gerry left for his afternoon rest and Dot and I were alone. She gulped a cup of tea and handed me a sheet of figures.

'See this payment for that large book order? It came in last month, so it counted against June's debts. He asked why I hadn't included it in July's figures. "We're dispatching the books this month – it should be here," he said. But it's been spent and GH doesn't see that.' She called him GH in private conversations. 'It's absolutely crazy. It's a kind of double accounting.'

Although Dot was on the Central Committee, I had always seen her as a back-room office worker who paid a few bills and managed payments at conferences. Now I began to realise how much Gerry depended on her, how pivotal her role in the Party's machinery was. Gerry screamed, denigrated her, but 'Mrs Gibson' was far more than a pen-pushing bill-payer. Political theory moved the Party, yes, but much hinged on money.

◀ *Labour Review* the WRP'S monthly organ of revolutionary Marxism, began in June 1977 to assist development of political theory

'Our accountant is dead. Someone else is living in his house.' Linda from Runcorn had helped prepare the company tax accounts but when she took them to the former League member who had audited them for years, she found that he had died eight months previously.

Dot put her head in her hands.

'How are we going to tell Gerry? How will we find a replacement?' She looked tired and panicky.

'Yellow Pages directory,' suggested Linda.

'Gerry won't trust just anyone …'

'It's a legal requirement. The last thing we want is the tax authorities snooping around.'

We heard the Granada arrive in the yard. The car-door slammed and Gerry came into the finance office. Dot came straight to the point.

'Our accountant has died. We'll have to find another.'

He took the news surprisingly calmly.

'Don't use a local one – they could be a security risk.'

Linda and Dot selected an accounts firm in central London and arranged a meeting. Gerry hated officialdom and made sure he was off the premises.

Richard Moss was a middle-aged man who spoke with a public school accent, but had an informal, friendly manner and seemed tickled by the thought of working with a Trotskyist organisation. He sat at my desk to look through the accounts.

'A lot needs sorting out here.' He leafed through the pages. 'I can arrange for one of our staff to come and work through the books here in your offices.'

Dot blenched. Gerry wouldn't like that. How much would it cost? Would it be a security risk? The only outsiders allowed into the Centre were technicians for the photocopier or the Muirhead picture transmitter. The window cleaners weren't even allowed to clean the *News Line* windows any more. Dot thought quickly.

'He could work upstairs in the archives, above this office. There's a back staircase to the finance hatch if he has questions.' And he would be out of Gerry's sight, I thought to myself.

So the friendly young accountant, Allan, was installed in a corner of the untidy archives to make sense of the inter-linked company accounts.

Richard Moss asked for a private discussion with me.

'New Park Publications owns the major part of these premises. I see you own the other half.'

'Yes, but that's not known by others who work here.'

'New Park pays the running expenses, but they don't seem to pay any rent.'

'No, there's no rent.'

'You allow them to use it free?'

'It's not "them". It's us. I'm a Party member and I see this as a Party resource.'

'I see.' He thought for a while. 'You know, I've told Mrs Gibson you need a dedicated book-keeper to work here part-time, maintaining the books over the year. We could even provide one. It would be much cheaper than an expensive accountant sorting things out afterwards.'

'What did she say?'

'She said Mr Healy wouldn't agree to that.'

'I'm sure she's right.'

'You see, Clare, this is not a small concern. This is Big Business. Some of your book-keeping is computerised, but it's not adequate for the size of New Park Publications' book-publishing activities and all the companies.'

This conversation made me begin to question how the finance office functioned.

Mike Banda and Dot had a meeting with me in his upstairs office across the path from the editorial offices. Below it was the bus-engine generator that would keep *News Line* production going in the event of a power cut. Each month Charlie ran it to check its function: a noisy, smelly operation.

◀ Power cuts could have threatened *News Line* production. With the help of a crane in the adjacent fire station, Dave Bruce oversees installation of a generator across the path from the editorial office

Mike spoke carefully.

'You've bought these premises' – he indicated the adjacent building – 'and we want to be sure that the Party is secure here.'

'As far as I'm concerned this will always be a Party building.'

'Yes, yes, but we would like a legal agreement.' I guessed Gerry was behind this suggestion because Mike was never this concrete. 'You and Dot should see our lawyer to draw up a legal document.'

Benedict Birnberg's offices were in a narrow building on Borough High Street. I was excited to be visiting this important civil-rights lawyer. Dot introduced me and explained our request.

'Wouldn't it be simpler to transfer ownership to the Party?'

'No. We can't do that.'

'The problem is that you can't have an agreement without a "consideration" to the other side. You can't, for instance enter a legal agreement to make yourself a slave. The agreement has to give you something.'

'We need some kind of document.' Dot was firm.

Birnberg had dealt with Gerry on a number of occasions and probably realised this strange request came from him.

'I'll draft something. But it won't be legally binding.'

An impressive legal document arrived that seemed to tie the building permanently to the Party. Only Dot and I knew it was no more than a vague statement of intent. I had no difficulty in signing it.

With a screech-and-clunk Charlie opened the gate to let me in. I saw Gerry's short, bulky figure in the yard, fastidiously tidy in his dark suit, white shirt and tie, looking like a retired wrestler.

'Ah, you've been to Cowley.' His small eyes sank in the fleshy folds of his chubby face below the smooth dome of his bullet head with neatly trimmed remnants of hair. 'Very important to keep up the pressure on Thornett.'

Another screech-and-clunk as Charlie spoke to an unfamiliar man.

'Please come up to the canteen and I'll tell Mrs Gibson you're here.'

Gerry looked uneasy.

'Who was that?' he asked on Charlie's return.

'He's from the catering supply company. He has an appointment to see Dot.'

Gerry shuffled off towards the *News Line* office. Charlie's face appeared at the finance office hatch.

'Dot, the bailiff is here again.'

Gerry certainly mustn't know. Even traffic wardens terrified him, apparently. Dot went upstairs to check which bill he was chasing this time and came back to fetch a cheque. She saw him off the premises with friendly chatter.

'Doesn't Gerry know we're behind with payments to some of our suppliers?' I asked.

Dot gave me a peculiar look.

'Well, yes and no.' She sat down at her desk. 'Actually …' She sucked one arm of her glasses. 'He hasn't a clue about the day-to-day cash flow.'

Sheila came in, always in transit. She never sat down.

'How much did the bazaar make in the end?'

'Well over £3,000.' Dot handed her a sheet of paper.

'Mmm. The women's clothes did well … and the refreshments.'

'But look here.' Dot showed her another sheet. '*News Line* figures for the weekend are down by almost the same figure.'

'Oh, come on. They just haven't paid the money in yet.' Sheila lost interest and went out.

Robert grinned cheekily.

'The entire London membership is at the bazaar and she still demands the same paper sales.'

Dot and Sheila worked well together but there were inherent tensions. Dot's domain was behind the scenes while Sheila's was the visible functioning of the branches and the excitement of campaigns. She spoke to leading members countrywide every day; she followed the branch debts meticulously. To her they encapsulated the throbbing life of the Party. This detailed knowledge made her powerful.

When the branch debts had finished printing on sprocket-fed continuous stationery I took them upstairs. Sheila was on the phone to a Party organiser, typing with one finger at the same time.

'He can't make the Central Committee because his wife's baby is due? Nonsense.' She stopped typing. 'Babies are born every day of the week. I'm instructing him to attend.'

She's bonkers, I thought, and put the debts on her desk as she handed me a list of increased *News Line* orders, always up, never down. The pressure to sell more papers, raise more money, recruit more members was relentless.

A comrade arrived at the hatch, agitated, asking to talk to Dot. She leaned forward to catch his low voice.

'Do we need to buy a new one out of the canteen money? Here, sign the petty cash slip and bring back the bill and any change.'

He thanked her and slipped away.

As the senior woman in the Centre who was there before Sheila and Aileen, Dot had a subtle power. She could advise on tricky internal negotiations or could get comrades out of a fix when something went wrong – a breakage, or an unexpected expense. The 'canteen money' seemed to be a general fund that she could use for small purchases without abusing her authority.

As she sat down, Vanessa arrived with the slightly distracted air of a serious revolutionary.

'I have some money for the development fund.' She scrabbled around in her handbag. 'I intended to pay it in for my branch, but …'

There was a palpable increase in Dot's tension. She felt Vanessa was always acting a part. The four cheques were each bigger than most branches dreamed of.

'Comrade Gerry has told me it should go in centrally and that branches should raise the fund from their own members and contacts.' Vanessa looked at us earnestly, nodding her head. 'We must recruit new members.' She wafted out.

Gerry left for his afternoon rest and Dot relaxed, becoming expansive.

'When I joined the Socialist Labour League and worked on campaigns, Gerry realised I was capable, so he brought me to work at the Centre. He needs people with ideas and abilities, but he wants *control*. He incorporates their ideas, presents them to the Party and sets about implementing them. That's his genius.'

'On theoretical matters too?'

'Oh, yes. He relies heavily on Mike and the university and college lecturers. Now he has the theatre and film people as well. He won them through his theoretical brilliance and then developed campaigns to incorporate their particular skills into Party activity.'

Dot assembled some papers.

'GH wants me round the flats at 3 o'clock to discuss the expansion plans.'

I had begun to realise that her relationship with Gerry was more complex than just his shouting and impossible demands. Occasionally he sat down in the finance office to talk things through with her like an equal colleague, discussing quite rationally.

When Gerry returned at 5 o'clock he came straight into the finance office, looked at me and made a shock announcement.

'I'm giving your car to Ted Knight.' Gerry had bought me a sporty, metallic blue Ford Fiesta XR2 with the insurance money after a drunk driver had demolished my previous car. 'Change the name on the registration certificate to your maiden name so no one connects it with the Party.'

Ted Knight, Labour leader of Lambeth Council, had previously been in the Socialist Labour League and had a continuing association with the Party.

'But it's my car … Surely Lambeth Council has a fleet of vehicles?'

'Oh come on, Clare, this is for the Party,' admonished Dot. Gerry saw that I was upset and tried to mollify me.

'Don't worry, comrade. You can have the beige Fiesta.'

Of course I conceded, but I felt resentful.

▲ Dot Gibson managed the Party's finances and companies

International Committee

The usual flurry of preparations was underway for a meeting of the International Committee of the Fourth International. Aileen photocopied documents, checked travel arrangements, organised accommodation. The security comrades made space in the archives above the finance office.

A week before the conference Dot and Aileen bought a length of brown corduroy fabric and ordered a single divan bed. Next day I found them on their knees in Gerry's inner office, scrabbling around with pins and fabric, covering the bed against the far wall. I burst out laughing.

'It's for Gerry to have a rest during the International Committee sessions.' Dot shoved a pin in the fold underneath one corner. 'He won't have time to go back to his flat. He's almost 70, more than twice the age of most delegates.'

Aileen stood up.

'Come on Dot, that'll do.'

'I'll take it home tonight and sew it.'

'Don't be silly. This is fine!'

'It needs to be done properly.'

By the next day the bed was tidily covered, with three matching cushions propped up against the wall, doubling as seating for Political Committee meetings.

Comrades arrived from Australia, Sri Lanka, Latin America, the United States and European countries. Two women comrades from Spain and Greece stayed in my flat, which barely had room for their camp beds. During the week we heard muffled voices above the finance office, chairs scraping and, occasionally, Gerry's forceful tones. We chatted to the delegates in the canteen over lunch, eager to hear what was happening in their countries. The German section was preparing to launch its own daily paper and there was a special buzz around its delegates: lithe, fair-haired Ulli and dark-haired, sombre Peter.

'Clare, where is …' Dot was trying to find something in the piles on her desk. 'Gerry wants me and Dave North to discuss the financial details with the German comrades.'

'Why don't the Americans start a daily paper?' I asked. 'They're the next biggest section and they already publish books.'

'That's a political decision for them and the International Committee.'

Dave North, leader of Workers League, based in Detroit, was a handsome, dark-haired man in his thirties with an unmistakable air of authority, but easy to talk to. He and Dot went upstairs for the meeting. She returned very worried.

'I don't see how they can do it. They only have 36 members – the cadres, that is, not the wider supporters. And they're all taking out mortgages and loans to pay for the expensive web-offset press.'

Aileen came in, looking weary.

'Dave has reported to Gerry and he's exploded. I've sent the German comrades in. He's controlling himself, but he's furious.

'Ulli and Peter have brought money with them and seemed to think they could raise the rest, over £100,000,' said Dot. 'But when I asked how many members they had, we immediately realised it was madness. They'll also have to pay for a bigger printshop, wages, paper, ink.'

'Why, oh why, didn't anyone ask that question a year ago before this was all decided?' Aileen shook her head.

Plans for the German daily paper were scrapped. The international delegations departed. Dot had to cancel the order with the press manufacturer, Solna GmbH in Germany.

'But you have signed a contract. We are already making the press,' said the horrified sales representative. 'There will be a penalty for cancellation.'

The penalty was £25,000. Dot swallowed two aspirins, gulped her tea, took off her glasses and put her head in her hands.

'Keep calm,' said Aileen.

'How do we find £25,000? This is crazy.' Dot threw her pen on the table and flung her glasses aside. 'We don't have the money.'

'Just come and tell Gerry. We'll work something out later.'

'They could go to court to bankrupt us.'

'Dot, calm down. We'll talk this afternoon.'

As Dot went out, Aileen turned to me.

'Clare, hang on to Dot's ankles. She's about to become airborne.'

We heard Gerry shouting. Dot went back and forth to his office. Then he stormed in.

'Where's Mrs Gibson?'

'In the toilet.'

He banged her desk and kicked the door.

'These are impossible problems. I have to deal with such backward comrades.' He kicked the desk. 'I can't work like this. I'm supposed to lead this movement and this is what I have to deal with.'

This was one of the worst rages I'd seen. He came over to kick my desk, picked up some books and brought them straight down on my head. It didn't really hurt but I was incensed.

'You can't do that. You know I had a fractured skull in the car accident,' I cried, glaring at him. He turned away, kicking Dot's desk again.

'You're so backward, you *made* me do it.'

Where had I found the nerve to shout back at him? Why was he blaming Dot, who had asked the concrete question he hadn't thought of?

We didn't see Gerry for a week. He retired to bed, leaving the problem to Dot and Aileen. They conferred in her office, made phone calls and worked something out, though I couldn't imagine what. Sheila stayed well clear at a sympathetic distance. Mike Banda was no use at resolving concrete matters.

Twenty thousand dollars

I don't know where the $20,000 originated. Perhaps a supporter had donated them. I learned about them indirectly after one of Gerry's sorties into the finance office.

'Get your dinner,' he told me and Robert. 'I want to talk to Mrs Gibson.' His voice had an ominous edge. He called her 'Mrs Gibson' to diminish her importance, with a slight suggestion of 'housewife' and the little things in life.

After Gerry had gone home for his afternoon rest, Aileen found Dot and me alone.

'Was it all right?'

'He just looked without touching.' Dot seemed exhausted.

'So he was wrong if he thought he would catch you out.'

'What did Gerry look at?' I asked.

'Some dollars.'

Dot walked across to the small, windowless room at the back, unlocked a filing cabinet next to the safe, pulled open the second drawer and took out a plump folder tucked at the back. She put it on my desk and unfastened it. Packed inside were bundles of dollar bills, fastened neatly with paper bands.

'He insists that no one else should know.'

'But they should be in a bank, accruing interest. Why are they in a filing cabinet?'

'Oh no. "You can't trust banks," he says.' Dot replaced the folder in its hiding place.

'Some very illogical things go on round here.'

Aileen nodded. I sensed that she and Dot had shared something very confidential.

I worked in my branch all day on Saturday and returned my car to the Centre after the evening pub sale. I found Dot waiting to give me a lift.

She drove in silence around Clapham Common to its southern edge, pulled up in the dark car park of the Windmill Pub and switched off the engine. I couldn't imagine what this was about.

'The Americans are here to discuss the Gelfand legal case and Gerry wants to give them the $20,000 I showed you.'

Gelfand was an American Trotskyist who was fighting a court case against the United States government and the American Socialist Workers Party, about government agents in political parties.

'Dave North is going back to Detroit on Monday, and we don't have the dollars.'

'How d'you mean?'

'Aileen and I spent them in several financial crises that GH couldn't handle. The dollars I showed you weren't real.'

'They were forgeries?'

'Not exactly. When we spent them we had to replace them with something in case Gerry asked to see them.'

'And?'

'Dave Bruce found some paper similar in thickness and texture to dollars and guillotined it to the exact size of $50 bills. Then we dyed the paper so the edges looked the same when they were stacked up together.'

'Dyed?'

'Some greenish ink that Dave found for us. Peter and our three sons helped. We dipped the "dollars" in the diluted ink and pegged them to clotheslines to dry, with newspapers all over the living room floor catching the drips. Then we bundled them up with real bills at the top and bottom and replaced the paper bands.'

'Wow.' I didn't know what else to say. 'Who knows about this?'

'Only Aileen and Dave.'

'And your family.'

'Well, yes.'

'Why are you telling me?'

'You have to help us.'

'Me? What can I do?'

'You have to get us $20,000. We have no one else to ask.'

I couldn't believe what I had heard.

'Where would I get $20,000?'

'Well, you would have to phone your mother in South Africa and –'

'And ask her for $20,000? But it's an enormous sum of money.' I shook my head. 'What on earth could I say it was for?'

'Aileen thinks you should tell her we need it for legal costs in the Gelfand case.'

Occasional figures flitted out from the murky shadows of Clapham Common as I struggled to think.

'I don't know if I can do that.'

'If GH discovers the money isn't there all hell will break loose. There'll be the most enormous political row, with unimaginable results.'

I believed her. I had witnessed Gerry's explosions over much smaller issues.

'Sheila's away this weekend. You can phone your mother from her flat. Aileen will give you the keys.'

Next morning I counted money like an automaton, panicky thoughts swirling around my head. I hoped Dot would have changed her mind overnight, but when the Political Committee meeting finished Aileen brought me Sheila's keys.

'I don't know how I'm going to do this …'

'Come on, Clare. Just tell your mother about the Gelfand case.'

Aileen had a way of making gigantic difficulties seem simple.

I walked home, skirting Clapham Common, seeking delays. I bought a pastry from the delicatessen, I waited for the lights to change before crossing at the tube station. I went upstairs to the top floor and made a cup of tea in my own flat. Then I went along the corridor to Sheila's meticulously tidy flat, with her kitchenette separated by a waist-high wall from the main room and a full-height wall differentiating the sleeping area. My flat is better, I thought. Tea in one hand and pastry in the other, I looked out of the windows at the hodge-podge of walls, pipes and rubbish bins that serviced the commercial buildings below. An uglier view than mine, but quieter. I was procrastinating. I sat down at the table to make notes.

Sylvia Franklin was secretary to the leader of the American Socialist Workers Party when Trotsky was assassinated by a Stalinist agent in 1940.

Later, court trials in the US revealed that she too was an agent of Stalin's secret police, the GPU.

Leaders of the Socialist Workers Party covered up for Sylvia Franklin and had secret dealings with US intelligence ...

Oh no, it was too complicated. I crumpled the paper and started again. And again. How could I explain why it was important to prove in court that United States government agents had infiltrated an American socialist party?

Trotskyist parties in different countries belong to the Fourth International. If one party has been infiltrated by agents it is dangerous for the whole international movement. Alan Gelfand has gone to court to prove ...

That was no good either. I would have to explain that the Socialist Workers Party belonged to a different Fourth International to ours. Much too complex.

Half-way through the afternoon Aileen tapped gently at the door.

'How are things going?'

'I can't work out what to say. It's impossible.'

'No it's not. Tell your mother how vital the court case is.'

'But she doesn't agree with us politically.'

'She'll understand that you need the money. Your parents responded in the past.'

At 5 o'clock I dialled my mother's number. She was pleased to hear from me and her voice reassured me.

'Mum, I need your help. We are fighting a court case in America about government agents in socialist parties ...' I gabbled on in a breathless flood, my heart pounding. 'We urgently need money for the next stage.'

'Oh dear. All that money making lawyers rich. A terrible waste. How much do you need?'

'$20,000, and we need it tomorrow.'

'Well, you had better ring Pamela from the trust tonight. I'll give you her home number. Ask her to ring me to confirm it.'

I was shaking with relief.

'This will of course come from your share, to be fair to your brothers and sister.'

My teeth were chattering as Mum told me other family news. I struggled to talk normally.

'Phone Pamela now,' she said as she rang off.

It had been so simple. Mum wasn't concerned about an incomprehensible court case. She was agreeing because it was important to me, her daughter. I felt a wave of love for her.

▲ My mother

'Hello, Pamela, I'm sorry to disturb you at home but my mother advised me to ring you tonight. I need $20,000 in cash tomorrow morning.'

Silence.

'$20,000?' Another moment's silence. 'I hope the bank even has that many cash dollars available.'

She agreed to phone me in the morning with the arrangements.

Next morning Dot arranged for Dave Bruce to drive me to Standard Chartered Bank in the City. He didn't ask why, we never gossiped about such things.

I showed the teller my passport, as Pamela had instructed. He fetched a prepared packet and counted the $20,000, in $50 notes, in front of me. I signed a receipt, put the packet in my bag and left, trying to look casual. It had taken barely ten minutes. Back in the waiting car, I locked the door, hugging the bag close to my body.

Gerry was in a meeting with the Americans: Dave North and Larry, a black comrade who never left his side, both dressed in impeccable dark suits. At four in the afternoon Gerry brought them into the finance office.

'Comrade Dot will give you the dollars,' he said grandly. He didn't seem to care that I was there.

Dot went into the back room, unlocked the filing cabinet and brought out the folder.

'Count them,' Gerry instructed.

Larry tucked the packet into his briefcase. He and Dave North said goodbye to Dot and nodded to me. A comrade was waiting to drive them to Heathrow.

As the door closed Dot put her head in her hands. Her whole body flagged as the tension dissipated.

'Clare, go and make us a cup of tea.'

Volume 38

The Marx Centenary March in 1983 was a jubilant affair. I missed Mike Banda's opening oration at Marx's grave in Highgate Cemetery because Sheila wanted me to drive her car to Alexandra Palace. The bus to come back was diverted because of the march, so I walked. I heard distant chanting, singing, and suddenly the march appeared round a bend, led by banners of the International Committee of the Fourth International and the Party's Central Committee, followed by an exuberant mass of red flags and banners. People watching from windows waved at the confident, thousands-strong column with myriad banners from trade unions, Party district committees, Young Socialist branches, international delegations. Call-and-response slogans and spontaneous singing of the *Internationale* created a celebratory atmosphere.

I spent the rest of the afternoon in the finance office, disappointed to have missed most of the march and almost all the speeches afterwards. That's how things were.

'We're going to have classes on dialectical materialism at 8am every Wednesday,' Robert told me when I arrived back from Cowley, 'starting with the section on Hegel's *Science of Logic* in *Volume 38*.'

A white number on the spine of the green dust cover identified Lenin's *Volume 38: Philosophical Notebooks*, a complex book of disjointed notes. On Wednesdays another driver went to Cowley, so I was able to attend the classes, crammed awkwardly into the editorial office. Gerry faced us sideways to a table, legs splayed to accommodate his round belly. The obligatory bottle of Perrier water was beside him, alongside his notes on small cards. He drew our attention to a passage:

▲ **March 1983**: To mark 100 years since his death, an international memorial march was organised from Karl Marx's birthplace in Trier, Germany, to a centenary commemoration rally in London

▶ **Karl Marx centenary commemoration rally**: A huge crowd surrounding Marx's grave at London's Highgate Cemetery heard Mike Banda trace the development of Marxism over the century since his death

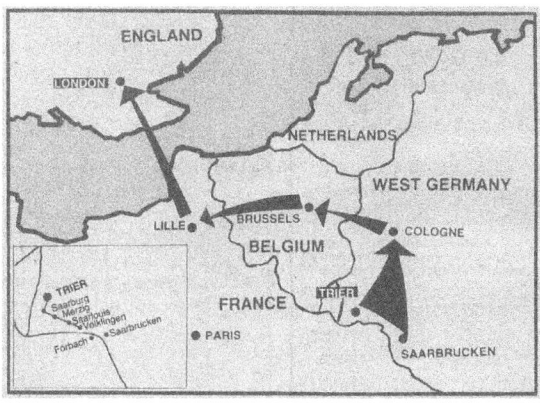

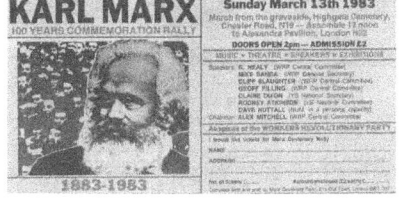

◀ Route of the international march

'I am in general trying to read Hegel materialistically: Hegel is materialism which has been stood on its head (according to Engels) —that is to say, I cast aside for the most part God, the Absolute, the Pure Idea, etc.'

It became more complicated. Gerry drew diagrams on the blackboard and I copied them.

'Well, comrades? Who wants to speak?'

Quiet Sri Lankan Sam made an interesting contribution. Gerry nodded approvingly, correcting one point before selecting another comrade, who stuttered through an interpretation of a particular passage.

'But comrade,' Gerry said, '*being determines consciousness.* You don't grasp this. That's why you make mistakes in your work. You're expressing Kantianism.'

The comrade tried again.

My mind wandered. Poor Lenin, grappling with Hegel's philosophy, exiled in Switzerland as the First World War began. Scribblings in his personal notebooks, underlinings, and double underlinings. He couldn't have known that years later someone would recreate the jumbled layout, word by jotted word, retaining interspersed German words, translating them in footnotes, to make a book for Russian workers, students and intellectuals to examine in

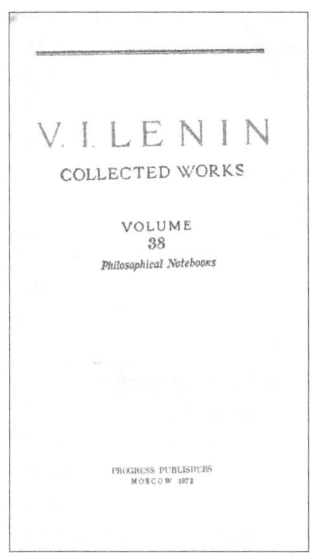

▲ The green dust cover for my copy of Lenin's Volume **38**: *Philosophical Notebooks* had disintegrated. Here is the title page

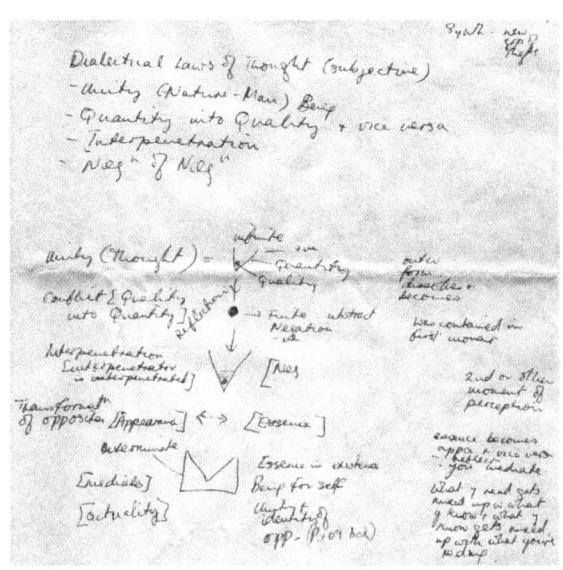

▲ My copy of Healy's incomprehensible philosophy notes

detail, to be translated into dozens of languages. He couldn't have imagined that the English translation would become a sort of textbook for our Party.

I struggled with the philosophy, grasping at nuggets: '*The most trivial examples – above and below, right and left, father and son, and so on without end – all contain Contradiction in one term. That is above which is not below; "above" is determined only as not being "below", and is only insofar as there is a "below", and conversely: one determination implies its opposite.*'

So far so good, but then: '*We term dialectic that higher movement of Reason where terms appearing absolutely distinct pass into one another through themselves, through what they are, and the assumption of their separateness cancels itself.*' Difficult to grasp.

Gerry seemed to present *Volume 38* as a handbook of applied philosophy, a sort of blueprint for the revolution. Vanessa grasped this better than anyone and Gerry encouraged her, making small refinements to her interpretations. As she rambled on in the class my mind wandered back to the distinct unease I had felt at the fraught, extended Party Congress the year before, when political differences not resolved over the weekend were thrashed out into the following week. Only those at risk of losing their jobs had been allowed to leave. Highly respected Cyril Smith, a statistics lecturer at the London School of Economics, had interpreted a passage in *Volume 38*, only to be bitterly attacked. Gerry had denigrated him, jeered, insisted that he reformulate, humiliated him for half an hour in front of the silent Congress. I had felt uncomfortable, struggling to grasp how Cyril was wrong. Then Gerry had slapped the table.

'Vanessa, what do you think?'

She had risen from the front row, tall and slender, with Cyril still standing to the right. With thoughtful concentration she had reinterpreted the passage.

'You see?' Gerry had turned fiercely towards Cyril. 'If she can do it, why can't you?'

She had said nothing different from Cyril, it had seemed to me. Tears were rolling down Cyril's face.

'Oh, now we've got the Wailing Wall,' Gerry had mocked, a shameless reference to Cyril's Jewishness. 'Sit down, comrade.' Gerry had looked round triumphantly. 'We'll take a break.'

A small seed of doubt had lodged itself in my thoughts at that Congress. Was this abstract philosophy a means to enforce Gerry's political viewpoint? Was Vanessa being used as his lieutenant in Party battles she was too naïve to grasp? I had pushed the thought away, but it remained troublingly in the back of my mind.

My thoughts jolted back to today's class as she finished speaking and Gerry looked round the editorial office for the next comrade. Please don't call me …

'So, comrade, you've prepared a presentation.' Gerry looked at Dave Bruce.

Dave proceeded to examine Hegel's *The Science of Logic* and explain his ideas and their context in the development of philosophy. It was really interesting and Gerry didn't attempt to correct him.

Back in the finance office Robert grinned.

'I persuaded Dave to stop reading books *about* thinkers and to read the thinkers themselves.'

'Safer than challenging Gerry on *Volume 38*,' commented Dot.

Finances deteriorate

We heard Gerry screaming across the yard after Dot had taken him the figures. She came back into the office, sat down, took off her glasses and put her face in her hands.

'If the world doesn't fit his expectations, it has to be made to do so. I can't do this any more.'

Gerry stormed in.

'You just don't check properly,' he shouted. With an aggressive lunge he swept the piles of papers off Dot's desk, scattering them all over the floor. He kicked the reinforced panel along the bottom of the door – fitted to repair damage from his previous kickings – and went out, slamming the door shut. He shouted in the yard. This was a full-scale row that could become violent.

We heard the welcome roar of the Granada engine as Aileen drove him to the flat for his afternoon rest. Dot relaxed slightly, put her glasses back on and tried to sort the papers I was picking up off the floor.

'Dot, just give him the figures he wants,' Aileen said when she returned.

'The whole thing is going to break down. As soon as some extra money comes in, like that large fund donation, he spends it on something else. I can't do this any more.'

'Yes, you can. We have to hold things together.' Aileen stood there, elegant and calm. 'If he realises the finances are collapsing he'll hit out at everything and everyone. All hell will be let loose.'

Dot sat crumpled at her desk, head in hands. Her lank, dark hair spread over her fingers.

'He's terrified of losing control.'

'We'll just have to hold on for the moment while we work something else out.'

On his return at 5 o'clock, Gerry accepted the revised figures.

'Why couldn't you do this before? Why do I have to put up with this fucking nonsense?'

The Political Committee left control of the Party's financial and business matters entirely to Gerry. Dot tried to discuss financial shortfalls with Sheila.

'There's just not enough to pay the bills.'

'We'll just have to make sure the branch money comes in.'

'That's not going to solve it. All our money is tied up in capital, all the premises – Runcorn, six bookshops, seven Youth Training Centres, machinery, books, the school …' Sheila was losing interest. 'And GH won't allow Runcorn to take in commercial printing.'

'But they print the Libyans' *Green Book*, and *Janamot*, the Tamil magazine.'

'Yes, political printing. Not nearly enough. The presses should be running all day with commercial jobs. Ray has given GH proposals, but he won't allow it.'

Now Sheila was really bored.

'I have to go. People will be phoning me.'

A major shock occurred. Only the leadership and a handful of us knew the details.

'Gerry's had a heart attack at the school. He's in hospital.' Dot was extremely worried.

I was aghast.

'Will he be OK?'

'Don't know. We're simply saying he's ill for the moment.'

How would the Party manage without Gerry? It was unimaginable. His political leadership was vital. My thoughts raced, I felt fearful.

Aileen phoned from Derbyshire.

'Get Dot to ring me back at this phone box. She'll have to come up here. I need some clothes and Gerry wants her to bring him the figures.'

'Figures, in hospital?'

'He thinks he can carry on as usual.'

Gerry was away for several weeks. Then he resumed daily Political Committee meetings and continued to oversee every detail of Party activity.

But we had seen his vulnerability. We had been compelled to imagine the Party without him. I felt something had fundamentally changed.

Money became ever tighter. Our catering suppliers demanded cash on delivery. Bailiffs called more frequently. Several book wholesalers refused to supply our shops, though we tried to keep the accounts live with small payments each month. The newsprint suppliers demanded prepayment, but we didn't have the money.

'You'll have to eat into the emergency supplies,' Dot told Ray in Runcorn. She turned to Aileen. 'He says Gerry will notice the stocks have dwindled when you go there on Thursday.'

Aileen took the phone, cool and authoritative.

'Come on, Ray, the reels of paper are stacked three high – shuffle them forward with the forklift truck so that Gerry won't see the gap at the back.'

One of the biggest book wholesalers stopped our account altogether. Bridget, who helped in the bookshops, went with me to their head office to negotiate, armed with a substantial cheque. The man sized us up carefully.

'New Park Publications is an important customer, ordering about £200 of books a day.' He looked at his sheaf of papers. 'And your Christmas orders run in thousands. We don't want to lose you, but you're not reducing the debt.'

We presented our proposals. Bridget's knowledge of the book trade was very convincing and he agreed to continue supplying. We returned in high spirits.

'Now we have to ensure we don't fall back on the agreement.' Dot said grimly.

The Reuters and Press Association news tapes, electricity, gas and telephone lines all had to be paid for. Fuel costs for the trucks travelling daily between London and Runcorn were substantial. Journalists had heavy petrol expenses, photographers frequently received parking fines as they covered urgent news events. The staff wage bill was enormous despite our low pay. Students' fees to the College of Marxist Education were swallowed up on more urgent debts but its bills still had to be paid. Dot and Aileen put a desperate proposal to me.

'Ask your mother to buy one of the Youth Training Centres from the Party, Nottingham, for instance. It would release capital to pay other debts.'

The woman at the family trust created a limited company called Copsecroft Holdings, similar to the Party's Copsecroft Limited, inconspicuous if anyone stumbled on the paperwork. So we had several thousand pounds to pay off some debts. A few months later Aileen and Dot asked me to buy the Upton Park bookshop.

My mother had resigned herself to my political involvement; the money had been earmarked for my inheritance and she felt I could choose how to spend it. But the incoming cash was only a temporary respite. The fundamental problem remained.

1984
MINERS' STRIKE

South West Africa

I was 39 years old. I had been a Party member for 18 years and I was completely committed to the coming revolution. My marriage had ended 12 years before and I had had no serious relationship since. I felt I must look around for someone who understood my commitment. But who? How? I splashed out on a bubbly perm and two-tone highlights in my hair. I ordered two Liberty dresses by mail order for £30, almost a week's wages each. I bought contact lenses. I was alert to opportunity.

I went on holiday to South Africa, eight years after the Soweto uprising and four since Zimbabwe's independence. I sensed greater confidence among Africans on the streets and in shops. But the war in South West Africa's far north continued and South African operations into independent Angola were an open secret. Suddenly the government released black nationalist leader Toivo ja Toivo from Robben Island jail.

'South West Africa was a German colony, governed by South Africa after the First World War,' my mother told me. 'It's a huge desert area, sparsely populated.'

With her encouragement I flew there for two days.

'Are you pleased that Toivo is being released?' I asked the cheerful taxi driver as we travelled through the dark veld from the airport into Windhoek.

'Very, very pleased.' He smiled joyfully.

Next morning, I saw a long queue outside the post office: white men in suits, black men in overalls, men known as 'Coloured', uniformed soldiers, 'Coloured' and white women and the distinctive Herero women in brightly coloured, long-skirted dresses with full-length sleeves and elaborate headdresses. Everyone chatted, complained and laughed together.

'It's for car tax, the last day,' the maid in the hotel told me.

'It's not like in South Africa,' I said. 'Everyone queues together.'

'*Ag, nee*, we have no apartheid here, you know.' I was pleased that she hadn't called me 'madam'.

Verandas shaded the pavements outside the shops. German names and architecture were evident everywhere. At a department store a 'Coloured' security guard inspected the contents of my bag, a stark reminder of the hidden war. Shop assistants effortlessly switched between German, Afrikaans and English.

A reporter at the local newspaper was happy to talk to me and suggested I speak to the representative of the national liberation movement, SWAPO.

'But they're a banned organisation.'

'The operational leadership is in exile. He's just a political representative.'

After making an appointment for the following morning I set out in my hired car to explore Katatura township. Its small single-storey houses laid out in systematic street plans, some dilapidated, many with flowers and even trees, looked similar to South Africa's black townships but no permit was needed to visit. A Coca Cola sign above a café proclaimed: 'Probably the best hamburgers in the world'. Children in school uniform were heading home; boys played football on the dust roads. People greeted me in Afrikaans, asking where I was from. I felt both wonder and anxiety. What harsher realities were concealed by the carefree atmosphere? I glimpsed colour television screens through open doorways. The township had *electricity*.

The small SWAPO office was opposite a massive German brewery. The representative was a man in his 30s who spoke with quiet authority. I told him I worked for a socialist newspaper.

'Toivo's release is a great victory, but we still have a long way to go.' He described the oppressive conditions in the territory and talked about SWAPO's aims, without mentioning military actions. 'I am watched all the time.'

I took notes for the article I intended to write for *News Line*. My political activity in London seemed remote from SWAPO's front-line struggles.

'Go and see the central prison,' he suggested as I left. 'Some of our people are political prisoners there.'

The jail was a sprawling collection of low buildings surrounded by high, barbed-wire fences and watchtowers at intervals, and a further, outer ring. There were queues at the entrance booths, mainly women, presumably waiting to visit incarcerated relatives or to hand over food or clothes. The atmosphere was a mixture of tension and mournful resignation. I felt like a voyeur and drove on.

As my thousand-mile return flight began, the shadows were lengthening on the endless Kalahari scrubland. There had been something deceptive, disturbing, about the seemingly relaxed city. My emotions were tangled up with the confusion in my own life.

We landed in Upington. A handful of new passengers boarded, watched by the first officer in epauletted shirtsleeves.

'May I look out?' I asked. 'I haven't been here for 30 years.'

He seemed surprised that I was old enough. I was wearing my blue floral Liberty dress, pretend-lapis-lazuli necklace and blue high-heeled sandals.

'It was a tiny *dorp* when my mother brought us to see the Augrabies Falls on the Orange River. Now it has an airport.'

'Flights to Europe refuel here because Johannesburg's altitude is too high to take off with full tanks and the countries further north won't allow us into their airspace,' he explained. 'I'll ask the captain if you can come into the cockpit to see the river as we take off.'

But it was already dark as we ascended and I couldn't make out anything. When the stewardess asked me to return to my seat for dinner, the captain invited me to stay for the rest of the flight. I was delighted.

Above the impressive panel of dials and instruments I had an unencumbered view of the dark sky, ablaze with stars, the blackness below punctuated with lights of small towns like Postmasburg, Kuruman, familiar from childhood journeys. We were flying north-east. To the left was impenetrable darkness over the desert, extending northwards into Botswana.

'Those lights to the south are the Kimberley conglomeration,' the pilot explained. 'About 200 miles away.'

'Kimberley's where I grew up.' This was really exciting.

'You can pick out the mines even at this distance. Wesselton is on the left.'

I felt I was floating on a magic carpet, looking down on a panorama of my childhood: the small towns of the Kalahari, Kimberley, the mine hooters at six each morning.

Suddenly my adult political consciousness intruded. The diamond mines, like the gold mines, used migrant labour from all over southern and central Africa, an opportunity to earn money, and also be exploited. I felt complicit in the political oppression linked to control of these resources.

As we descended towards Johannesburg a dark area of smog appeared below, stretching far and wide, dimly illuminated by security floodlights on the main roadways.

'That's Soweto. They cook with wood fires.'

'Terrible. A million people live there, without electricity.'

'Give us time,' said the first officer defensively. 'We've started electrifying but it will take a few years.'

'Yes, I've heard that.' I reined in my indignation, and looked at Johannesburg's brilliant lights ahead. I noticed a bright geometric layout.

'Look, there's the runway. Aren't I clever.'

'*You're* clever? What about us? *We* found it.'

We laughed like old friends and then both men became absorbed in communicating with the control tower, reading instruments and flicking switches.

I floated into the terminal flanked by the pilots in their peaked caps and gold-trimmed jackets.

'Are you *sure* you're all right getting back into town?' the first officer asked. I detected a hint of invitation.

'Quite sure,' I replied, smiling. A romantic fling was not what I was looking for, and Soweto's security lights, faintly suggestive of concentration camps, had pulled me back from my reveries to South Africa's realities.

My mother was waiting to meet me.

'I've had an amazing two days,' I said.

My secret flat

I was restless after my South African holiday. I dreaded Gerry murmuring, 'See me at 3 o'clock', but fortunately, it didn't happen often. I wanted to find a way to develop a relationship with someone, but how? Our lives were under constant scrutiny and I knew Gerry wouldn't sanction any liaison.

▲ April 1984: Jubilant miners cheer the announcement of the no-ballot decision on strike action by the National Union of Mineworkers' executive

The 1984 miners' strike over pit closures began. It was the biggest working-class action I had ever experienced, with mass flying pickets and support groups all over the country. The full force of the capitalist state was mobilised against them, billions of pounds were spent. It felt like the beginning of revolutionary struggles. How would these developments affect our lives? How had things been in the Russian Revolution? I began reading about the lives of Russian and German women revolutionaries. From Bolshevik Alexandra Kollontai I moved on to Clara Zetkin, Rosa Luxembourg, Larissa Reissner. They had affairs, passions, fallings-out. I saw no parallel with our ascetic lives and the disapproving control over us women at the Centre.

A Mozart piano concerto wafted out of the security office next to the kitchen as I made tea for the finance office. I listened, entranced. Charlie was bent over a piece of equipment on his workbench.

'I set the timer in my room in Orlando Road to record it from the BBC. The aerial on the roof has perfect reception. Shall I make you a copy?'

'Music was the biggest thing in my life outside schoolwork when I was a teenager, but now I don't even have a tape recorder.'

'Shall I look out for a second-hand one?'

On Saturday morning Charlie knocked on my door. He was allowed keys to the outer and landing doors because of his security responsibilities.

'I've found a good tape recorder and it's not expensive. Shall I buy it for you?'

My view of Charlie was beginning to change. His German precision and insistence on rules had previously irritated me but Dot had defended him against my complaints.

'He works closely under Gerry. His technical knowledge is needed for security issues and electronic projects.'

Now he and I discussed music while the cook clattered oven trays and the potato peeler thundered away. A gentle friendship developed as I learned more about him.

'I seldom get home. I often sleep in my office when the other full-time security guards are away.'

'Do Gerry and Sheila know that?'

'Of course. They have decided that I must stay at the Centre. Saturday is the only day for myself, after Comrade Healy has left. I go out, or run five kilometres round Clapham Common. I'd like to run the marathon one day.'

A German delegation stopped in London on the way back from the College of Marxist Education. After lunch Charlie came to see Dot.

'They've gone to the British Museum. I wanted to go with them.'

'You should have asked.'

'I did. The other guard said he would cover for me. But Sheila refused point blank.' He shook his head. 'They're my long-time comrades and I never see them.'

Next day Janet found a wallet on the pavement opposite our alleyway. It contained a few notes and Charlie's security pass.

'It's unlike him to be careless.'

'Ah,' said Dot. 'He's upset about Carmen, his girlfriend in Germany. She became pregnant while recovering in a convalescent home and the comrades say she's retreating politically.'

Dot helped Charlie write a memo asking permission to visit her.

'Better say it's to see your family.'

'No, the comrades will inform Gerry I've visited her.' He was defiant. 'If he says no, I'm going anyway. They're hounding a hard-working comrade who's been in the movement a long time.'

Charlie had seen Carmen only during her brief political visits to England, but had remained admirably loyal. I listened with sickening disappointment as I was forced to recognise how I had come to feel about him. Surprisingly, Gerry agreed that he could go. I struggled to erase him from my thoughts for the five days he was away. He returned in a buoyant mood and showed us pictures of Carmen by a lakeside. I tried to be pleased, but I was also sad.

And yet our discreet conversations in the canteen continued as if nothing had happened. When the guard on the gate prepared to escort me home Charlie said, 'I'll go. I need some fresh air.' We chatted easily as we walked and then stood talking outside the flats as the late-night traffic roared by. This was safe – no one would question why we were there. We talked for about 20 minutes, not wanting to stop.

My one-room flat had been my home for nearly 16 years. I had made it attractive with floral curtains and bookcases under the windows. On the orange wall demarcating the kitchen area my school painting of a tree-encircled playing field hung above my Chinese lacquer cabinet. The facing wall was deep turquoise; table lamps gave soft lighting. Rules in the flats had become stricter and men were allowed into the building only to see Gerry.

'I wonder if I could get a flat of my own somewhere else,' I said to Dot.

'GH would never agree. There'd be a big row, a security investigation.'

I felt dispirited and spoke to Aileen.

'Why not? You'd have to do it secretly and still keep your flat at 155a. You'd have to be very, very careful.'

My last flatmate had not been replaced and I realised I had ideal conditions. Because of my early-morning trips to Cowley – in bed at nine, up at four-thirty – no one disturbed me at night, or even knew if I was there.

My branch area was safest to look for a flat because I knew it intimately and central Party workers were unlikely to come there. I viewed the basement flat of an elegant house in Aldebert Terrace, two blocks from Dorset Road estate, where we had lots of *News Line* readers. Steps led down to what felt like a secret place. The bedroom on the left looked out on to a raised flowerbed and the pavement above. The main room had double doors to a small patio edged with greenery from the elevated adjacent garden. The kitchen also opened on to the patio, the bathroom was beyond. Liberty curtains framed the patio doors, giving a feeling of luxury. It seemed perfect. I rang my mother.

'I'll tell the trust to pay you £34,000.'

When the cheque arrived Dot looked thoughtful.

'You'll pay a deposit, but completion of the purchase will take a while. What will you do with the rest of the money in the meantime?'

'I could pay it into the Party for the interim.'

'It would really help the cash flow.'

The day for completion arrived. I transferred the money I had held back into the solicitor's account and told Dot I needed the rest, but she didn't seem to register. At lunchtime I had an anxious phone call from the owner. I was cross and passed Dot a note, worried the money had been swallowed up in Party debts. But she arranged it with the bank manager and the following day the sale went through.

My own flat: empty, bare, the smell of new carpeting, waiting for me to imprint my personality. I sat on the floor with my back against the wall, looking out at the concrete patio and the green bushes beyond. I could scarcely believe this was mine.

I needed furniture. I could bring a few kitchen utensils, perhaps a chair, but the Clapham High Street flat had to remain unchanged to avoid suspicion. At Arding and Hobbs department store in Clapham Junction I ordered a double bed and chose a pleasantly tactile fabric with a beige and blue leafy design for unlined bedroom curtains, which they made up free. I bought net curtains for daytime privacy. A small kitchen table and stools from a second-hand shop provided somewhere to sit and a few days later a compact rattan three-piece suite arrived with a green-and-brown, oriental bird-design akin to the Chinese lacquer cabinet I hoped to bring one day. The flat was gradually becoming mine. But when would I dare sleep in it?

Only Dot and Aileen knew my secret. When they came to inspect I had fabric with a brilliant-green jungle pattern laid out on the floor to make lined curtains for the patio doors.

'It would be a big risk to stay here very often,' said Dot. 'How would you get to the Centre to collect your car to go to Oxford?'

'Oh, I've sorted that out. I pointed out it's unsafe for me to walk alone to the Centre at four-thirty in the morning so I now park near the High Street.'

We laughed.

'Get Charlie to come and assess the security', suggested Aileen.

'You think it's OK to tell him about it?'

'Come on, he knows half the stuff that goes on at the Centre is nonsense. He won't talk. And he can replace the curtain rail for you.'

'Can he?'

'Of course. He can do anything.'

I told Charlie I had a secret flat which needed security checking 'against burglaries and surveillance by the State'. We agreed he would come on Saturday, when he was out running.

He carefully assessed windows, door-frames, the bar on the bathroom window, possible access from neighbouring houses. He examined the patio doors. His tall, robust figure was silhouetted against the bright light; I noticed his tousled light-brown hair and his muscular legs, unfamiliarly exposed in running shorts and trainers.

'Listen, you're not just here to assess security.'

News Line circulation

'The Political Committee has appointed you *News Line* circulation manager,' Gerry informed me. I suspected Dot was involved in the proposal as she had often said it was ridiculous to have no circulation manager for a daily paper.

'Start immediately. Investigate where the branches sell the papers, see what the problems are, discuss ways to expand the sales.'

'Will I still do the Cowley sales?'

'Yes, and you'll continue in the finance office. Keep in touch with the branches by phone and by letter and visit a different area each month. Give me a detailed itinerary beforehand.'

I felt rather daunted.

'Get the German' – he meant Charlie – 'to fix you up a new telephone line.'

I was duly made an alternate member of the Central Committee and attended the daily Political Committee meetings when I wasn't driving to Oxford.

▲ I am now listed as Circulation Manager

I tackled my new responsibilities diligently. I asked every branch to complete a form detailing how many daily deliveries they had, what door-to-door canvasses, factory and high street sales they did, how many people were involved in selling the paper. A gloomy picture emerged: often it was only the active cadres who did sales; some branches never did door-to-door sales and seldom increased their daily deliveries. Active cadres rushed round, before and after work, doing deliveries as well as all the other activities involved in Party-building. Instead of being a means to expand and recruit new forces into activity, the paper had become a burden, treated as a 'debt' by Sheila, who was haughtily sceptical about my new role. She was in touch with the branches all the time, why did it need me as well?

I developed some new procedures: posters to put in newsagents, leaflets to distribute at trade union conferences, badges for the miners' pickets to wear alongside their plethora of other support stickers, and large, day-glo orange shoulder bags with *News Line* screen-printed on them, really helpful for delivering papers. I had video copies made of the film about *News Line* for informal meetings in readers' homes, to encourage more involvement in sales. I wanted to issue the 60 loudspeaker systems bought for our election campaign so that branches could hold open-air meetings, but this didn't take off. It wasn't easy to rally exhausted members who were campaigning daily to support the striking miners as well everything else.

Carefully stored in the warehouse were 60 moped bikes which Gerry had bought in one go. Branches often requested one.

▲ *News Line* 4th June 1984

'It would really help increase deliveries. They take ages on foot.'

'I'll ask. Sheila issues the bikes.'

Therein lay the problem. Sheila didn't issue the bikes. Her criteria for awarding them were unclear, but the branch had to increase its *News Line* order and membership first. So the seldom-issued bikes stayed year after year, a tantalising expression of our back-to-front methods. I complained to Dot.

'Sheila's method of Party building is exhortation and haranguing, not tackling concrete issues. My responsibilities as circulation manager conflict with hers.'

'Be careful, get Gerry to back everything you do.'

My guide was Lenin's small book, *What is to be Done?* which described the role of a national newspaper. I empathised with Lenin's struggle to gather seething groups scattered all over Russia into a coherent revolutionary movement, which I explained to branches:

'For Lenin the newspaper was not just concerned with narrow, local trade union issues, but gave workers a national perspective and brought revolutionary theory into the working class.'

I described the organisational structure he saw forming around the paper.

'Workers would send in reports, a network of supporters would sell the paper, it would be a nucleus to bring people together in a revolutionary group. In this sense the paper would be the *organiser* of the revolutionary movement, and this still applies today.'

Each day *News Line* reported on the miners' actions and the huge police resources being mobilised against them. Fleet Street, meantime, poured out hostility and lies. Prime Minister Margaret Thatcher's government was better prepared than Heath's had been in 1974: it had North Sea oil and stockpiled coal; riot police trained in the widespread inner-city rebellions of 1981 were mobilised from all over the country; and the mineworkers' union funds were sequestrated. *News Line* stated: 'The miners face a bourgeoisie with colossal experience, a state far better equipped and more centralised than anything which faced the workers in Tsarist Russia'.

In Nottingham I attended a miners' mass meeting in the City Hall. *News Line* was well known so we were welcomed. We sat in the balcony overlooking the seething crowd of 2,000 miners who chanted and sang boisterously as they waited to hear their leader, Arthur Scargill.

'They're like football fans,' I said to the comrade next to me.

'They *are* football fans,' she laughed.

▲ **June 1984**: Hundreds of police charged miners' pickets at Orgreave coking plant. Horses were also used in vicious charges against the miners, escalating police procedures which had begun in the 1977 Battle of Lewisham and were developed further during the inner-city riots of 1981

▲ Orgreave pickets carried a telegraph pole to defend themselves against police attacks

'There have been scenes of almost unbelievable brutality. The intimidation and brutality that we have seen here today is reminiscent of a Latin American police state.'

Arthur Scargill, NUM president

An altercation broke out in the tier below us, with shouting and swearing. Scargill jumped down from the platform and made his way through the packed seats. After heated discussion a man was escorted out of the hall, to cheers and whistles.

'A journalist from Fleet Street,' Scargill reported, to more cheers.

A month later I visited Glasgow. We were trying to expand our influence in the Communist Party-dominated coalfield, some distance from the city. I was met off a late-night train by Simon, Party organiser and journalist.

'I'm doing an early morning sale with Willie. Keep the car and meet me at the offices at ten,' he said.

I overslept. I imagined Simon's withering reaction: *The miners are locked in a life-and-death struggle and you can't even get up in the morning.* He could be quite intimidating.

I hurried. I consulted the map at red traffic lights, ready to turn left. The lights changed and the van in front moved off rapidly. Its back doors swung open and a tray of meat slid on to the road as the oblivious driver sped on. Should I stop and pick it up and pretend to follow the van? But I was already very late. Fear of Simon's whiplash comments overrode my sense of initiative. As I drove on, I felt guilty. Simon was going to the coalfields that afternoon and there was enough meat in the tray to feed 20 miners' families.

I reached the office an hour and a half late.

'Hello,' said Simon. 'Did you find the way all right?'

▼ Miners' wives at the Bilsthorpe strikers' canteen

The Party opposed branches being sucked into the vast movement of support groups who supplied the miners with food, clothes and money. But I found that branches, particularly those near the coalfields, were uneasy about this policy and some just ignored it. A comrade from Reading told me about the trades council collecting clothes and food.

'Sheila sent a minibus crammed with bags of stuff from the Centre. I was so embarrassed. It was all jumble, old clothes.'

'Was nothing useful?'

'It felt like the Party was completely unaware that the miners were ordinary people, just like us, with the same needs, with new babies like mine that needed nappies; growing children who needed shoes, schoolbooks, shampoo, coats. And we sent … jumble, scruffy old cast-offs.' He shook his head.

'But a revolutionary struggle won't be won with trade union consciousness. The miners need more than clothes and food.'

'Well, it seemed like the Party in London was completely out of touch.'

In December I visited Murton in the Durham coalfield and stayed at the home of Dave Temple, Party Central Committee member, tall, with a quick mind, a highly respected leader of the Durham miners,.

'It's ridiculous to reject the miners' support groups. Without them we would starve, we couldn't fight on.'

'But aren't they just the expression of the spontaneous consciousness of the working class? We know revolutionary consciousness doesn't arise spontaneously – that's fundamental to Marxist theory. We need to recruit miners into the Party and set up community councils, like "soviets", to give organised support to the miners.'

'The support groups could become community councils if the Party fights to win influence in them. I'll take you to our village community centre. It's owned by the miners' lodge and you'll see how things work.'

I was troubled that Dave questioned the Party's policy.

The large, modern hall was thronged with families eating a substantial meal cooked by miners' wives and supporters. There were organised activities for the children. Returning pickets were welcomed with a plate of hot stew. Pride in the actions of husbands, brothers, sons and fathers was evident in the laughter and warmth. I feared I was being seduced by the power of 'spontaneity'.

A van arrived full of boxes that were carried into a back room.

◄ Miners' children enjoy their Christmas party in Dodworth, South Yorkshire

'They're from the support group in Middlesbrough,' a woman told me. 'We've given them the names of every child and they are preparing wrapped presents for each one, so the bairns *will* have a Christmas.'

'You're only the second comrade from the Centre to visit us in all these months,' Dave said as he dropped me at the station.

'Surely the Party leadership discusses strategy with you?'

'I go to London for Central Committee meetings and Mike Banda visited us once. The *News Line* photographers have been several times.' He shrugged. 'I'm in regular contact with the journalists and with Sheila, of course. I occasionally talk to Gerry. But no other Central Committee member has been here.'

Something was not right.

M1 motorway

Aileen fetched me to see Gerry. He was sitting in the antechamber between her office and the windowless back meeting room. Papers and a cup of tea were on the small table beside him.

'You're to go as co-driver with Aileen every fortnight to visit her mother in Nottingham, starting this Saturday.'

I stood awkwardly in front of him, rather bemused.

'You'll stay overnight and drive back early the next morning for the Political Committee.' He dismissed me and turned to his papers.

We left for Nottingham after Saturday's Political Committee meeting. I relaxed into the broad, leather passenger seat.

'Shall I drive on the M1?'

'No need. I'm quite happy driving with no one shouting at me. Don't you realise, you're only here as my chaperone.'

'How d'you mean?'

'Gerry thinks I might get up to mischief, so I need a minder. Since you're allowed to drive the Granada, you're the obvious choice.'

She selected a music tape. The car had several desirable gadgets and a mobile radio so the Centre could contact her if necessary.

'We'll go to the school first and make sure everyone sees us, in case Gerry checks.'

We turned off the motorway after Derby, drove through Ashbourne and on towards Parwich, the nearest village to our College of Marxist Education. The route was very familiar after eight years and today I particularly noted the beauty of the rolling hills. From a smaller, tree-lined road we turned into the driveway of the solid, elegant house with its lawns, large trees, and sweeping views beyond the neighbouring farm. The lecture was still in session so we waited in the canteen while Annabel, the manager, made us tea and brought Aileen the student list.

'When the comrades arrive from Scotland we'll be completely full.' She handed a file of invoices to Aileen. 'It would be good to pay this one as soon as possible.'

We heard chairs scraping in the main lecture room and Annabel rose to check the stew. A branch secretary from the Eastern Region came in for kitchen duty and greeted Aileen cheerily before a guarded expression spread over his face.

'Is Comrade Healy here?' His eyes moved to the door of Gerry's flat, beyond the canteen.

'No, we're going to see my mother.'

After lunch and a scheduled phone-call to Gerry Aileen dropped me at Derby station, as agreed earlier.

'I'll collect you from your flat at quarter to eight tomorrow morning.'

The fast train took me to King's Cross. The tube journey to Stockwell was risky, but I had my story ready. I would say I had been taken ill and had come back ahead of Aileen. I couldn't risk doing branch work so I spent the evening in my flat reading Clara Zetkin's biography, listening to Beethoven's second piano concerto and looking forward to Charlie sneaking out to join me.

▲ Alan Thornett

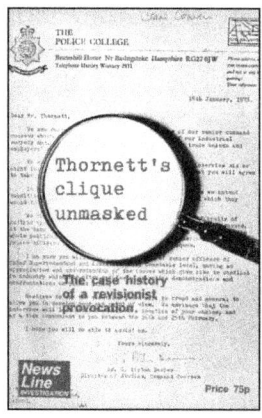

◄ The Party's rebuttal of Thornett's views

On these fortnightly journeys Aileen and I had time to talk and ponder what was really happening in our lives and in the Party. We were the same age but she had grown up in the Party and knew it intimately.

'Peter Fryer was *The Newsletter*'s first editor. He joined after the *Daily Worker* rejected his reports on the 1956 Hungarian revolution and the Communist Party expelled him.'

'What became of him?'

'He left over explosive disagreements with Gerry. Paul and I had both trained as journalists and married very young so we were brought to London to work on *The Newsletter*. I edited the youth paper, *Keep Left*.'

Like a child fascinated by stories of her forebears, I was hungry to hear more.

'The real danger came from Alan Thornett's 1974 political challenge to Gerry. When Sheila and I went to an aggregate meeting in the Western Region we found they all supported Thornett. It was a big shock.'

'I remember the campaign against them: pamphlets, aggregate meetings, the Congress in Battersea whose venue was secret until half an hour beforehand, but they still found out. It was bizarre, our own comrades leafletting outside. They claimed Gerry had been drunk at some meeting, but I've never seen him drinking.'

'He doesn't now.'

'Dot told me she insisted he must stop drinking if he was to defeat Thornett.'

'Maybe she did. It was the biggest fight of his political life. They'd have liquidated the Party into syndicalism and we'd have become like the other left-wing fringe groups: petty-bourgeois talking shops, fellow-travellers of social democracy.'

'That's all Thornett's group is now.'

'I don't know if it could have been done differently. We certainly rode roughshod over the Party constitution. Thornett wasn't allowed to appeal to the Central Committee, only one or two hand-picked members heard him. Gerry was terrified of them addressing a full congress. Who knows how the vote would have gone.'

'Well, we won in the end.'

'We paid a price. We lost much of our industrial wing and members all over the country.'

We delved deeper into the political malaise inside the organisation. Looming large were the financial problems.

'Dot lives in constant fear it will all fall to pieces,' I commented.

'Well, it could. Gerry's primitive business ideas have controlled the finances for too long. Whenever Dot tried to tell him differently there was a violent explosion. He's hit her plenty of times. Any changes have been achieved by a careful strategy to make Gerry think it was his idea.'

'But why has no one else questioned the finances?'

'Come on, you know Gerry keeps the financial control strictly to himself. No committee manages it. The company directors are paper officials.'

'When bills are paid late, surely someone guesses there's a deeper problem?'

'They concern themselves with their own fields of work. Sheila has enough difficulties with her Party-building responsibilities. Mike Banda busies himself with theoretical issues and lots of reading. Alex makes international contacts and writes in the paper. The Redgraves believe everything Gerry tells them. Others don't have the confidence to question anything and leading comrades outside London don't ask.'

'Shouldn't Dot prepare a report to the Political Committee – or directly to the Central Committee – explaining how serious things are?'

'There would be a volcanic row. Gerry would say Dot had hidden things from him. She would be scapegoated, charged under the constitution and the Party would back Gerry.'

'But the whole thing will collapse if a creditor takes us to bankruptcy court.'

'That's exactly the problem. So what do we do? We have to protect the Party for the coming mass struggles, hold things together until the political situation brings new forces into play.'

Underpinning all our hopes was the belief that we had moved into a revolutionary period, reflected in the miners' powerful strike.

'You manage to remain calm whereas Dot is often close to panic.'

She shrugged.

'If the finances collapse, Gerry will blame Dot, me, Sheila, probably you, too. He would lash out everywhere and do even more damage.'

The tape had finished playing. Aileen inserted another, driving at 80 miles per hour. I gazed at the train overtaking us alongside the motorway.

'Gerry's violence – why doesn't anyone intervene?'

'Violence has been the hallmark of Gerry's leadership for years. Lots of political differences have been settled by beating someone up, or threatening to.'

'I've never actually seen him hit anyone. I know about Dot's pierced eardrum, the lacerations to her leg and the hospital's incomprehension that she wasn't going to press charges against the perpetrator. And you wore huge dark glasses for two weeks.'

'Gerry gave me an enormous black eye. And he seriously injured my back when he struck me with a broomstick. That's why I regularly have to see an osteopath.'

I already knew this but I still found it shocking.

'He throws plates of food at me if he's in a tantrum, but I've learned ways to protect myself when he's like that.'

Sending me as Aileen's co-driver was one of the most unwise decisions Gerry Healy ever made.

Political Committee meeting

The Political Committee assembled in Gerry's inner office. There was a hierarchy in the seating arrangements: Gerry's small desk was in the corner next to the door, facing the divan sofa-bed on the far wall. Alex always sat on his right, Sheila next to him; Mike Banda sat opposite. Aileen sat on the other side of the doorway, ready for any errand. The leading Young Socialists and I sat on the uncomfortable sofa-bed. Everyone else – Dot, Corin, Vanessa, Dave Bruce and anyone else who was invited – slotted into available chairs.

As the last participants came in Gerry poured a glass of Perrier water, looking sterner than usual. Mike arrived in his usual untidy clothes, and slumped into his chair. Alex strode in, with a dramatic haircut that would have made an Australian sheep-shearer proud. We looked at him, startled. Through the open windows of the antechamber came derisive shrieks of laughter in the yard from Charlie and Phil Penn, who maintained the car fleet. I didn't dare catch Dave Bruce's eye; I looked down at my notes, stifling an overwhelming desire to giggle and felt the comrade next to me tensing, clutching her notebook.

There was no hilarity in the ensuing meeting. Gerry gestured to Mike.

'Make the opening political report.'

'The Bonapartist state …' He talked for ages, until Gerry intervened.

'That's enough.' He looked directly at Aileen. 'Well, comrade, what do you think?'

She began to make a political point, but Gerry interrupted angrily.

'You refuse to grasp the dialectical method in your practice. Why do you insist on sticking with these bourgeois ideas?'

Something must have happened, but I had no idea what. Gerry insisted she explain herself and then attacked everything she said. Vanessa listened intently and tried to support Gerry, but he restrained her with a raised hand. He glared at Aileen. Tears were running down her face, but he persisted. Suddenly she stood up and rushed out. Barely pausing for breath, Gerry looked at Dot.

'Go and fetch her back.'

We waited in taut silence. It was uncharacteristic for Aileen to lose her composure. We heard wails and sobbing coming from the women's toilets in the yard. After a few minutes Dot returned alone.

'She won't come back.'

'We have this kind of bourgeois opposition at the heart of the organisation.' Gerry thumped the desk. 'We'll go on without her. Alex, continue.'

'… one of the most turbulent periods in British history … 200,000 miners …' It was as if nothing had happened. I couldn't concentrate; I was very upset.

'Mrs Gibson, go and find her,' Gerry directed as the meeting broke up.

Aileen had left the Centre, said the night guard, Shiraz, a handsome Pakistani who worked closely with Gerry on mysterious projects.

'I heard her crying. She was really distressed. I took her up to the security office to phone her brother-in-law and waited outside with her till he picked her up.'

The Political Committee assembled as usual next day. Gerry looked at Aileen.

'Comrade, do you want to make a statement?'

Her face was expressionless.

'I give an undertaking that I will do anything Comrade Healy requires of me.' She seemed distant, as if she didn't see us.

There was a brief pause.

'Why did it all take so long?' Gerry looked at her sternly and then turned to one of the journalists. 'Comrade, report on yesterday's miners' meeting.'

Everything seemed to have been smoothed over. So what had the row been about? Something was going on that I couldn't fathom.

My mother visits London

When she visited London my mother was delighted with my flat. I invited her and my cousin Susan to lunch and bought paté and lettuce to start, a jar of sauce for spaghetti bolognese, and fruit for dessert. I laid the table with scarcely used wedding presents from 16 years before: hunting-scene table mats from Susan and turquoise table napkins from an aunt. My first attempt at entertaining was successful.

Later that week Vanessa invited us to supper, presumably on Gerry's instruction.

'I've bought fish,' she said. 'Enjoy your sherry while I put it in the oven.'

Twenty minutes later she was expertly filleting the whole fish, subtly flavoured with herbs and fine slivers of onion, accompanied by salad and new potatoes.

▲ With my cousin Susan at our family reunion at Lancaster Gate Hotel in 1984

'Elizabeth, I'd like to invite you to the British première of my new film, *The Bostonians.*'

'From the Henry James novel? I'd be delighted.'

We had prominent seats next to Vanessa for the film about feminist women in late 19th-century Boston, which seemed remote from my life. When the lights went up Vanessa was enthusiastically applauded, and stood to bow in acknowledgement. To my surprise, Mum invited her to the family reunion I had organised for my southern-hemisphere siblings and a cousin who happened to be visiting London at the same time, along with their counterparts in Britain. When I told Gerry, his face spread into a satisfied half-smile and his little eyes looked thoughtful.

'We'll send a *News Line* photographer to take pictures for your family.'

For this historic gathering I made a slim dress with narrow straps from the Hawaiian fabric that my sister had given me and bought a little white jacket to cover my bare shoulders. I had my hair done; my nails, lipstick, earrings and high-heel sandals were in the same red as the hibiscus flowers on the dress. I arrived early to check the arrangements at the Lancaster Gate Hotel, near where my mother, sister and younger brother were staying. The long dining table was elegantly set with flowers and sparkling glasses and a pianist was playing as the 12 of us assembled in the first floor lounge. Photographer Sean Smith arrived and I introduced him to my mother.

'I suggest you all stand over here. Vanessa, you're best at the back, Clare's mother in the centre. Move in a little closer, please.' Sean's professionalism helped everyone relax.

The evening was a success. I showed Gerry the pictures, aware that his scheming was intended to ease family money coming to the Party some day. He had no idea it was already happening.

To introduce Charlie to Mum I arranged another Saturday lunch and included Dot and Aileen to make it less intimidating. Charlie was late.

'We'd better start without him.'

I was disappointed. He arrived 15 minutes later.

'You're late.'

'You said 1 o'clock.'

'I said 12.'

'It was definitely one.'

He was sure he was right. It didn't occur to him just to say sorry and it didn't occur to me that he might have been nervous. I was relieved he had arrived and everything went well. Mum invited Charlie and me to see *The Caine Mutiny* in the West End, starring and directed by Charlton Heston. The play was about the trial for mutiny of naval Lieutenant Maryk on the American ship, *Caine*, just after the second world war. During a typhoon he had relieved Captain Queeg of command on the grounds that he was insane. At the trial the captain appeared to be a capable commander, a firm, decisive leader, albeit tough on military discipline. Then Maryk described in detail some petty, vindictive actions by Queeg. We listened intently.

'There was the missing strawberry incident,' said Maryk. Queeg had launched a full search of the ship for a secret duplicate pantry key he imagined the thief must have possessed. Charlie nudged me in the ribs. Gerry had often reacted disproportionately to similarly small incidents.

Under cross-examination Queeg was asked to justify his actions and became nervous and irritable. We listened with growing recognition, nudging each other at each revelation. Queeg became enraged, ranting that he was surrounded by disloyal officers. My heart was thumping, I couldn't believe what I was hearing.

After Maryk was acquitted, his Jewish defence lawyer regretted the destruction of Queeg, a career military man who had helped stop Nazi atrocities.

We applauded vigorously, but I was disturbed by the lawyer's regret.

'I never thought there could be another person like Gerry,' I said to Charlie as we drove home. 'I thought his angry outbursts were because of the enormous burden of political leadership.'

Charlie shook his head.

'The captain was mentally ill.'

'Are you suggesting Gerry is mentally ill?'

'I don't know. His reaction to small things is paranoid.' He tapped the dashboard. 'And his son has a serious mental illness.'

'But he's built this large international movement. He's a powerful leader. A mentally ill person couldn't achieve that.'

The life I was leading required subterfuge. Twice a week, when I wasn't going to Oxford, I left my car at the Centre for the other driver, slipped into Clapham Common station and travelled to Stockwell, a short walk from my flat. I had a story prepared: 'I need to leave an urgent message for someone in my branch.' I devised another charade in case I returned home with a comrade from the flats: I surreptitiously tucked my handbag under the car seat and walked upstairs with a cloth shoulder bag – the popular woven Greek kind – to give the impression that I had all my paraphernalia. Once inside I listened for a few moments to be sure no one was on the landing and went back downstairs, holding only my keys. My story would be: 'I left my handbag in the car.' I then drove to Stockwell but never parked outside my flat, always in the next road. I would say that my car had broken down.

▲ Charlie in our secret flat in Stockwell. Behind him are the green tropical-patterned curtains I had made myself

Charlie and I ignored each other all day except for work communications. Occasionally he managed to leave the Centre at night, but things could go wrong. Late one Saturday night Sheila sent someone to his room in Orlando Road but he wasn't there.

'See me first thing on Monday to explain yourself,' she instructed him the following day.

'Tell her you went to the all-night cinema in the West End,' Aileen advised quietly.

Fortunately Sheila didn't enquire in detail but she made it clear that Charlie had no right to be away from the Centre, ever.

We became bolder as time went on. When I was supposedly in Nottingham we ventured to the West End, confident in the teeming crowds that we wouldn't meet Party cadres, who would all be doing pub sales in working-class areas. Our enjoyment of Mozart's glorious music in the newly released film *Amadeus* was heightened by its illicit aspect.

'I want to show you something,' Aileen said as we headed to Nottingham.

She pulled up outside a terraced house near Sloane Square, behind Peter Jones department store. She unlocked the glass-panelled front door, passed numbered doors inside and went into a sizeable first-floor room with a patterned carpet and tall windows to the back, heavy with maroon curtains. The furniture was old-fashioned: a double bed, two armchairs, a table and chairs, small cooker and a sink. The shared toilet was in the corridor.

'This is *my* secret flat. I sneak off here from time to time.'

Aileen was at Gerry's beck and call virtually 24 hours a day and bore the brunt of his frustrations and anger. It was good that she could escape somewhere.

'Someone joins me here sometimes.' She smiled.

I looked at her, amazed.

'Who?'

'Oh, I'm not saying.'

'You don't mean Paul?'

'Oh no, our marriage has been in the doldrums for ages.'

Who could it possibly be? Shiraz, the security guard? How could she conduct a secret affair in her constricted life? Even within our tight-knit relationship some things weren't disclosed.

As I passed Gerry in the warehouse he glanced around and then edged over.

'See me at 3 o'clock.' he said in a brisk undertone.

I didn't want sex with him. Several months had passed since he had last summoned me to his flat. I felt distaste and irritation at his cloak-and-dagger way of making the arrangement when he knew I would have to tell Dot where I was going.

Promptly at 3 o'clock I pressed his buzzer at the street door and went upstairs.

'Sit down, comrade.' He sat in the chair opposite the sofa, wearing slippers. Braces held up his trousers over his rotund belly. 'You can have your car back. Ted Knight can't drive it any more.'

◄ Ken Livingstone and Ted Knight were co-editors of the left-Labour weekly paper *Labour Herald*, which was typeset and printed by Party companies. Here they hold the paper, barely visible, at its launch on May Day 1982

My surprise must have shown.

'A letter in the *South London Press* has disclosed that the Leader of Lambeth Labour Council is driving a car belonging to "a prominent member of the Workers Revolutionary Party". There'll be questions in the council and the press will blow it up into a scandal.'

I was pleased.

'Take off your dress.'

I suppressed my revulsion as he slipped the braces off his shoulders.

'I know Ted Knight used to be a member, but I don't understand our relationship with him now,' I said to Dot.

'We cooperate with him to produce *Labour Herald*.'

I knew that our comrades typeset the weekly paper in Grafton Litho's small premises, just beyond the main gate.

'But *Labour Herald* is not our paper, we don't control it.'

'A paper representing Labour's left wing around Ted Knight and Ken Livingstone is vital to counter Kinnock's right-wing leadership inside the Labour Party.'

I was still unclear.

'Do we subsidise the production of the paper? Who pays our comrades' wages?'

Dot shrugged. I was asking more than she was prepared to divulge.

I collected my car from Lambeth Town Hall. It had a few scrapes and dents, reeked of smoke, and had litter scattered on the floor and back seat. I drove it into the warehouse for Phil to check over.

'The pocket in the door has been used as an ashtray. It's full of fag ends.'

'Don't worry I'll clean it up.'

It looked perfect when Phil gave it back. He was very skilled.

As I pulled up at the traffic lights on the Vauxhall one-way system, a man on the opposite pavement called out to me, with a big grin on his face. I wound down the window.

'I know whose car that is. It's the Leader's car.'

I smiled wanly. Oh no it's not.

1985
CLARITY

Alex Mitchell, Gerry's right-hand man, suddenly disappeared. Aileen phoned the Australian section; letters were sent, but he didn't respond. His partner, Judith, was distraught.

Norman and I had a quiet conversation at the finance office hatch.

'He's been Gerry's closest confidant.'

'With unparalleled freedom of movement as *News Line* foreign editor and wide contacts outside the Party.'

'Good looks, charisma, a knack of worming his way into everyone's confidence. His disappearance certainly raises questions.'

'Or he just couldn't stand the heat of the revolution.'

Alex Mitchell ▲

I asked Charlie why he thought Alex had disappeared.

He shrugged.

'Working on security, we keep our eyes and ears open. We have no fixed ideas. But I really scared him when I was testing our new parabolic microphone on the bridge between the Young Socialists' office and the archives. Alex and another journalist were walking up the alleyway, talking quietly, about 50 metres away. I heard every word. When I repeated the conversation to Alex afterwards he was shitting himself.'

'Did he say anything suspicious?'

'It was nothing, but he wasn't happy to know he could be overheard.'

I laughed, thinking we would never see Alex again.

Ten months into the miners' strike, in bitter weather, Aileen and I settled into the Granada's warm comfort. The motorway verge was mid-winter bare, the fields in the distance looked frosty in the bleak morning sun. I must have travelled this road 100 times, it was familiar, neutral, and encouraged reflection. I felt unsettled. A tumultuous working-class struggle was taking place, but were we equal to our historic responsibilities?

'We're a long way from being in the leadership. Miners' families eat potatoes or starve while the trade union and Labour leaders betray them, and we're told to keep away from the support groups. But branches outside London disagree,' I said.

'Gerry thinks the Party will liquidate into a morass of syndicalism.'

'The Seventh Congress documents, the stuff about "the individualist idealist approach to practice is the most common idealist error" – what the hell does that mean?'

Aileen smiled.

'Our policies are way off beam, but it won't be easy to change them.' She had learned over years not to panic.

'In the secrecy of the technical office Robert says that he and Dave Bruce discuss taking on Gerry's philosophy.'

'If Dave challenged Gerry's analysis the full Party machinery would be brought down on him, as happened to Thornett. Gerry would crush him, with Mike Banda's and the Redgraves' support. He'd call in the intellectuals.'

'I suppose most members would support the leadership.'

'They would only ever hear the leadership's position. The issues would never be properly discussed.' She shook her head. 'Gerry has defeated all past political opposition, he's a consummate political fighter, the most experienced. We have to think of something else.'

It became clear that Thatcher would defeat the miners. The frenzy at the Centre was becoming worse and Gerry's explosions were more and more frequent. 'Where's the Kraut?' he would yell, or 'Fetch Dave Bruce'. He shouted at Dot and Aileen, occasionally at me, and criticised everything Sheila did.

Aileen returned from dropping Gerry at his flat. She tossed her keys on to the table and sat down, looking worried.

'I think Gerry is plotting to sideline Sheila. He closes himself in with Mike in his inner office, or at his flat, all the time. He probably thinks she's organising a faction against him.'

'He's leaning on Mike much more since Alex's disappearance. Have you warned her?'

'She dismisses it. She's over-confident.'

'Hmm. How can we find out what they're discussing?' Dot sucked one arm of her glasses, her thinking habit.

'Charlie tells me who leaves the Centre in the afternoon so we can try and work out who else might be going to Gerry's flat.'

Dot put her glasses down.

'Surely Charlie can work out some way of listening in to what they're discussing?'

'Shh! You mean bugging his office?' I laughed out loud.

'Why not? GH is in danger of smashing up all sorts of things if he moves against Sheila.'

'I have thought about it.' Aileen looked out of the window. The frosted lower panes obscured the view, but the brick wall and windows of the main building across the yard were visible through the upper panes. A Hiace van was parked to the left, close up against the window. A soulless, workaday view. 'I'll ask Charlie if it's possible.'

'You won't mention it to Sheila, will you?' I asked.

'Absolutely not.'

Next day Gerry hounded Aileen relentlessly. He followed her into the finance office, screaming. He looked angrily at Dot, thumped the desk and kicked the door. Aileen looked pale and drawn. When I took him some figures in the late afternoon he was in the passage between the small kitchen and Aileen's office. I saw that she had pushed her desk forward to block the doorway and was standing defensively behind it. Dot had her back to the staircase and was shielding herself with a chair, its legs pointing towards Gerry. She signalled to me to keep away from him. He was shouting and flailing like a fish trapped in a bucket.

When he had stormed off to the *News Line* office Aileen handed me a £10 note.

'Quick, go and buy me a small bottle of brandy.'

'Brandy?'

'Go on! He's driving me up the wall.'

The cook came in.

'I've put the chops for supper in your fridge,' she said.

'They'll probably end up on my head,' said Aileen.

When it was time to drive Gerry home her office reeked of brandy.

'It's OK, he has no sense of smell,' she said in an alcoholic haze. 'Don't worry. I can still drive. It's the only way I'll survive this evening.'

A small group was beginning to coalesce, five of us, aware that something, as yet unformulated, had to be done. We never met together but discussion circulated between us as we kept the mundane machinery of the Centre running day to day: finance, security, technical equipment, providing for Gerry's needs. Aileen talked to Dot when Gerry was out. Dot talked to me when we were alone and to Dave Bruce in the quiet evenings. Aileen talked to Dave when he drove her to her osteopath appointments, and to me when we drove to Nottingham. We each separately talked to Charlie.

Robert shared Dave's political assessment and spoke blasphemously in the confines of the finance office about errors in the Party's analysis, but he was unpredictable. He could open his mouth at the wrong time. One or two other trusted, long-standing comrades were also concerned about the state of the Party. But Dot and Aileen proceeded very cautiously, they couldn't risk Gerry sensing a whiff of the group organising against him.

Charlie opened the gate to let Aileen drive out. She wound down her window.

'Did it work?' she asked almost inaudibly, looking straight ahead.

'Everything is in good working order,' he replied in his formal manner, as if he had repaired a cupboard door. 'I have been checking it this morning.'

As we drove down the alley a big smile spread over Aileen's face.

'He's done it.'

'Done what?'

'Last night I left the window to the ante-room unbolted so Charlie could climb into Gerry's office to attach a bug under his desk.'

'How? Surely the guard at the gate would have noticed?'

'He must have crept behind the vehicles in the dead of night.'

'My God. That doesn't say much for the security at the Centre.'

We both laughed.

Gerry suspected an opposition, but he was looking in the wrong place.

The revelation

Nothing suggested this trip to Nottingham would be different from any other. It was a misty morning and the roads were clear. We listened to a Bruce Springsteen tape, excited that Charlie had successfully bugged Gerry's office.

'I suppose he'll listen in and, when he hears a private conversation with Mike, he'll press the button to record.'

'My God. They'd be furious if they found out.'

'No one else has the technical knowledge to find a bug. Only the four of us and Dave Bruce know about it and we'll keep it that way.'

A few miles after Watford Gap service station Aileen made a casual remark.

'You do realise Gerry has a whole queue of women.'

I looked at her, puzzled.

'How d'you mean?'

'When the women from the *News Line* offices or the Young Socialists go round to his flat in the afternoon, it's not to discuss Trotsky or *Volume 38*.'

I watched the road, struggling to understand. She waited a few moments.

'The divan in his inner office – do you really think he rests on it?'

'The divan bed?'

'He has sex with every woman he can.'

My stomach tightened.

'Gerry? Sex? Who with?'

'Everyone. With me for 20 years.'

Aileen, too, had sex with him? My teeth were chattering and I had to put my hand up to still them.

'I don't understand.'

'It's hard to grasp, I know.'

I watched the lorries in the slow lane. A large removal van, a car transporter with two layers of shiny new vehicles. Gerry had sex with other women? I had always thought I was the only one. Two horse boxes travelling together. Did Aileen know about me?

'What do you mean "everyone"?'

'Every woman he can possibly get. He views all the young women at the Centre as potential sexual partners. He's done it for years.'

She must be mistaken. It couldn't be true.

'Surely someone would have guessed?'

'Oh, he's very clever. He manages to hide it from everyone.'

By the time we passed Leicester Forest East service station I had grasped what she was saying. But I was thrashing around, trying to convince myself she was mistaken. She pressed the button to replay Bruce Springsteen.

'Have you always …' I stuttered. 'How long have you known?'

'Only since Gerry's heart attack, when Dot and I began comparing notes. I was stuck in a hotel near the hospital. Gerry expected me to stay with him all day but the ward sister wouldn't let me, thank goodness.'

'Fuckin' hell! I should hope not!'

'Dot brought finance figures and clothes for me. We walked the length of Dovedale, talking. Suddenly all sorts of things gushed out of her, as if she couldn't suppress what she knew any longer.'

'But are you sure? I mean, surely you know everything Gerry does?' I was stuttering again. 'You cook for him, wash his clothes, run his errands, fix meetings.'

'He makes the arrangements for the afternoon discussions in his flat, not me. I don't know who he's seeing, unless I bump into them when I collect him at 5 o'clock.' She paused. 'I always presumed he was having political discussions. He has men comrades round as well, remember.'

I breathed out slowly, aghast.

'Didn't you suspect anything?'

She thought a while.

'When I was convalescing in 1981 after my operation, I sat on the top landing at the flats, under the skylight. I could see the stairs leading down from Gerry's floor. An International Committee was underway and I noticed women leaving his flat, from Spain, Germany, Greece, Peru …'

'But surely they were there for political discussions about their sections?'

'Well, maybe. But it felt odd. And I didn't dare discuss it with anyone.' She thought for a long moment, staring at the road ahead. 'And there was a silly occasion when I was cooking supper while Gerry and Alex looked at early editions of the Sunday papers. Alex opened the fridge and found a black bra, which he handed to me, grinning saucily, murmuring, "This isn't mine. It must be yours." I had no idea where it came from.'

I was too shaken to find this amusing. An incident came to mind: Gerry had called me into his office to hand me an earring, saying conspiratorially, 'You dropped this yesterday.' But it wasn't mine, and I'd soon forgotten the matter.

We drove in silence. Then Aileen spoke again.

'There was the matter of a leading Young Socialist in the 1960s. Gerry had an affair with her that became very messy. The membership never heard the details because it was referred to the Control Commission to investigate. Mum was on the commission, but she won't say anything about it. It was very unpleasant.'

I tried to picture Gerry as a younger man embroiled in an affair that went wrong. But Aileen was describing something seedy: he was married; his children must have been nearly as old as the young woman involved.

We arrived at the College of Marxist Education and went through the usual ritual of lunch with the students so they could vouch that we had been there. I tried to behave normally, but I ate very little and struggled to talk to the comrades at my table.

I boarded the train at Derby station, battling to still my turbulent thoughts. The pounding rhythm of Bruce Springsteen's *Born in the USA* went round and round in my head.

Could anything I knew confirm what Aileen had said?

I had once taken a file into her office knowing she was out and had passed a Latin American comrade in the passageway. Gerry had emerged from the ante-room adjoining Aileen's office with a triumphant leer on his face that had changed to a hostile snarl when he saw me. Yes, that had been strange. The divan bed in the inner office … I shuddered with distaste.

When I reached home I flung off my coat and put on Shostakovich's first cello concerto, but the disturbing, troubled music increased my distress. I changed to Mozart's piano concerto No. 21 and lay on the bed, hoping it would calm me.

I had some serious thinking to do.

I thought back to an incident in the early 1970s along the Blackwater Estuary in Essex:

> *I am in the back of the car, Gerry in front, Aileen driving. He has invited me to accompany them on a sortie away from the thousand-strong Young Socialists' summer camp. A grey day in early August; a vast clouded sky above. No one speaks. We meander alongside the estuary. 'Pull up here,' Gerry says at an isolated spot, a broad expanse of flat, marshy land, interrupted by rivulets of water and mud. Scarcely a breath of air. Squawking birds soar high in the sky.*

He walks out along a spit of land projecting into the marsh, surveying the huge openness. Aileen and I wait silently by the car. He seems tense and lonely. I think I can feel his strain. The summer camp has been difficult. Disagreements with the French delegation are close to the surface amid whispers that there could be a split. In the huge marquee the assembled Young Socialists, League members, trade unionists and international delegations listen to lectures on the world situation: the Vietnam war; Stalinism propping up imperialism; social democracy's bankruptcy. The French introduce a somewhat different perspective but the Greek, German and American sections support us. Big issues are at stake and the future of the Fourth International depends on the outcome. Gerry's interventions are decisive. No one is his equal, he bears an enormous historical responsibility for the theoretical struggle.

The camp is reinforcing my determination to become a revolutionary cadre, to play a role in the revolution. I feel privileged to be here on the estuary with this great man. I wish I could make his burden easier.

I jolted back to the present-day reality.

For 20 years Gerry Healy has dominated my life. His analysis of the Rhodesian situation had convinced me to join the movement in the first place. I had been inspired by the large, modern organisation he had built to fight the capitalist system, rotten to the core, ripe for overthrow. I'd lived through massive events: May-June 1968 in France, the Vietnam war, the dollar coming off gold in August 1971, the docks strikes, miners' strikes, Britain's 'winter of discontent', and now the developing revolutionary situation. Gerry had analysed these events and forged our policies … *but he's not doing so well on the present miners' strike.*

I felt disturbed, angry. I couldn't read. I couldn't listen to music. I decided to vacuum the carpets, hoping the physical task and the gadget's reassuring growl would help marshal my thoughts.

Gerry criticised me, taught me, encouraged me.

I moved into the passageway. *He leads the fight in the historical tradition of Marx, Engels, Lenin and Trotsky. And he turned to me for love and comfort.* Or that was how I had seen it.

I felt cheated, betrayed. I wanted to scream, smash something. I shouted a repetitive torrent of frustrated swear words from my limited vocabulary: 'You fucking bastard, fucking arsehole …'

I yanked the hoover cable to reach the corner.

I needed to completely reassess my view of Gerry, already tarnished by the idiosyncratic behaviour I had seen at the Centre. I unplugged the hoover and took it through to the living room.

One night, in his flat, he had told me:

'I was a seaman before the war. I saw Hitler coming to power.'

'You were in Germany?'

'I saw it, I was there.' His inscrutable expression had suggested superior wisdom.

But Aileen had dismissed this account.

'Nonsense, it's a fantasy. He's taken it from a book written by someone else.'

I had heard him speaking at a large rally in the Conway Hall.

'They wouldn't conscript me during the war. They didn't want a dangerous communist in the army. "Good," I said. "Give me a nice big factory to organise instead."'

The audience had laughed. I never learned where he had been in the war.

I put the hoover away, made a cup of tea and flopped on to the sofa. My thoughts were in chaos; I felt disgust, betrayal, disbelief. Aileen had opened my eyes to something tawdry, repulsive. Who was Gerry, really? Why had I been so deluded as to imagine that his perfunctory coupling was about 'love and comfort', that I was the only one?

I had always seen Aileen as an important political leader. She accompanied Gerry to meetings in Canada, America, Europe, Australia; to meet PLO leader Yasser Arafat, Colonel Gaddafi in Libya and Arab leaders in Syria, Lebanon, Iraq. She had enormous respect and authority in the Party. But only in recent years had I realised how intimately she was expected to wait on Gerry: prepare all his meals, make his bed, wash his dirty underpants, iron his vests and shirts. She even measured out his Milk of Magnesia. 'I once mixed toothpaste with water when it had run out and I'd forgotten to buy more.' She was on call via the intercom system throughout the night. Why hadn't anyone questioned Gerry's exploitative relationship with her?

I covered my face with my hands. I wanted to cleanse it, wipe something off my skin.

And what about the young women in their teens or early 20s with whom Aileen suspected he was having sex? He was over 70, old enough to be their grandfather. Surely they wouldn't agree to sex with this physically repulsive old man? Aileen must be wrong …'Clare, do you think he gives them any choice?' she had said this morning. I was a sophisticate from the 1960s sexual explosion, 20 years older than many of them. But these were young women on the cusp of adult life. I was appalled.

It was all too awful to contemplate. I decided that when Charlie arrived I wouldn't mention Aileen's revelations. Not yet, anyway.

My confusion

I tried to behave towards Gerry as before but now I watched, observing seemingly insignificant things, questioning everything. A cold anger and revulsion underpinned all my daily work. I continued discussing with Aileen.

'Two years ago, Mike and Sheila sent Charlie to Syria as Vanessa's bodyguard when you and Gerry were away. Gerry was furious on his return. Why?'

'He probably thought they would have an affair.'

I could think of few things less likely.

'Is Vanessa one of the women Gerry has sex with?'

'I don't know, but the desire is certainly there. I've seen the way he looks at her.'

'And what about Sheila?'

'I can't believe he hasn't tried with her in the past. But she seems to have some hold over him, as if she knows something he wants to keep secret. I can't work it out.'

There were subtle intersections I had not been aware of before.

'And Janet, why does Gerry never, ever have any conflict with her? She was a leading member when I joined.'

'I can't remember how I know, but one day, years ago, she found a hotel bill in his desk, made out for Mr and Mrs X, the name of a woman comrade working at the Centre. Janet challenged him and kept the bill as evidence. It gave her a certain kind of protection.'

'Oh God, it's so full of intrigue. So she knows about Gerry's sexual proclivities?'

'Well, when Gerry sees the children to give them pocket money, she never lets her daughter go in alone. She always stands in the doorway.'

'She's a child.'

'Yes, but she'll grow up.'

I learned that Aileen's secret lover was Peter Jones, the full-time lecturer at the College of Marxist Education.

'After Gerry's heart attack I had to stay near the convalescent home in Derbyshire. I was bored out of my mind. Pete and I got talking and that's how it started.'

'Does he know what you think about Gerry?'

'Oh yes, he's long dismissed Gerry's theoretical stuff.'

I needed to tell Charlie about Gerry's sexual activities but I was worried how he would react. I made tea, put on Beethoven's violin concerto, one of our favourites, and sat next to him on the sofa.

'I have to tell you something really difficult about Gerry.'

'Go on.'

I put my mug down and took a deep breath.

'He has sex with lots of women in the Party, you know, when the girls go round to his flat in the afternoon …'

I stopped to see his reaction, but he just looked at me, listening, so I rushed on.

'It's been going on for years, with everybody' – my heart was thumping – 'including me. It, it doesn't happen very often. It's quick and secretive, he calls me round maybe once every two or three months, but not late at night any more because I go early to Oxford and he knows I have to sleep, and anyway I'm not in the flats, though he doesn't know that.' The words tumbled out chaotically. 'It's not because I want it –'

I suddenly felt soiled, like used goods. All society's stereotypical judgements rushed into my mind and I stopped. Charlie shrugged and took a sip of tea.

'Yes, well, he's a fucking bastard. His relationship with people is very strange.' He stared at the opposite wall for a long moment. 'He wants everybody to be afraid of him. He always wants to be in control.' Another sip of tea. 'I see things at the Centre that no one else knows about. Nothing surprises me any more.'

His matter-of-fact reaction overwhelmed me. Relief flooded through my body. I clutched my solid, comforting mug and took a deep gulp of tea. I felt intensely grateful.

'What do you see?'

'Oh, I don't know. Listen to the violin, this is a lovely bit.' He waved his hand in time to the music, conducting an imaginary orchestra. 'I mean, Gerry's an important political leader, but I realised long ago that he's also crazy.'

He was quiet for a moment.

'Security is a serious issue. The state observes us, they infiltrate agents and informers into the Party, they tap our phones. And the Stalinists also want to know what's going on inside our organisation. We have to protect ourselves against all that. But Gerry has paranoia. He has ridiculous ideas. We've all kinds of security equipment –' He stopped to conduct again.

'You mean, like the telescopic mast towering above the canteen?'

'Well, that's for radio reception. There's lots of other stuff. But in security' – he looked directly at me – 'the principle is: Don't-tell-people-if-they-don't-need-to-know.'

'OK, OK.'

'Gerry sent me to scan the Libyan embassy for bugs. He thinks we have more sophisticated equipment than the government of a country. Crazy.'

'Did you find any bugs?'

'Of course not. It was ridiculous.'

When Charlie left early next morning, I gave him a big hug.

'Thanks.'

'What for?'

'For your understanding about Gerry's sex stuff.'

'But I haven't done nothing.' He was grinning broadly as he slipped through the door.

A particularly ludicrous row took place. Charlie was summoned to the Political Committee, accused of an incomprehensible security breach, to do with a fire escape. Gerry demanded he write a statement about his political position.

'What was that all about?' I whispered to Aileen later.

'When we came back to the Centre last night, Gerry headed for the *News Line* offices but they had finished the paper early and the warehouse far door was barred.'

'So?'

'I suppose he wanted to arrange to see one of the women comrades at his flat and he was thwarted by the bar. He was yelling and screaming.'

For nearly a fortnight Charlie's 'security breach' dominated the Political Committee meetings. The non-discussion went round and round, punctuated by Charlie's self-flagellating memos written with Dot's secret help, only to be rejected by Gerry and recomposed for the next day. I now assessed everything as revolving around his sexual obsessions.

Gerry was as brittle as tinder. The security guard brought a half-empty bottle of Perrier water to Aileen.

'We've no more for Gerry's meeting and the off-licence isn't open yet.'

'Great. Another flashpoint for a senseless row.'

She took the bottle and filled it with tap water, took an unceremonious swig to check it was still sour and bubbly and handed it back.

'This will do.' We giggled at her initiative.

In the final desperate weeks of the miners' strike the atmosphere at the Centre was tense and sombre. Financial strains were becoming unbearable. Dot worried all the time; her hair was lanky and unwashed, and she wore the same clothes for several days. Before meeting the bank manager she put on a bright red gash of lipstick – to give her courage or to impress him? It looked garish. Payment demands threatened supplies. Aileen continually bolstered Dot to stop the hysteria just below the surface breaking through. 'Clare, hang on to Dot's ankles.'

Only we three knew how dire the finances were. Our hopes that large battalions of workers would come into action and change class relationships hadn't happened in support of the miners, so when would it?

'We need a cash lump sum *now*.' Dot looked grim.

'That won't resolve anything,' I said.

'It would buy time.'

'We need time to formulate another plan,' Aileen insisted.

We secured a loan on my building in the Centre, negotiated through a bank in Frankfurt for £69,000. The secret, fragmentary discussions continued between the five of us: Aileen, Dot, Dave Bruce, Charlie and me. How could Gerry be reined in? Who among the flawed leading members could forge a new leadership? Which women and girls were caught up in his sexual excesses and how could he be stopped? What about the finances?

Alex Mitchell suddenly reappeared from Australia, his wings clipped, slightly shamefaced, but slotting effortlessly back into the entourage that supported Gerry, writing silver words in *News Line*. Whispers about him continued, never voiced openly.

We had to think carefully and proceed with caution.

Two important things happened: the miners' strike ended on 3rd March 1985, and I became pregnant.

We prepare to act

The year-long miners' strike – heroic, bitter, inspiring – was over. As 200,000 miners marched through the pit gates behind their colliery brass bands, heads held high, I felt fury at the trades union and Labour Party leaders who had betrayed them. I felt burning hatred for Mrs Thatcher. Gloom pervaded the Centre.

'A defeat for the miners would be a catastrophe for the whole working class,' *News Line* had said previously. 'The miners by themselves cannot defeat Thatcher and the combined forces of the capitalist state. The choice is simple: see the miners' union destroyed or fight for a General Strike.'

But the Trades Union Congress had not called a General Strike. They had never intended to. There was to be no storming of the Winter Palace, no period of 'dual power' between the working class and the capitalist class. The template of the Russian Revolution would not be repeated here in Britain, or not yet.

The Party now turned to campaign for the release and reinstatement of miners who had been jailed or sacked during the strike. Sheila oversaw arrangements for marches through the coalfields and industrial areas to a final rally in Alexandra Pavilion.

Dot and I were in a permanent state of watchful, taut anxiety, discussing continually when we were alone.

▼ Miners' march in London in summer 1984 at the height of their year-long strike

▲ An attentive audience at the Young Socialists' 25th annual conference. Healy would be considering who could be brought to work at the Centre

'You know how GH sees the marches?' She took off her glasses. 'He'll bring a new crop of young women who've proved themselves in the campaign to work at the Centre, more potential sexual victims. We have to act soon.'

'How?'

'I don't know.'

Aileen and I tried to work out which women were, or had been, sexually involved with Gerry. 'He would like to have sex with every woman around him, but he avoids those he feels are dangerous.'

'Dangerous?'

'Those he fears might blab, or aren't fully committed to the Party, or intellectual women. He has to be sure they're under his control so he plots very carefully and he's prepared to wait years. Believe me, he spends every minute of the day thinking about it.'

'That can't be. He has all the political thinking and writing to do.'

'Clare, I've been watching him. Sex dominates his life: planning his next assignation, identifying someone new, building her up, attacking her political weaknesses at the same time, until she's in his thrall.'

Dismal raindrops obscured the windscreen.

'He manipulates lives, he breaks up couples by sending the man away as a Party organiser, so the relationship becomes impossible.'

I knew of two such couples, Aileen listed others.

'And he destroys relationships, usually through rows with the man, who becomes a political pariah and even leaves the Party.'

I suddenly faced an awful realisation.

'Oh, God, yes. That's what he did. My marriage, he deliberately broke it up.'

I grappled with this painful thought: I had been duped, manipulated. The back-and-forth of the windscreen wipers seemed to be mocking me.

'How have you and Paul survived?'

'Gerry's tried to drive him out, but he refuses to go. Editing a newspaper is every journalist's dream and he won't give it up, thank God. He's my protection against Gerry invading my flat at any time he likes. And Gerry needs him. Who could replace him on the paper?'

'Does he know Gerry has sex with you?'

'Absolutely not.'

We considered women who had left the Party, perhaps to escape Gerry's sexual attentions. I remembered a girl in the flats and her look of fear when she was summoned late one night to see Gerry for what I had assumed was a deserved reprimand.

'Oh, fuckin' 'ell. It's awful. And remember the comrade who took an overdose in my flat, the trip in the ambulance?'

The rain stopped as we turned off the motorway.

'Dot is looking for an opportunity to ask two or three of the girls, separately, if Gerry's had sex with them. It's delicate and dangerous. She must be careful.'

It had been more than two months since Gerry had last called me to his flat. The whole seedy set-up disgusted me, the more so now I was pregnant, which Aileen didn't yet know.

'I don't want to have sex with the old bastard any more,' I said.

'You won't be able to stop it.'

'I'll tell him I have some medical condition.'

'You won't get away with it. He won't accept it. You remember that Political Committee meeting where I cracked up?'

'Of course. I couldn't understand what was going on.'

'I had refused to have sex. But I realised I wouldn't be able to withstand the non-stop rows and the whole committee being wheeled in against my fabricated political position. My life would have been unbearable, so I gave in.'

'Jesus Christ!' I covered my face with my hands.

She moved lanes to overtake.

'Paul visited me in hospital after my operation in 1981 and told me: "Congress has just voted to give Gerry unlimited powers." "Well," I said, "they've just signed my death warrant."'

The Central Committee meeting on 27th April underlined the hopelessness of a political challenge to Gerry. Mike Banda's opening report, evaluating the political situation after the miners' strike, set the scene for Gerry to attack Sheila as a 'subjective idealist'. Tensions between him and Sheila had been building up for weeks, apparently over arrangements for the jailed miners' march but in reality over deeper, never-expressed issues. He moved her suspension from the Party on spurious charges, which was ridiculous. She was one of the most important members of the leadership and she fought back. Then Stuart Carter, a young Central Committee member from Manchester, spoke.

'I don't agree that Comrade Sheila is damaging the Party. She's been organising the march arrangements very efficiently.'

Uproar broke out. The usual people rallied to the attack: Mike Banda, Corin, newly-back-in-the-fold Alex. But Stuart stood his ground, even when Sheila accepted she might have committed some procedural error. I wondered where his courage came from to oppose Gerry's ludicrous allegations. I listened to the barrage of pseudo-analysis of his political position with stifled fury coupled with admiration for his principled stand. As the bellowing continued, Gerry stood up and punched Stuart in the face. No one objected. I noticed the expressionless profiles of Aileen and Dot in the rows in front of me; Dave was to my right further along the row. I dared not look at him.

We couldn't support Stuart. It was too early, we weren't ready. I looked down at my notebook, remembering Oliver Cromwell's advice, often quoted by Gerry: *Trust in God, but keep your powder dry*. With bitter resentment I voted in favour of Stuart's suspension 'for opposing the Central Committee's authority to discipline its members and rule on their conduct'. Well, at least our powder was still dry.

When the meeting ended I passed Dave on the staircase. We exchanged glances. 'Jeee-sus Che-rist,' I muttered under my breath.

We knew we had to act soon.

▲ In front of the Central Committee banner Dot Gibson (left) talks to Sheila Torrance. Corin Redgrave is behind the banner on the left

Dot snapped the finance office hatch closed and slid the bolt. I could see she was itching to tell me something.

'I asked one of the girls if GH had approached her for sex. She said yes, and she hated it. She was quite upset.'

I recoiled at the thought of the young woman being pawed – and penetrated – by a lecherous old man, this unattractive, malodorous bully.

'Does she know of any others?'

'She hasn't talked to anyone else.'

'Will you ask them?'

'If I have an opportunity.'

A second girl* confirmed that Gerry had sex with her too; a third said he had approached her, but had backed off when he realised she was under the legal age.

---

*   The awkward references to 'first girl', 'second' and 'third' are to preserve their anonymity

'They won't tell anyone you've asked them?'

'Oh, no. They know their lives would be turned upside down if GH found out.'

In his flat, after a brief discussion about my work Gerry uttered the unwelcome words:

'Take off your dress.'

'I'm afraid I can't.' I looked straight at him. 'I have a gynaecological problem and the doctor has told me I mustn't have sex.'

His face showed disbelief as he moved towards me. I raised my hand to stop him.

'No, the doctor insists.'

As I rebuffed him I sensed nervousness in his demeanour. Why? He bullied others, why was he unsure with me?

I left feeling triumphant, but uncertain if it was permanent.

I was thrilled to be pregnant and noted the small, subtle changes in my body.

'I won't tell anyone until the amniocentesis test confirms there's no abnormality,' I said to Charlie. 'Not even my mother.'

'When people notice you're getting big they'll ask who the father is.'

'I'll just say it's secret. They'll never guess about us.'

We laughed.

An early morning philosophy class on Lenin's Volume 14: *Materialism and Empirio-Criticism* forced our plans to crystallise. Gerry called on Robert, who talked about the materialist Feuerbach, for whom 'the thing-in-itself' was a world existing outside us, completely knowable, in direct opposition to idealist Kant's 'abstraction without reality'. Gerry's face was a solid mask, as if he'd lost the thread. He didn't criticise Robert but shifted the ground to talk about 'subjective idealism' damaging our Party. He suddenly turned on Dot.

'Mrs Gibson, I want to inspect the finances. I'm not happy with the way they are conducted. You'll need to prepare a full report.'

◀ Lenin's Volume 14: *Materialism and Empirio-Criticism*, distinguishable by the number 14 at the top right corner of the green dust jacket

Back in the finance office Dot was very agitated. When Aileen fetched her to see Gerry she rose, picked up her papers, then flung them back on the desk.

'This is it. He'll find out what's going on. He'll appoint someone like Vanessa – God help us – to look at the books. He'll see we have no money.' She pushed the piles of papers further back on her desk, shoved the phone to the right, lined up her pens and pencils with a clatter. 'He'll have me prosecuted so he can appear squeaky clean, as if wicked Mrs Gibson had been duping him all along. This will be the end.'

'Dot, calm down. Don't lose your nerve now.' Aileen was insistent.

'It's a powder keg. It'll all come out –'

'This is not the time to panic. He hasn't even worked out how to investigate yet.'

As Dot went through the door, Aileen looked at me.

'Clare, for Christ's sake, hang on to her ankles.'

Robert started counting the money.

'We could sell some of the bookshops, and the trucks we don't use; give up the third factory unit in Runcorn.'

'Shut up, Robert. That's not helpful right now.'

Various plans criss-crossed our secret, five-cornered discussions as we conspirators exchanged information.

> **Dot**: 'After GH's heart attack I suggested locking him in his flat until he resigned from the leadership.'
> **Clare:** 'What?' (Laughing.)
> **Aileen**: 'It wouldn't have worked.'
> **Dave:** 'I'm writing something to expose his political bankruptcy.'
> **Aileen:** 'Come on, Dave. You know he'll be able to defeat a direct political attack.'
> **Dave:** 'But half the comrades at the Centre know he's bonkers.'
> **Aileen:** 'I think I should write a letter exposing his actions with the women and disappear until the dust settles.'
> **Dot:** 'It should be *me* who writes the letter and disappears.'
> **Aileen**: 'The finance regime is too complicated. He'd be able to twist it.'
> **Charlie:** 'I listen to his private meetings. He thinks Sheila is working against him.'
> **Dot:** 'She thinks she can hold her own against him.'
> **Clare:** 'You haven't told her about our discussions?'
> **Dot:** 'No. She suspects nothing.'

Aileen: 'If Gerry gets even a whiff that we're working against him we'll all be out, expelled on trumped-up charges.'
Charlie: 'I don't hear suspicions about any of you.'
Dot: 'We're the "little people" who do the back-room jobs. He believes the plot against him will come from leading members, the political ones.'
Clare: 'If we reveal his sexual habits surely the Party will respond?'
Aileen: 'It's the only way. I'll expose the details and then disappear.'
Dave: 'You'll have to disappear for a very long time. You won't be able to come back, you know.'
Clare: 'Where will you go?'
Aileen: 'To the secret cottage in Derbyshire that Pete and I have.'
Dot: 'When will we do it?'
Dave: 'What about the day after the rally at the end of the Justice for Miners march, 1st July?'
Charlie: 'I'm ready.'

Dot and I were alone in the finance office when Aileen came in, wearing a beautiful top embroidered with a sophisticated appliqué design. Her hair and make-up were impeccable, as always, but she looked weary.

'Are we doing the right thing? We're all too close to it. My mother's with us in principle but there's no one else to check with. They'd go straight to Gerry, every single one.'

'Well,' said Dot, 'I've told Norman about GH and the women. He was horrified, angry, distressed that he might have been complicit, like when he's had to drop women at the flats to see Gerry.'

Norman was older than Dot, a long-standing comrade from Yorkshire, trusted by the Party Congress, which had elected him to its independent regulatory body, the Control Commission. He helped Aileen with some of the running around, like buying Gerry's smoked salmon from Harrods – or rather, he bought it locally and transferred it into a Harrods bag. From his workbench for *News Line* dispatch at the bottom of the canteen stairs he observed everything.

'He knows we want to move against Gerry, but I've given him no details. He gave me unconditional encouragement.'

'His validation is really important,' said Aileen.

We were living in a fevered atmosphere, trying to keep up the appearance of calm normality: light-hearted banter with Robert as we counted money in the mornings, chatting to Janet about her children, dealing with comrades' queries at the finance hatch. Charlie opened and closed the main gate, worked on electronics in the security office next to the canteen, supervised the night guards, responded to Gerry's yells, listened to his secret meetings. Dave worked on little-understood technical projects in his office at the bottom of the alleyway. Aileen carried out the usual routine tasks for Gerry: summoning comrades to his office, preparing his meals, typing his philosophical notes, recording the bookshops' daily sales figures, accompanying him to meetings. Meanwhile, she drafted a letter and planned how to disappear.

On Thursday 27th June the Political Committee received a letter from Bob, one of the Runcorn printers, saying that Norman had criticised the Party and Comrade Healy.

'Where is Harding?' asked Gerry. 'Get him in here.'

'He's in Bournemouth, on the sales team at the Trades Union Congress.'

'Tell him to come straight back.'

When the sales team rang me I asked for Norman.

'You have to come back to London. Gerry wants to see you.'

'What about?'

I looked round to check no one was at the hatch.

'Bob has reported that you have disagreements. You'll have to explain yourself tomorrow. You'll be collected at the station and you'll have to stay in your flat till the meeting.'

'I'll be there. I'm ready.' He was enthusiastically defiant.

Friday dawned, three days before our action planned for Monday 1st July. What if we failed? Did we have a fall-back plan? I drove back from Oxford in an agitated frame of mind, knowing Norman was being interrogated by the Political Committee. Would they succeed in bullying him into submission?

Back in the Centre, I made tea in the deserted canteen. Charlie sidled out of his security office, grinning.

'Norman really fought back. Mike Banda got angry and so did Alex. They've set up a sub-committee to continue the inquiry tomorrow: Mike, Alex and – guess who – Dave as well.'

We laughed quietly under cover of the humming the tea urn.

The letter

We five conspirators met together only once, late on the Saturday night before the Alexandra Palace rally to welcome the Justice for Miners march. I knocked at the second-floor flat of Dave Bruce's partner in a red-brick council block in Camberwell, glancing over the balcony at a train passing on the same level. Charlie and Aileen were already there, chuckling at a witty crack from Dave, despite the tension of the occasion. Dot arrived with her husband Peter, a long-standing Party member and leading trade unionist on the buses. I watched them sit down, appreciating the solid authority Peter brought to our gathering. 'To me as a teenager they were a glamorous Cockney couple, lively, active,' Aileen had told me.

Aileen handed us each a final copy of her letter, which we read in silence. Peter spoke first.

'This is dynamite. I'll hide our copy at home in the rubbish bin – under the bin-bag. If Gerry decides on a raid they'll never think to look there.'

'You've added the list of names,' I said. It was a shock to see mine among them.

'Yes, 26 women we're sure of. Some are from the past.'

'There are probably more,' said Dot.

A slow train rattled past.

'I've put letters in sealed envelopes addressed to each Political Committee Member. They're hidden behind saucepans in the small kitchen. I'll come back after tomorrow's rally, around midnight, and put them on their desks, so everyone will have a copy even if Gerry tries to suppress it. I've done envelopes for Corin, Vanessa and the *News Line* comrades to leave with the night guard.' She looked at Charlie. 'You'll be on the gate in the morning, won't you?'

'Of course.'

We thought for a few moments. Dave looked at Aileen.

'What are your exact plans for Monday morning?'

'Gerry will be picked up from the flats by Phil Penn. The minute the car leaves I'll go downstairs to Stonhouse Street where my brother-in-law will be waiting. He'll bring me straight to Clare's secret flat for about half-past seven and I'll hide there until he can drive me to Derbyshire after work.'

'So, when we arrive for the Political Committee at eight Gerry may not yet realise you're not turning up,' said Dave.

A door slammed outside and we heard voices passing along the balcony. We were all wrapped in our own thoughts.

'Have you said anything to Paul?'

'No. But I'll see him in the pub after the rally to forewarn him that something unspecified is going to happen. I owe it to him. We've been married for more than 20 years.'

Another train sped by and the surface of my tea vibrated.

'What if the Political Committee decides to ignore the letter?' asked Charlie.

'Well, they can't.'

'Everyone at the Centre will wonder why you've disappeared.'

'I've told two of the girls to tell their parents about Gerry at the rally tomorrow,' said Dot.

'But they don't know what we're planning?'

'Of course not.'

'Earlier this evening I met the third girl and her father.' said Dave. 'We arranged that he'll come in on Monday morning and demand to see Mike Banda to tell him about Gerry's depraved approach to his daughter. He'll demand a Control Commission inquiry.'

'And surely the other parents will do something.'

'There's also the inquiry into Norman's statement, which is scheduled to continue on Monday. It's driving them mad. They can't understand why he won't recant.'

We laughed nervously.

'In Monday's Political Committee meeting,' said Dot, 'I will appear distressed, worried about Aileen, and ask permission to phone her sister.'

'I'll express outrage at the letter's contents,' said Dave.

'Me too,' I said.

'Charlie, how's the bugging equipment?'

'It's working perfectly. I'll record everything.'

We had prepared as much as we could. Now we had to go through the Alexandra Palace rally and wait for Monday morning. We left one by one to avoid attracting attention.

Alexandra Pavilion

The March to Release the Jailed Miners processed triumphantly up the hill to Alexandra Palace, led by Murton Colliery's brass band. Applauding crowds greeted them in the sweltering heat as they headed into the Pavilion.

In the back-room finance office, I plugged in the counting machines and

made ready for an intense day. Jean Kerrigan had been instructed to help Dot and me as Robert was needed to steward. The office would also be Sheila's headquarters and Gerry would wander in from time to time.

I peeped into the hall. Giant photos of about 40 jailed miners, mostly young, many smiling, looked down on the assembly beneath a slogan 'RELEASE THE JAILED MINERS!' This was repeated on a massive red banner behind the speakers' platform alongside the logo of a miner behind bars and 'REINSTATE ALL SACKED MINERS'. Banners from the Edinburgh, Liverpool and Swansea marches were displayed in front of the

▼ The 4,000-strong audience at the Alexandra Pavilion rally

stage; a profusion of decorative miners' and other union banners lined the back wall. Four thousand exuberant people found seats, chattering, greeting each other.

Gerry was sauntering around the hall. I felt a nervous tightness in my stomach. *Tomorrow we begin the action to bring him down.* He greeted comrades with a little wave: *the great man acknowledging his followers.* Aileen hovered nearby.

Returning to the finance office I was startled to find that the steward stationed outside was the father of the third girl. *He's coming to the Centre tomorrow to demand a Control Commission, but he's not aware that I know.*

A continual stream of Party members brought us their branch money. The heat was unbearable. Aileen sent a steward to find an electric fan, which she positioned near the seat kept clear for Gerry. As we counted the money Sheila was talking to a comrade from Yorkshire.

'You still owe for 20 tickets and last week's *News Line*. Go and get it.'

'It's back in Leeds with another comrade.'

'It has to be clear before the end of the speeches. Work something out.' She turned to a Scottish comrade and consulted her lists. 'OK, you're clear. Please fetch Paul from Leicester.'

Above the rattle of the coin-counter we heard frequent applause. We took turns to go and listen for a few minutes. Mike Banda's speech was powerful, as was to be expected.

'Thatcher launched a merciless assault on every single basic democratic right of the working class. The miners were not defeated, they were betrayed.' Energetic applause. 'Their year-long undefeated strike drove back the concentrated strength of the repressive apparatus of the capitalist state and

▲ A speaker from the government's intelligence and security organisation GCHQ described their months-long battle against withdrawal of their trade union rights. Above: picket at Downing Street in February 1984 while Thatcher reiterated her insistence on a non-union spy centre

completely disrupted their strategies.' More applause. 'New layers of workers are preparing to struggle against the capitalist Bonapartist state.'

'Undefeated' strike? And who understands what 'Bonapartist' means?

The range of speakers was impressive: several miners, wives of jailed miners, speakers from Women Against Pit Closures, Ted Knight, leader of rate-capped Lambeth council, a leading print worker, the seamen's union leader, and a speaker from the government's listening post, GCHQ in Cheltenham, where they were fighting for trade union rights.

I heard part of Gerry's rousing speech.

'Thatcher is preparing now to take on the printers, the miners over pit closures, all sections of the working class,' he said, waving his arm emphatically, index finger pointed upwards. 'She wants a class confrontation and she must get it – we must give it to her.' Stormy applause. 'Only the organisation of the General Strike can prepare the struggle for power.'

The audience was wildly enthusiastic. *You're a charismatic speaker, but you're a fucking bastard, a bully.* In the rows in front of me I

▲ Gerry Healy speaks

noticed several of the women on Aileen's list. *Loyal comrades whose lives you've messed up. Just you wait!* At the back, Aileen's face was impassive. I tried to imagine her thoughts. Dave Bruce was in Clapham in case of a technical breakdown on *News Line* production. Charlie was near the door, supervising the stewards, every inch the security man: tall, light-blue shirt, two-way radio attached to his belt. He wasn't even listening to Gerry. I went back to the finance office and gave Dot a significant look.

'Go and listen for a bit.'

Sheila stepped up to the platform to take the collection after Gerry's speech, when the audience's enthusiasm was at its peak.

'We start with £100 from a trade union branch which supports our campaign for the jailed and sacked miners. Are there any other donations of £50 or over?' Stewards stationed in all the aisles took cheques and notes up to the platform while Sheila kept a running total. 'The Tory government is now coming for the rest of the working class and a major confrontation is ahead. Can we see the £20 notes?' She was very experienced at cajoling large collections from audiences: £10, £5 and soon-to-be-withdrawn £1 notes, ending with loose change collected in white plastic ice-cream tubs. As I fed the takings into the coin-counter Gerry came in with a confident smirk on his face. *You're pleased with yourself now, but your hour will come.*

A cast of actors ended the rally with a *Review of Labour History*. Matthew Kelly played a butler; Ian Charleson was a Scottish soldier returning from the war; David Calder played Marx. I couldn't relax, because of the gnawing tightness in my stomach. *Will our plan work? What can go wrong?* We began packing up the finance office as the audience booed portrayals of the class enemy. Aileen came in and exchanged a silent glance with Dot and me. My heart was pounding. *Jean is oblivious to our extreme tension.* Robert and another steward loaded equipment and the heavy leather briefcases holding thousands of pounds into the car. *Robert doesn't know either.* Charlie came to check that everything was under control, issuing instructions to stewards standing by the car, too busy to catch my eye. I felt a terrible excitement.

Aileen and Gerry left swiftly at the end. *After Gerry dismisses her she'll go and meet Paul in The Plough, she'll take the car back to the Centre, she'll distribute the envelopes.*

Back home, I had a cool bath and a cup of tea. My thoughts were in turmoil. A *brilliant day. It's an honour to be part of this working-class movement, I'm proud of our Party. But – we're going to deal with the old bastard.* Nervous, excited, determined, I fell asleep.

1ST JULY
TURNING POINT

The sound of a key in my front door took me by surprise. It wasn't yet seven-thirty, 15 minutes before I needed to leave. In marched Aileen, pale and drawn, followed by her brother-in-law Dan. I'd forgotten that her timetable ran earlier than mine.

'Hullo Clare,' said Dan cheerily.

I grabbed my clothes and went into the bathroom. It was already very hot. I threw on my red-and-white sundress, flat Indian thong sandals and red earrings, of course.

When I came out Aileen was sitting on the sofa, leaning her head on one hand.

'Make yourselves tea. There's bread, butter's in the fridge and a few other things. Just help yourselves.'

She waved dismissively. Her thoughts were elsewhere and she looked very tense.

'We'll be OK.' Dan was calm, in control of the situation.

Everything appeared normal as Charlie opened the gate at the Centre. Clutching my envelope, I waited in the yard for the Political Committee to start. One of the journalists was reading something, presumably Aileen's letter; Dot flitted between the finance office and the small kitchen, fetching things and making tea for Gerry. When Corin arrived Charlie handed him his letter. He strolled in and tore open the envelope. I went over to him.

'I found this letter under my flat door,' I lied, waving my piece of paper. Corin glanced at me and then read his copy. Without a word he folded it up, replaced it in the envelope and moved away. I couldn't guess his reaction.

Dave Bruce arrived, huffing and puffing.

'This is outrageous. This is a scandal.' He too was waving a piece of paper.

Alex was next. Charlie handed him his letter and Corin moved towards him. Sheila came down and went straight into Gerry's office, followed by Mike Banda, who had come through the warehouse from his office. Sheila came back to speak to Charlie.

'Where is Phil Penn?'

'He dropped Comrade Healy and went back for Aileen, like normal.'

A few minutes later the Granada drove up the alleyway and Charlie swung open the large double gates. Vanessa arrived at the same time. We moved aside to let Phil park in the designated place alongside the crewbus so that Gerry would have access straight into the passenger seat. Phil was alone. Sheila came out.

'Where's Aileen?'

'I don't know. She's not at home. I waited as usual and then I buzzed her flat. Paul said she had already gone out, he presumed to meet me.'

Sheila went back into Gerry's office. A few minutes later Dot called us into the meeting. I took my place on the divan along the back wall, facing Gerry in his corner to the left of the door. He sipped his tea as he watched us file in. As always, Alex sat on his right, then Sheila, with Mike opposite. The nervous tightness in my stomach was almost unbearable; adrenaline rushed through my body; I was tensed for action. Three youth comrades sat next to me.

'Dot, sit there.' Gerry pointed to the chair Aileen usually occupied, to the right of the door. His voice was calm and authoritative. 'It seems that Comrade Jennings has decided not to attend this meeting, but she's left a letter. Alex, read it out loud.'

> June 30th 1985
>
> *To the Political Committee*
>
> During the course of action on the Manchester Area certain practices have come to light as to the running of Youth Training by a homosexual and the dangers this holds for the party in relation to police provocation. I believe the Political Committee was correct in stating that a cover-up of such practices endangered the Party from a serious provocation.[*]

---

[*] Aileen Jennings wishes to make clear that she totally disassociates herself from the homophobic sentiments that were involved in the Party's 1985 actions over the Manchester Youth Training Centre and apologises unreservedly for the first paragraph of her letter

Having realised this I must therefore say to the Committee that I can no longer go on covering up a position at both the office and in the flats at 155 Clapham High Street which also opens the Party to police provocation; namely that whilst for 19 years I have been the close personal companion of Comrade Healy I have also covered up a problem which the Political Committee must now deal with because I cannot.

This is that the flats in particular are used in a completely opportunist way for sexual liaisons with female members employed by the Party on *News Line,* female members of the International Committee and others [26 individuals were then named].

On any security basis one of these or more has to be the basis of either blackmail by the police or an actual leak in security to a policewoman. I am asking the Political Committee to take steps to resolve the position for the Party in the present political situation.

In 1964, after the Control Commission of Investigation Comrade Healy gave an undertaking that he would cease these practices, this has not happened and I cannot sit on this volcano any longer.

Yours fraternally, Aileen Jennings

A moment's silence followed.

'This is a provocation,' said Vanessa.

'But it's true,' I bleated.

'It's outrageous,' shouted Dave. 'Totally against revolutionary morality.'

'Ah, so we're moralists now!' retorted Corin.

'Where is Aileen?' wailed Dot. 'Something must have happened to her.' Silence. 'Please can I go and phone her sister?'

'Stay where you are,' instructed Gerry.

Confused discussion broke out. Alex, floundering, rather uncertainly poured scorn on the letter. Vanessa said something high-sounding. Mike pontificated. Corin expounded on petty-bourgeois morality. Sheila was silent, superior, annoyed. Dave kept saying that Gerry's behaviour was scandalous. I put in my tuppenceworth – my name was on the list, after all. Gerry said nothing.

'I want to phone Aileen's sister. Something must have happened,' moaned Dot.

'I'd like to hear what Comrade Jennings has to say about it,' said Sheila's protégé from the London District Committee, Richard Price. He imagined Aileen would be back for a rational discussion.

No one said the allegations were untrue. No one even questioned them.

I watched Gerry's impassive face while the mayhem raged. He was listening, looking round the room, the experienced political fighter trying to work out what was really happening, who was involved.

'We had an important rally yesterday,' said Mike. 'We need to distil the lessons from the whole experience of the Justice for Miners march for next Saturday's Central Committee meeting. This is a diversion.'

'I propose we take a vote,' said Vanessa.

'What on?' demanded Dave.

'That Comrade Jennings' letter is a provocation and should be ignored.'

'All those in favour,' said Gerry in a matter-of-fact voice. Virtually everyone raised their hands.

'Against?'

Dave and I voted against. Dot kept moaning in distress and didn't vote either way.

The committee had decided that Aileen's letter was so unimportant that it should be ignored.

'Who wants to begin an assessment of yesterday's rally?' Gerry still seemed calm.

Alex rose to the occasion. I felt sick. Is Gerry going to be able to hold things together? Or have we – maybe – succeeded in scuppering the ship? Is Alex just rearranging deckchairs on the *Titanic?* I wasn't at all sure.

When the meeting broke up my legs were shaking, my teeth were chattering, I was completely drained of energy. I noticed the father of the third girl waiting in the yard, but found little comfort. No one on the Political Committee had questioned whether the young women were willing sexual partners to Gerry, so why should they care about his daughter?

I sat down at my desk. The phone rang and I had to take a deep breath to calm myself before answering it. I heard Charlie's quiet voice.

'Well done. That went really well.'

No phone call could have been more welcome.

Sheila followed Dot into the finance office.

'You'd better phone Aileen's sister.'

Dot sat down weakly, looked up the number in her address book and dialled.

'Hullo, this is Dot. Aileen hasn't come in to work. Do you know where she is?' She shook her head, looking up at Sheila. 'No, Paul doesn't know either. Please ring me if she contacts you.'

Dot blew her nose tearfully. Sheila's face hinted at impatience with this emotional reaction. I wondered what she thought about Aileen's sex list. Had she ever been one of Gerry's sexual partners? Her name wasn't on the list as Aileen hadn't been sure.

'Maybe her mother knows something.' Dot dialled the number and handed the phone to Sheila.

'Hullo Mickie. Aileen hasn't come into work and we're a bit mystified. Has she said anything to you? Well, if she contacts you please ring me.'

Dot continued sniffing.

'I don't know what to think,' she said, shaking her head. 'Clare, stop counting the new money. Please go with Robert to bank yesterday's money.'

We took a third comrade to help with the heavy bags. I was relieved to briefly escape the Centre and exchange commonplaces with the bank teller.

'This is a lot of money even for a Monday. Did you have something on this weekend?'

'A big rally. About 4,000 people.'

Back in the finance office I could hear people coming and going in the yard, but I had to concentrate on my work and answer queries at the finance hatch. Dot and I never seemed to be alone. She was called into Gerry's office several times by the young comrade fielding calls at Aileen's desk. Lunchtime in the canteen was bizarrely normal as no one outside the Political Committee guessed that anything unusual had happened or that Aileen had disappeared. But there were turbulent undercurrents. Youth comrades on the Political Committee had seen the names on the letter. What were they thinking? What had happened when the third girl's father saw Mike Banda? What was Paul Jennings thinking?

In due course Phil Penn drove Gerry to the flats for his afternoon rest.

'Gerry wants me to go round,' Dot murmured as she assembled her papers. 'He'll be fishing for background information about Aileen's disappearance.'

At the end of the day I rushed home. Dan had just arrived to drive Aileen north. She seemed tense, exhausted, and listened anxiously to my description of the Political Committee meeting.

'Strangely, the rest of the day seemed completely normal in a superficial sense.'

'It won't stay like that, believe me. The fuse has been lit. Give it time.'

She knew Gerry through and through; she understood how things worked within the Party and her certainty was reassuring.

'We'll head off for Derbyshire now,' said Dan, calm and relaxed.

I wondered when I would see Aileen again.

The following days

One of the youth comrades spoke to Gerry as she came into Tuesday's Political Committee meeting.

'I have a statement to read.'

Gerry glanced up at her and then looked round the room.

'We have a big agenda today and you're not actually a member of the committee.' He seemed to sense a problem. 'We'll take it at the end of the meeting. Wait outside, comrade.'

The whole meeting was taken up discussing the political implications of the seven-week Justice for Miners campaign. It was very interesting but it felt unreal. The only reference to Aileen was to confirm who would work at her desk 'until she returned'. I pitied the young comrade selected.

The discussion ended and Gerry pointed outside.

'Call the comrade.' Dot summoned her. 'You have a statement to read.'

She stood in the doorway to the inner office with the light behind her, clutching her papers. She glanced at us before proceeding.

'Comrade Aileen Jenning's letter is true – '

Instantaneously, Sheila interrupted. She looked at her watch and shifted in her seat.

'People are phoning me. Can't we take this tomorrow?'

There were murmurs of agreement and Gerry waved his hand to dismiss her.

I was furious. The comrade had written a courageous statement and Sheila had intervened to suppress it.

I missed Wednesday's Political Committee meeting because I went to Oxford.

'Did she read her statement?' I whispered to Dot.

'No. Mike persuaded her to destroy it.'

'Oh bugger. That's a blow.'

'GH is very edgy. He's discussing with Mike, Alex, even Sheila. He calls me in quite often. I let him think I'm trying to help him get to the bottom of things. He's still trying to work out who's involved.'

'He doesn't suspect you?'

'Not at the moment.'

I would have enjoyed the irony if I hadn't felt so helpless. Nothing seemed to be happening after two whole days.

'Actually, he suspects everyone. He only trusts any of us up to a point.'

'Does he think Sheila's involved?'

'I don't know.'

'Where does she stand on the sexual stuff?'

'She won't discuss it. I think she believes it's a side issue.'

'What happened with the third girl's father on Monday?'

'Mike took him in to see Gerry and there was shouting but I don't really know what happened.'

Thursday's Political Committee took a new turn. It was dominated by a row with Charlie over trumped-up allegations that he was endangering the Centre's security. Gerry seemed to be reclaiming absolute authority as he harangued Charlie, demanding answers to pointless accusations. Two whirring fans, moving back and forth in the oppressive heat of the confined space, created a lurid ambience. I felt pure hatred as I watched Gerry in full spate: *this is how you operate – thrash around at anything you recognise as a danger; fabricate a political misdemeanour; blow it out of all proportion and bring in the whole committee to bully the comrade.* I marvelled that his finely tuned political antennae had sensed Charlie's involvement in a challenge he knew to be serious, but didn't yet understand.

Mike, Alex, Sheila and Vanessa all joined the attack. Charlie defended himself, but the issues were irrelevant in this ridiculous frame-up. Disciplinary charges were proposed against him and I voted in favour – opposition would have been tactically disastrous – but I felt like a louse.

The scene was set for Saturday's Central Committee meeting with resolutions to ignore Aileen's letter and to discipline Charlie.

Central Committee

The weather was hot and stormy. Arriving Central Committee members congregated around the steaming tea urn in the canteen: Dave Temple from

Durham, comrades from the north-west, Jim Bevan from the giant Port Talbot steelworks. I nodded to Peter Jones and Peter Gibson, the only other people complicit in Aileen's disappearance, but we avoided talking to each other. The father of one of the girls mentioned in Aileen's letter stood by the window. What was he thinking?

We assembled in Sheila's office with all the windows open. Occasional thunder rumbled, strategically placed fans whirred in the forlorn hope of reducing the heat. I was anxious, a lot was at stake.

The chair ran through the absences.

'Comrade Aileen Jennings has taken off without an explanation,' he said.

'Taken off': the phrase used disparagingly about those who couldn't take the strain and ran away. How outrageous to suggest that of Aileen. There was a rustle of surprise in the meeting. I seethed inwardly and kept my eyes on my notebook.

'She left a letter, but the Political Committee has decided it was a provocation and asks the Central Committee to endorse that decision while we investigate and report back. Is that agreed?'

The letter wasn't even read out. I couldn't believe it. Would it ever surface again? I barely listened to the long political report about the Justice for Miners march or even the interesting discussion that followed. I was worrying about the letter being suppressed.

We moved to the next item on the agenda, the charges against Charlie. He came in looking confident, neatly dressed in an open-necked shirt and dark trousers. His light brown hair was combed to one side, his moustache was neatly trimmed. He towered over Gerry and Mike at the top table, clutching the notes he had prepared.

Mike described the background and read the charge: to expel Charlie for dereliction of duty and send him back to Germany.

I was horrified. This wasn't what we had discussed at Thursday's Political Committee meeting. Had they changed the charge at Friday's meeting when I wasn't there? What was going on?

Charlie defended himself. Alex weighed in. Gerry threw in a few attacks. Sheila added more. Charlie refuted their statements defiantly. My God, this is a kangaroo court. They've already decided the result, I thought.

It came to the vote.

'The charge has changed from what we discussed at the Political Committee,' I ventured apprehensively.

'It's the same in essence,' ruled Mike. 'All those in favour?'

I voted against. I was incensed.

'Call the other guards,' directed Gerry.

One was a tall Australian, the other a black Geordie, who had a judo black belt. Both were full-time security guards who'd been away on the march but were now back at the Centre. Trifling with either would have been unwise. Gerry spoke directly to them, pointing to Charlie.

'Go home with this man and supervise him packing up all his possessions. Then take him to Victoria station and put him and all his gear on a train to Germany. He's been expelled. Dot will give you the fare money.'

They nodded and gestured to Charlie to leave with them.

'Don't think you can crawl back to your section in Germany,' Gerry shouted after him. 'We'll ring Essen tonight to tell them to have nothing to do with you.'

The meeting broke up. I went downstairs to the finance office, shocked and distressed; I felt a bleak emptiness and sat down at my desk, trying to control my despair. A key turned in the lock and the door suddenly flew open. Gerry came in, followed by Mike and Cliff Slaughter.

'Why did you vote against the resolution to expel Charlie?' demanded Mike belligerently.

'Because it was different to what we had discussed in the Political Committee meeting.'

The space between the doorway and me was blocked by three big men looming over me: Cliff very tall, Gerry squat and bull-like, Mike large in all dimensions.

'But you're bound by the Political Committee decision,' said Cliff.

'Surely the Central Committee is higher than the Political Committee?'

I was really frightened. I didn't know if Cliff was prone to violence but I certainly knew that Gerry and Mike were. If they hit me would I tell them I was pregnant?

'You're a piece of shit,' said Gerry. 'Go home to your flat.'

I needed no further bidding. I went to the Clapham High Street flat in case Gerry summoned me later on. I opened the windows for air; I'd forgotten how impossible the traffic noise was. I had had my secret flat for exactly a year and I didn't like coming back to this dreary reminder of a bygone existence.

I opened the built-in wardrobe and from the inner drawer took out the telephone we had secretly installed for Aileen's use. I lay on the bed and dialled her number in Derbyshire.

'The meeting just brushed over your absence. Pete will tell you when he's back.' My voice wobbled. 'But they voted to expel Charlie and they're sending him back to Germany tonight.'

'Maybe Gerry's just threatening.'

'No, no, they're packing all his things now, as we speak.'

'He's sent people to the airport before and then summoned them back at the last minute.'

'This is for real. He knows that somehow Charlie is connected with your letter. He's flailing about, trying to work it out. He's banned Charlie from contacting the German section, he's driving him out of the revolutionary struggle.'

'Clare, don't worry. He'll come back.'

I was too absorbed in my own distress to consider how Aileen was faring in her isolated hideout.

'They couldn't send Charlie to Germany,' Robert chuckled as we counted Sunday morning's money.

My hopes rose. Perhaps he had been reprieved.

'There was no train to Frankfurt, so they brought him back and kept him under guard overnight at our place at 180b Clapham High Street.'

'And now?'

I couldn't sound too eager because Robert didn't know about our secret relationship. He laughed derisively.

'There's a train this morning. They've taken him to Victoria again.'

I spent a miserable day in my branch, talking to members and readers, knocking on doors, but the nagging thought was always there: Charlie's gone. What will happen to our relationship?

I popped home in the afternoon. The phone was ringing as I opened the front door. I rushed to answer it.

'It's me.'

'Where are you?'

'Ramsgate.'

'Oh, I'm so pleased to hear you. What's happening?'

'I've got a return ticket. I pointed out that it was cheaper than a single and would save the Party money. Listen, the train back to London goes in 20 minutes. Can you pick me up?'

I arrived precisely on time under the overhanging canopy at Victoria Station. Charlie slipped out from behind a newspaper stand with only a case and a shoulder bag.

'Is that all your luggage?'

'The boxes have gone on to Frankfurt.' He tossed the case into the boot and climbed into the back of the car. 'I'll duck down in case we're seen.'

Back in the flat I threw my arms round him.

'I was scared I'd never see you again.'

'Don't be silly. What's the point of going to Germany? I'm banned from my comrades in Essen. My Frankfurt relations haven't seen me for seven years. I can't suddenly arrive and expect them to put me up.'

'What'll you do now?'

'I've no idea.'

In case the exposure of Gerry's sexual practices stalled we had planned that Dot would inform the Political Committee of an 'income shortfall'.

Gerry exploded.

'Why have you kept this from us? I don't trust your figures any more, Mrs Gibson.' Then he turned to me. 'Comrade Clare, prepare a report on the results of the *News Line* price increase. I can't trust the figures any more. This all needs investigating.'

A 'finance committee' was set up, with ice-cold Corin Redgrave in charge. It included Mike, who lived entirely in the realm of ideas and polemic, and Sheila, who had chosen to ignore the financial problems despite Dot laying them out to her two years before. One of the committee's first actions was to launch a £100,000 Emergency Fund. The appeal appeared in *News Line* on 8th July: 'The urgent need for this special fund arises directly from the rapid deepening of the world political and economic crisis and its impact on Thatcher's Britain, the weakest link in the imperialist chain.'

It went on to refer to the 'undefeated strength of the working class and oppressed peoples of the world' and their 'unbreakable resistance to the ruthless policies of Reagan, Thatcher, Botha', creating the conditions 'for unprecedented revolutionary struggles'.

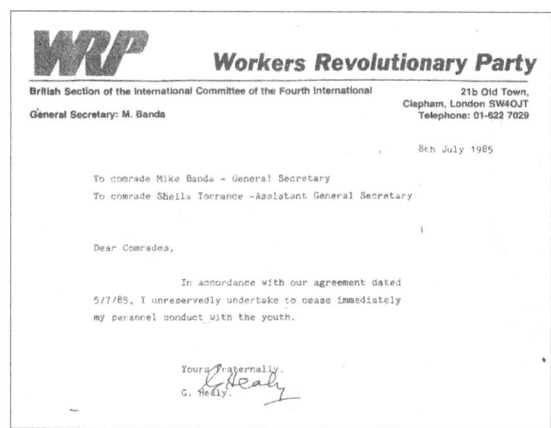

Meanwhile Mike and Sheila negotiated a weaselly agreement with Gerry:

> 8th July 1985
> To comrade Mike Banda – General Secretary
> To comrade Sheila Torrance – Assistant General Secretary
> Dear Comrades,
> In accordance with our agreement dated 5/7/85, I unreservedly undertake to cease immediately my personel (sic) conduct with the youth.
> Yours fraternally,
> G. Healy

This pathetically inadequate undertaking was presumably designed to forestall the demand for a Control Commission investigation from the third girl's father, who had confronted Mike on 1st July. Effectively, the two most important leaders were bolstering Gerry's authority.

It was decided we would say Aileen was 'away' if anyone asked. A comrade who worked in the Brixton bookshop, rang me about a book order and then asked a nervous question.

'Why do we have to give the daily sales figures to someone else? Where's Aileen?'

'She's away at the moment.'

'How long for?'

'I don't know.'

'She didn't tell us she was going away.'

'No.'

'Is she ill?'

'No, she's just away.'

'Is she all right?'

'I expect so.'

A few days later the comrade didn't turn up for work. The bookshop manager spoke to her branch secretary.

'It seems she has flown home to New Zealand. She was very worried about Aileen and scared something sinister might have happened to her.'

On 10th July I presented my report on the previous month's *News Line* price increase. The weekly income had increased by under £500.

'That can't be right,' said Sheila.

'You've been covering up the situation,' said Gerry, looking at me angrily. 'I want you out of the finance office. Go and do your work upstairs in Sheila's office.'

I was appalled – but worse was to come.

'And we don't want you in the Political Committee meetings any more. Alternate members of the Central Committee don't have an automatic right to attend.'

This was a blow. I would no longer hear what was going on. As the meeting broke up, Gerry called me back.

'From now on I want a memo from you every day about where you'll be going when you leave the Centre.'

On 11th July the finance committee called a meeting of all staff at the Centre. Extra chairs were crammed into the canteen. Sheila, Mike and Corin sat at the front; Gerry did not attend. You coward, I thought, you want to absolve yourself, and let the committee take the flak. We were each handed a list of 24 proposed staff cuts among 100 or so Party employees. To my surprise I was not included but Aileen was. So were three girls who had confirmed Gerry's sexual activities to Dot, along with Vanessa (I hadn't known she was on the payroll – why on earth was she?) and others whose work was deemed dispensable. Wages of the two comrades who worked undercover on *Labour Herald* were henceforth to be paid by the paper itself, unashamed confirmation that the Party had been subsidising the left-Labour publication. Incomprehensibly, Charlie's name was not on the list. Did comrades know he had been expelled? Had they even noticed that he was gone? Bitter fury welled up inside me. A mere five days since he had been thrown out and he was already considered a non-person.

Mike addressed the meeting.

'The Party faces a financial crisis: we are losing £20,000 a month in running costs. Last weekend's Central Committee empowered the new finance committee to investigate and make plans to overcome the problem. As well as launching an Emergency Fund, we are forced to make staff cuts and we will ask you to vote on these proposals.'

When he had finished there was silence. Someone asked why Aileen's name was on the list. Corin answered.

'Aileen Jennings is no longer working here. She has not been heard of since 1st July.'

He elaborated no further on the sudden disappearance of a leading, life-long member. I struggled to contain the hatred bubbling inside me. The meeting remained silent. Then *News Line* journalist John Spencer spoke.

'Hang on, you're asking us to vote that comrades should lose their jobs. We can't do that. It's no different from asking miners to vote for pit closures and for their colleagues to lose their jobs. This is totally contrary to basic trade union principles.'

There was discomfort at the top table. Sheila spoke.

'We have to find a solution to this financial problem –'

'Comrade, you can't ask us to vote for other comrades to lose their jobs.'

Mike marshalled his political authority.

'This financial crisis has been kept from us by the comrades working in the finance office. Comrades must understand that we don't want to do this but we face the threat of multiple bailiffs' demands and legal action for huge unpaid bills.'

There was another spell of troubled silence.

'When will it happen?'

'Everyone will be given a month's notice.'

The proposal was agreed in a rather disorganised vote. The atmosphere was sombre as comrades returned to their work. I sidled over to Dot.

'Why aren't I on the list?'

'Sheila said we couldn't sack you. You've given too much money to the Party.'

Gerry instructed me to write a memo describing my discussions with Aileen on our fortnightly trips to Nottingham. I fabricated an anodyne account:

12.7.85
To Comrade Healy, CC Department
Resumé of conversations I had with Cde Aileen Jennings during the trips as co-driver to Nottingham in the last year.

During the journey, as we both tended to be very tired, we often slept when not driving, though sometimes there were conversations.

These dealt mainly with the struggles of the Party, the particular issues that came up during the miners' strike, how to turn the branches to campaign on *News Line* circulation, international developments, and specifically the political situation and its history in Portugal after my return from there. We sometimes discussed our childhood and earlier periods in the party.

Clare Cowen

As part of the daily charade of submitting memos, I wrote a second memo asking for permission to go to an unspecified hospital appointment the following day.

When Corin called me down to clarify something I found him working at my desk in the finance office. The cheek of it! I felt tension in the room as Janet and Robert slogged away silently at the routine money counting and Dot tried to continue her work. Corin mistrusted everything and seemed to think that Dot was being obstructive. I noticed her frustration at his attempts to reduce the complex finances to a crude balance sheet.

'He has no financial training – but of course he's read *Volume 38*,' said Robert dismissively as he brought the debt print-outs upstairs to me.

I was summoned to a finance committee meeting in Mike's office to answer incredulous questions about the family money I had put into the Party. Corin interrogated me with frozen disdain and I answered truthfully, but volunteered no additional information. Other comrades working at the Centre realised I was under some kind of disapproval, but didn't know why. They avoided my table at lunchtime and limited discussion with me to *News Line* circulation issues.

The next few weeks were bleak. Isolated in Sheila's office, I had to listen her haranguing phone calls all morning. She considered me a political lightweight and disagreed with the concept of a circulation organiser anyway. I had no opportunity to talk to Dot or Dave and I didn't even have Robert's irreverence to lighten the day. Each evening I phoned Aileen with little to report. Her exclusion from the political organisation she'd been in since childhood was complete. Charlie was in hiding, angry at being spat out by the movement he had joined as an apprentice, conscious that violence would be used against him if he were ever seen.

Almost every day Mickie phoned Gerry's office, or Mike or Sheila, pretending anxiety, asking for news of Aileen. I feared the letter would never see the light of day. Supported by his henchmen and women on the Political Committee, it seemed Gerry would remain in charge.

The exceptional heat continued. I had never felt so despondent.

The bookshops

On 21st July I was called to a meeting with Gerry in the antechamber to his inner office. Something was different in his attitude, he seemed uneasy. Mike was present, as if to support him.

'There have been security complaints about you, comrade.'

What on earth was he concocting against me?

◀ Our six bookshops were the public face of the Party.

▼ Here England and West Ham soccer star Trevor Brooking signs nearly 600 books plus brochures and programmes for ardent Hammers supporters at the Paperbacks Centre, Upton Park, east London, November 1983

'We have decided to remove you from the finance department because you are implicated as a cause of the Party's finance crisis. We consider you unreliable with money.'

Jesus Christ – what was he talking about?

'We are removing you from any work to do with the bookshops. We don't even want your suggestions about how to handle the accounts.' He glared at me angrily. 'And you won't be able to go to Oxford for the Cowley sale any more. We can't waste all that money on petrol.'

I was delighted. What a relief to stop getting up at four-thirty in the morning.

Gerry looked at the window panes behind me. He wiped his chin in a characteristic gesture, feeling his way, his jaw jutting out. I wondered what was coming.

'We have a proposal,' he paused, 'for you to take over all the bookshops and run them separately. You could purchase the whole chain for £100,000.'

I was flabbergasted. A minute before I had been a security risk, unreliable, the cause of the financial crisis, banned from work on the bookshops. Now he was suggesting I take them over, the public, flagship face of New Park Publications. My surprise must have been evident.

'Of course you would have to go to South Africa to speak to your mother. And the Party's accountants – who are they, Mike?'

'Richard Moss and Company.'

'You would have to discuss with them how to do this. Of course they would still be Party bookshops even though you owned them.'

This is barmy, I thought. It's fantastical. Do they really think my mother would agree to pay that kind of money? And they're groping in the dark if they think this will resolve the Party's finances.

'I would need to speak to the family trust to see if it's possible.'

'Do so as soon as possible, show them the New Park Publications accounts. You have permission to speak to the accountants. Make whatever arrangements are needed.'

I discussed the proposal with Richard Moss.

'My gut reaction is that this is a good suggestion. At the moment your finances are inextricably tied up with an organisation over which you have no control. This would give you financial independence.'

I couldn't quite picture Gerry letting me run it as an independent business, nor did I see myself as a businesswoman, but I listened.

'However, the bookshops underpin New Park's finances. If they were taken away New Park would be left in penury. The other companies in the group would have to be made profitable, otherwise your £100,000 at breakfast would be gone by lunchtime.'

'How could we make them profitable?'

'Look, Clare. Astmoor Litho, Copsecroft Ltd, Grafton Litho, the film company, the *News Line* – they could all be profitable if Astmoor could provide services outside the organisation.'

'You mean commercial printing?'

'Yes, indeed. You need to get key people round the table to rationalise things. I've told Dot but she says it's impossible to convince the directors to discuss it.'

Richard agreed to accompany me to the meeting with the family trust. He wore a smart pin-stripe suit. I wore normal summer clothes: a flowing Indian skirt, a loose aquamarine crocheted top, high-heel sandals and the essential earrings. I had my hair done beforehand to give me confidence. I felt ambivalent about the proposal, but if there was enough money in the trust it might help resolve the Party's financial crisis.

The trustees, a man and a woman, met us in an air-conditioned, fourth-floor meeting room. Richard and I sipped coffee as they pored over the accounts from two years previously.

'What proportion of the company do the bookshops take up? The profit of £24,000, is this from the shops or from the company's other activities? And how were the previous year's losses turned round?'

Fortunately Richard could answer these points. At last the trust manager looked at me.

'We need to see up-to-date valuations on the freehold and leasehold properties; we also need to know details of the stock values and fixed assets and we need to see last year's accounts and the drafts for this year.'

'Is my buying the bookshops a potentially feasible project?'

'We would have to be sure of the correct valuations and the purchase would have to take the form of a "trading trust" owned by us on your behalf. Obviously we would have to speak to your mother, but yes, it sounds a viable proposition.'

I typed a report to the finance committee. The thought of owning the bookshops was quite daunting and I half hoped it wouldn't happen, but I wanted to help sort out the Party finances. A few days later Gerry called me to his office. This time he had Corin with him.

'I've read your report. Arrange to visit your mother in South Africa to discuss the proposal.'

'When should I go?'

'The finance committee needs time to prepare the accounts. Go some time after the end of September.'

I had at least two months and a lot could happen in that time as things were beginning to unravel in unexpected ways. By wearing loose clothes I was successfully keeping my pregnancy secret, although Dot and Aileen now knew. But if the mid-August amniocentesis test indicated the baby was all right I would tell my mother, and the Party.

Perhaps Charlie could come with me to South Africa – secretly, of course.

After numerous phone calls and a surreptitious trip to Victoria, Charlie received his boxes back from Frankfurt. He put away his clothes, arranged some books and technical instruments, and put one remaining box in a corner: all his worldly possessions.

'I've given this address to the Aliens' Registration Office in Holborn. Now I need to find a job, urgently. I only had £13 in my pocket when they took me to Victoria.'

'They didn't give you any more?'

'Not a penny. Seven years working for the Party in England and they chuck me out just like that. The Jobcentre says I need my P45 to show I've left the job.'

He phoned Dot at home, the only way to keep in touch.

'Hello Dot. Yes, yes, I'm OK. But I need my P45 … I see … pretend you're posting it to Frankfurt but sneak it to Clare. OK.'

He put down the receiver and looked out wistfully at the fading light on the patio.

'I'd love to go to Frankfurt first to see my family.'

'You have a brother?'

'And my aunt and uncle who brought us up. And some cousins.'

'You never went to see them on your holidays?'

He laughed scornfully.

'My "holidays" were a week in Derbyshire at the school – where I still had to do guard duty. My rushed trips to Germany were when Gerry sent me to buy security devices. Twice they wouldn't let me back into England.'

'Why not?'

He shrugged.

'I was undesirable, or something. One time, Aileen had to fly to Essen, as my employer, to demand that they let me back in. The captain allowed me on the plane but couldn't guarantee what would happen in London.'

'Well, you got back in.'

'Another time, when they were holding me at Heathrow, I heard them on the other side of the partition saying, "You know who's coming now? Vanessa Redgrave. They're sending in the big guns. We'll have all the press here." So they let me in.'

'Why didn't you visit your family on these trips?'

'Never any time.'

'Well, go. I have some Krugerrands and silver coins that my father gave me. Sell something in the West End.'

Charlie returned from Frankfurt with German sausages and his aunt's home-made jam and cakes. Then he looked for a job.

'I'm starting at a rather disorganised TV repair shop on Lavender Hill, owned by a Jamaican man. At first he thought I was a tax inspector.'

The undemanding job gave him time to look for something better. He went for an interview in far-away Tottenham at a mobile radio company.

'The chief engineer pointed to a workbench and said, "This new Marconi 2950 test set combines all the dozen or so pieces of test equipment I use over here. It cost £12,000. See if you can use it to repair this radio."'

'Did you manage?'

'Of course. Come on, I was trained in a German apprenticeship. I looked at the instruction manual and proceeded. They offered me the job on the spot.'

A new pattern established itself. Charlie left at seven in the morning and returned 12 hours later. I no longer went to Oxford but I did early morning sales around Vauxhall or the sub-district *News Line* deliveries before going to the Centre at nine for the day's work. In the evenings I did branch work, as I had done for years, but returned home to Charlie in our secret flat. No one at the Centre guessed how my life had changed.

Political discussion

The Central Committee reconvened on 27th July, four weeks after Aileen's letter had been tossed aside like waste paper. Gerry was still in charge, but the leadership was in a flurry over the financial crisis, whose magnitude they hadn't yet grasped.

I sat near the open windows towards the back, where I could observe everything. I felt a gnawing anxiety, worried that we had lost the initiative.

Mike Banda had submitted a political document for discussion, 'The campaign for the United Front', apparently arising from heated discussion on the Political Committee. He outlined the developing world slump, the United States' trillion-dollar indebtedness and the possible collapse of world oil prices.

'Imperialism faces an undefeated international working class. In South Africa a civil war situation is developing: the industrial proletariat is defying the racist imperialist state and creating a virtual dual power in the townships.'

He turned to Britain.

'The Justice for Miners' March and rally of 30th June revealed the huge potential to build a United Front of all working class organisations against the Bonapartist state. We are not abandoning the *strategical* questions – General Strike, Workers' Revolutionary Government, Community Councils – but they must not obscure the central tasks of achieving a tactical and operational unity.'

Was Mike proposing a United Front because our call for a General Strike during the miners' strike had failed?

▶ London march against the Thatcher government's plans to abolish the Greater London Council and six other metropolitan counties

'We must not leap over the finite contradictory developments of the masses and replace it with one-sided revolutionary jargon,' he concluded.

Sheila, of all people, led criticism of the document. Who on earth had helped her prepare her attack? She had barely read a book, she never spoke on political questions in Congresses and Central Committee meetings, yet now she was taking on Mike Banda's huge knowledge.

'Comrade Banda has missed out the government's strategy to smash the youth, who are a vital part of *our* strategy.' She went through Mike's document page by page, and then spoke about Ken Livingstone, the left-Labour leader of the Greater London Council.

'When Livingstone moved to the right we *should* have criticised him. We compromised our position.'

The meeting stirred. Trade unionists and even Party members had questioned *News Line*'s uncritical support for Livingstone. I had not guessed that Sheila shared this view.

'It would be *wrong* to work for the return of a Labour Government instead of posing the question of a Workers' Revolutionary Government. Mike denies the independent revolutionary role of the working class and underestimates the role of the Party.'

When Sheila finished everyone shifted in their chairs, stretched, yawned in the stifling afternoon heat. A comrade opened a window wider, another adjusted the fans.

Two clearly different positions had been presented. I had never heard this kind of discussion on the Central Committee before. Corin criticised Sheila for not starting with 'the nature of the period'. But when another comrade said we should re-examine our attitude to trade union leaders who made agreements with the government, Gerry intervened.

'We have not made a mistake on Livingstone. We have to establish the concept of things in their relations and not rush things.'

Pseudo-philosophy to justify betrayal, I thought contemptuously.

Richard Price, Sheila's protégé, entered the fray.

'Many workers are raising the question of Livingstone. I don't see how not criticising him "establishes the concept of things in their relations". Of course centrists like Livingstone will vacillate. And Mike's document downgrades the question of revolutionary leadership, of the Party's role.'

Dave Bruce welcomed the Political Committee's decision to have the discussion, 'with no railroading. There *can* be genuine disagreements amongst communists.'

During the break, we continued talking informally outside, in the yard's fresh air. The bullying atmosphere and log-jam of unchallengeable positions that had usually characterised discussion seemed to have loosened.

But Gerry was not going to be swayed by the wind of free debate. When we returned he attacked Sheila with a vengeance.

'You say we have nearly 10,000 members, but I don't trust your figures. The finance comrades hid financial problems from this committee. Now we must check that you haven't done the same. We need a complete re-registration of all members.'

I caught Dot's eye but hastily looked away. The Committee agreed the re-registration proposal. My God, I thought, comrades may hope it will enable reality to return to the membership figures in their own regions but they have no idea how fraught a question this is. They haven't witnessed the uproar, hysteria, bullying and tantrums Gerry throws when Sheila's membership reports don't meet his demands. They only experience Sheila's exhortations to recruit, recruit, recruit. Now the true membership position will be exposed.

August heat

Sheila sent a letter to all branches about re-registering the membership, presented as a positive step.

> Because of the large increase in membership over this past year, the Central Committee decided to organise a re-registration of members starting August 1st 1985 …
>
> The vast number of new recruits were won during the period of the miners strike and out of the impact of our national marches to release the jailed miners. It is essential that every effort is made to re-register all of them and to assimilate them into the Party, in particular the youth.

August's unabating heat added to my unsettled anxiety. Gerry seemed still to be firmly in control; comrades continued to avoid me; the young women whose names were on Aileen's list retreated into themselves; and the financially illiterate finance committee floundered around, trying to understand the complex network of companies, suppliers and bank accounts.

A London aggregate meeting was called to prepare the active membership politically for the re-registration campaign and the Emergency Fund. The guards cleared space in the warehouse, arranging chairs in the front and benches behind. Over 100 were expected.

Mike's opening report rambled volubly over the 40th anniversary of the Hiroshima atomic bomb, the United States' budget deficit, the revolutionary situation in South Africa, Bonapartism in Britain, the 1937-1945 United Front in China between the Kuomintang and the Communist Party, our struggle for a General Strike, the objective changes that created the possibility of a United Front in Britain. He descended into colourful demagogy.

'We are no longer rowing around in a placid lagoon, it's more like a ship that has gone out into stormy seas. At times this requires a forced march, sacrifice from every comrade. Let's achieve the Emergency Fund, and even get commitments up to £200,000. There is plenty of money in and around the working-class movement.'

Corin was more concrete.

'We raised £100,000 pounds for the *Observer* libel case and we can do it again. We're in the deepest crisis precisely at the point where we're recruiting more members and selling more *News Line*.'

Sheila appealed to the meeting for a collection.

'Conditions for the Party are unprecedented. Our debts arose over a long period of time, out of the political situation, but the Party wasn't ready and able to meet up with the speed of political developments. We have written off branch debts to the tune of hundreds of thousands of pounds. If we had had that money we wouldn't have a financial crisis now.'

I marvelled at Sheila's ability to concoct a political explanation for the financial crisis and, at the same time, blame dedicated comrades for branch debts resulting from the Centre's unrealistic demands. She was now squeezing more money out of the same comrades for a collection that wouldn't reduce their branch debts.

As the meeting broke up some comrades looked longingly at the scores of moped bikes stacked tightly against the back wall, perhaps wondering how much their purchase had added to the financial crisis.

The date for my amniocentesis scan arrived. I submitted a memo to Gerry asking permission to attend 'a hospital appointment'. Sheila was genuinely concerned.

'You haven't got some dreadful illness, have you?'

I laughed.

'Oh, no. It's just routine tests.'

I had been able to conceal my thickening waist. No one believed a woman at the Centre would become pregnant, particularly me, because I was older. Dot had relayed a recent remark of Gerry's: 'Clare Cowen, she's over the hill.' But everyone would eventually know.

I watched the monitor, thrilled to see the tiny heart beating as the sonographer scanned my belly.

'Everything looks completely fine. I can tell it's a boy.' She inserted the amniocentesis needle. 'This will be tested and we'll contact you in about three weeks. Now go home and rest.'

I lay on the bed, watching the net curtains fluttering gently in the open window, observing the feet of occasional passers-by on the pavement above. What would I do if the results showed abnormality? I pushed the thought away, considering the exciting and daunting prospect of the baby who would change my life unimaginably.

In mid-June *News Line* had celebrated ten years of the College of Marxist Education with a four-page, pull-out section, a rousing account of how and why the school had been established, the renovations, the dramatic police raid and the *Observer* libel case. Each day thereafter a full-page advert for summer schools continued:

The Process and Practice of Cognition: A series of four studies – fortnightly courses. Tutor G. Healy
1. From the History of Philosophy / 2. Practice and Cognition / 3. Disclosing the 'cell' of dialectics / 4. The Syllogism of Necessity.

The theory of the Workers Revolutionary Party and tactics in the British socialist revolution. Tutor Peter Jones
1. A study of Lenin's 'What is to be Done?' (revolutionary theory, spontaneity …) / 2. The Workers Revolutionary Party and the United Front tactic / 3. Trotskyism and the crisis of Stalinism / 4. The struggle for power in Britain: the decisive revolutionary role of the Workers Revolutionary Party
  £98 for two weeks, £50 for one week (including VAT)

'You'd better go to the school next week,' Sheila directed. Oh joy, Gerry wouldn't be there so we would study Marxist classics instead.

The beautiful countryside surrounding the school was a welcome break from the Centre's suffocating atmosphere. I arrived early from a *News Line* circulation meeting in Manchester and chose a bunk bed next to a window in one of the women's dormitories, intending to relax for the evening.

'Come and watch television when my children are in bed,' said manager Annabel, who knew about Aileen's relationship with Peter Jones and had helped find their secret cottage.

We watched a stupid film about a man cheating on his wife. When she asked 'Who is that woman?' he answered with another question. 'Which woman?' 'That one over there.' 'Over where?' We giggled at his success in avoiding answers.

Peter joined us when he returned from Aileen's hide-out.

'Can I visit her while I'm here?'

Annabel thought for a moment.

'I'll have to work out an excuse to go somewhere.'

I was chatting to a Scottish comrade over breakfast when Annabel came over.

'Clare, please come with me into Ashbourne to collect some supplies. There's just time before the lecture.'

We drove along winding, narrow country roads, between indistinguishable, undulating fields, through unidentifiable crossroads, to a secluded hamlet. Aileen's hideaway was a plain, ground-floor flat, converted from the adjoining house. She looked drawn and had abandoned elegant dressing.

'My goodness, they'll never find you here.'

Annabel put a box down on the kitchen table.

'I've frozen you some meals from last week's menus.'

We drank tea and ate biscuits while Aileen took up her crochet work.

'I do a lot of embroidery to fill the days.'

I tried to think what to tell her beyond what we'd discussed on the phone.

'The Trotsky anniversary rally went well, with the usual stirring speeches. Corin is unearthing financial transactions; they're all trying to find ways to raise money. Gerry is still in control and seems to think he can weather it all.'

'He may put up a good front, but he'll be in a panic. He knows he won't be able to keep the sex questions under wraps forever.'

'He's supposedly stopped his "personal conduct" with the girls.'

'Don't you believe it. He can't do without it, it feeds his control obsessions.'

'They still haven't noticed that I'm not living at the flats. I always have a story prepared in case I'm questioned. Did you see that film on TV last night?'

'The cheating husband?'

'Yes – that's the way to do it. Answer every accusation with another question.'

We laughed as Annabel and I stood up to leave.

Over the week, camaraderie developed as we shared cooking and cleaning rotas, ate meals, and discussed the texts. The classes were in the main lecture room with the door and windows open to the garden. Between sessions, we sat on the grass studying the books, distracted by the rolling hills, distant bleating, farmyard noises and the seductive summer breeze. In the library the airless heat made staying awake difficult.

A comrade from Clissold branch, in Sheila's north London fiefdom, asked a question.

'Are we really in a revolutionary situation?'

Would Peter dare to explode this central tenet of our policies?

'Let's see how Trotsky characterises a revolutionary situation,' he said calmly.

We turned to the page he identified. Yes, the economic conditions certainly seemed to be present in Britain. Trotsky continued:

> But the revolutionary situation begins only at the moment when the proletariat begins to search for a way out, not on the basis of the old society but along the path of a revolutionary insurrection against the existing order. This is the most important subjective condition for a revolutionary situation.

'Well the miners' strike was the beginning of a "revolutionary insurrection", wasn't it?' persevered one comrade.

Others demurred. Peter referred us to other passages and left us to draw our own conclusions. There was some thoughtful discussion over lunch, but nobody dared to conclude explicitly that the Party's analysis was wrong.

I was packed, waiting to return to London in the crew bus arriving with the next week's intake, saying goodbyes tinged with regret that our group would never reassemble again. Annabel called me up to her flat.

'The comrade who's just collected members took me aside. She and her husband are long-standing Party members.'

'I know them well.'

'Their area organiser asked them if they knew anything about Gerry's relationships with women because he had heard some bad things.'

'What things?' I was excited.

'He mentioned the Control Commission in 1964 over Gerry's affair with a leading Young Socialist member and said he was asking for a Control Commission investigation again, now, into Gerry's relationships with youth comrades.'

'Christ, his daughter is on Aileen's list. What did you say?'

'I was careful. I agreed this was worrying. They told me a Young Socialist from their area had gone to work at the Centre and then had inexplicably left the Party, quite suddenly, and they had never understood why.'

'Fuckin' hell.' I shook my head. 'Has he spoken to other comrades?'

'Who knows?'

I travelled back to London in a frenzy of agitation, but I couldn't say a word to anyone else in the crew bus.

The two Americans were standing in the yard as I came through the gate: Dave North and Larry, in smart dark suits, reminding me of the Mormons who proselytised around London in white shirt and tie plus name badge. I stifled my irreverence, Dave was an important Trotskyist leader. Larry, who never left Dave's side, was black. Were Mormons ever black? I said good morning and asked after a comrade who had worked with us.

'She's having a baby.'

This was a big surprise.

'Is that good news?'

'A new life is always good news.' Dave smiled.

I wondered if life was more normal in the Workers League's Chicago headquarters than in ours.

Dot found me alone at my desk and we hurriedly exchanged news.

'The father of the first girl has been talking to comrades in the provinces,' I burst out.

'And he's sent a letter asking for a Control Commission investigation.'

'Really? When will it happen?'

'Oh, the Political Committee will drag it out and find ways of preventing it.'

'That's against the constitution.'

'Of course it is. They're feeling the pressure.'

Dot wiped her face.

'GH laid the financial difficulties before the International Committee meeting and spun a complex story about how it had come about.'

'Did he blame you?'

'It was much more elaborate. He couldn't let them think he had lost control. He needs me in place because he knows I'm the only one that actually understands it. All the sections pledged to raise money.'

'My God, we're supposed to be the powerful centre of the Fourth International.'

'Everyone's gone now.' She was sucking the arm of her glasses. She looked tired.

'Did anyone ask about Aileen?'

'Dunno. I was only there for the finance discussion.'

'How would they react if they knew about the sexual stuff?'

'Who knows?' She walked to the window overlooking the warehouse roof and then turned back, drawing a breath.

'I need to take figures to GH in the flats.'

'Does he still trust you?'

'He does and he doesn't. He thinks I'm keeping him up to date on the political machinations behind the scenes. I let him believe I support him while I try to probe what his plans are. I've known him for many years, remember.'

'Oh, Dot. I don't know how you can keep up such a charade.'

'Mum's sent a formal letter to the committee,' Aileen told me on the phone, 'saying she's had no contact with me since I disappeared two months ago and demanding to see the letter she believes I left.'

'Ooh, that's good.' After a lifetime in the Party Mickie's austere authority was unchallengeable. 'The mother of the second girl is also demanding a Control Commission investigation – that's three parents asking now. And Charlie has sent a letter demanding his wages in lieu of notice.'

I knew the appearance of 'business as usual' at the Centre was deceptive, but I could only guess at the underlying currents. Were ordinary staff members aware of the crisis engulfing the Party leadership? Sheila's relations with me became increasingly icy as Corin unearthed new details about my financial involvement. I hated her 'leadership by telephone', I pictured Corin's grey presence looming over the finance office, I took care not to be seen talking to Dot. Occasionally I met Robert making tea in the empty canteen.

'Mike Banda has challenged Dave Bruce to write a document explaining his position on the United Front,' he told me, rubbing his hands and grinning. 'It'll come to the next Central Committee.'

The results of my amniocentesis test were positive. Charlie gave me a big hug.

'You won't be able to hide it much longer, you know.'

I phoned my mother, feeling rather nervous.

'Are you sitting down? I'm ringing to tell you I'm pregnant. And it's a boy.'

'Well, darling, that's nice to hear.' Mum seemed bemused.

Now I had to inform the Party. Gerry was lecturing at the school, so I told Sheila. She didn't congratulate me, but she wasn't unfriendly.

'It's due in January? I'll inform the Political Committee.'

Suddenly everyone seemed to know. Norman Harding said how pleased he was and two of the young women excitedly demanded to know who the father was. Even some of those who'd been keeping their distance made friendly comments. Gerry, on the other hand, dismissed me with a wave of his hand when he returned from the school.

SEPTEMBER
CRACKS APPEAR

The agenda circulated for the Central Committee hinted at disarray in the leadership – it had the date as Saturday 8th September, but Saturday was the 7th. The meeting promised to be lively: continuing discussion on Mike's document and Dave Bruce's counter-document; a finance committee report; and my report on *News Line* circulation.

Corin, chairing, began with attendance at the meeting. As two late comrades from Scotland sidled into their seats, the father of the first girl stood up at the back.

'Comrade Aileen Jennings is still not here and the committee has had no explanation for her absence. I understand that she sent a letter. The committee should hear it.'

'The Political Committee decided the letter was a provocation and that was endorsed at our July meeting.'

But the father was insistent.

'Comrade Jennings is a long-standing, leading Party member. Her letter should be read to this committee. I'm proposing that as a motion.'

There was irritation at the front of the meeting, and Corin moved quickly to curtail discussion.

'We'll take a vote. All those in favour of reading Comrade Jennings' letter.'

The vote was six for and 27 against, with one abstention. I voted for the motion and carefully noted the others: the father, Dot, Peter Gibson, a leading Young Socialist, and Robert. Peter Jones was presumably keeping obscure his link with Aileen and Dave Bruce was tensed for the coming political discussion. The abstention was a young woman from Yorkshire, another leading Young Socialist.

Still under attendance, Mike Banda made a shock announcement. He was wearing his usual, rather scruffy, open-necked shirt and loose-fitting jacket. A lock of his black hair flopped over his forehead as he leaned forward, looking down at his hands. He spoke slowly, in a subdued tone.

'Comrade Healy is not present today. In consultation with him the Political Committee has agreed that he should retire from the leadership of the Party.'

A sharp intake of air rippled through the meeting,.

'This is because of ill-health and age. Comrade Healy will be 72 in a few months and he has had poor health over the last two years.'

He looked up. Every comrade was watching him; some appeared stunned. Political Committee members, who had had forewarning, looked sombre. I felt relief that something was finally happening. Mike looked down again and became emotional.

'For all these years Comrade Healy has been my political father. He taught me everything politically after my arrival as a young man from Ceylon with my brother Tony.' His voice was breaking. 'But now he is my political brother. The time has come when I have to take up my political responsibilities.'

He regained his composure, leaned back and gave a reassuring wave of his hand.

'Comrade Healy will continue on the finance sub-committee and in an advisory capacity on *News Line*.' His tone was more confident. 'The Party will not be bereft of leadership. In the last 35 years Comrade Healy has trained a cadre and laid the foundation for the leadership that must now take over.'

A light breath of air came through the open windows as we grappled with the implications of this momentous announcement. The silence seemed to contain confusion, emotion, anxiety. Corin took charge.

'Are there any questions?'

'Is this happening straight away?'

'Yes, as of yesterday.'

'What will happen about cadre training?'

'The Political Committee will discuss this. Cadre training and security will be the responsibility of the Central Committee Department.'

What would this grandly titled 'department' now be, I wondered? It used to consist of Gerry and Aileen, but not much was left now.

▲ Cliff Slaughter

'Is it right that Comrade Healy continues to work on finance and the *News Line* if he's not in good health?'

'He will work in an advisory capacity. He feels he still has an important contribution to make in those areas and he wishes to continue.'

As if to reassure the meeting, Sheila spoke.

'Comrade Healy has fought for this movement for 49 years and his contribution deserves to be celebrated. In due course we will organise a public meeting as a tribute to him.'

Only a few months previously Gerry had been manoeuvring ruthlessly against Sheila, I reflected ruefully.

The troubled silence was eventually broken by Corin.

'I will take a vote to accept the proposal that Comrade Healy retires from the leadership. All those in favour –'

The hands went up slowly, unwillingly.

'Any against?' He looked round and wrote down the figures. 'That is 30 for the resolution and five against.'

Miner Dave Temple, Peter Jones, Cliff Slaughter and two others had voted against. Some other issue was at play here.

'Comrades, why have you voted against the resolution?'

Cliff rose to his feet immediately. He was one of the Party's theoreticians, well-respected, a university lecturer, tall, with an imposing physical as well as intellectual presence, one of the Communist Party members who'd broken with Stalinism after the suppression of the 1956 Hungarian Revolution. His interventions at Congresses and classes were always interesting, but I hardly knew him as a person and I always felt nervous of my own political ignorance in the face of his vast knowledge.

'This retirement resolution is a shabby compromise, whose aim is to avoid an investigation into some of the comrade's activities in the Party.'

Sheila looked across at Mike with an irritated expression. Her view of Cliff was that he could talk and write, but never *did* anything; he was annoyingly able to resist her demands for frenzied activity. She turned to glare at him.

'You're casting serious aspersions on the comrade's huge contribution to this movement.'

Cliff was angry.

'Those serious aspersions arise out of the comrade's actions. I am proposing a Control Commission to investigate the issues.'

Mike Banda knew how to contain the challenge.

'There is a proper procedure under the constitution to request a Control Commission. I propose this discussion is deferred to the Political Committee.'

Corin moved swiftly to a vote. Robert, the youth comrade from Yorkshire and I joined the five to vote against deferral. But 27 members of the committee supported the leadership.

▲ Dave Bruce

The political discussion began. Dave Bruce presented his document with his usual intensity, starting from the economic crisis racking the world capitalist system. Then he directly attacked the vacuity of the mantra quoted in all our work: that we were living in a *revolutionary situation*. He called Trotsky to his aid:

'To confound an initial stage of radicalisation, which is still half-pacifist, half-collaborationist, with a revolutionary stage, is to head towards cruel blunders.'

In his soft Scottish accent he demolished the Party's glib characterisations wonderfully. He described the historical background to the United Front tactic in turbulent Europe before the second world war, then he attacked our decision not to expose Ken Livingstone's role in the rate-capping struggle.

'We left the membership with no answers to the questions asked by every class-conscious worker who follows our Party. If this is the "United Front" in practice, then it has become a mockery.'

He questioned our shallow call for a General Strike during the year-long miners' strike.

'Every basic right of the working class is under attack by Thatcher's government: education, health, welfare, pensions, unemployment benefits. Our documents talk of ruling-class plans for a Pinochet-style regime. Do we really believe a General Strike, by itself, will defeat that?'

After Dave had finished, Sheila weighed in.

'Comrade Dave is challenging the whole historic preparation of world Trotskyism, led by Comrade Healy, for the revolutionary situation which we are now in, and the turn to the struggle to take power, for a Workers' Revolutionary Government.'

Mike, Corin and some others spoke with more depth and theoretical finesse, expanding or disagreeing with Dave's historical references. Alex, floundering on the history front, spoke about current issues. As the discussion forged on, I tried to visualise the Party without Gerry's leadership. I looked around at my comrades, evaluating their flaws, egos, inadequacies, inflated hopes. Who on this committee could lead a Workers' Revolutionary Government? And what would such a government *do*? Dave had highlighted that we had no *programme* for a revolutionary government. We called for nationalisation of South Africa's banks, but barely mentioned the same for Britain. It was all left to the nebulous future.

It was decided the Central Committee would reconvene in a fortnight to continue the political discussion.

Next on the agenda was the finance sub-committee report, presented by Corin.

'We are losing £20,000 a month on running costs.' He mentioned a projected budget for the bookshops, and asked the committee for authority to raise money through events, printing, future fund appeals. Then he revealed that mortgages and loans had been taken out by 'the finance department'. Strangely, he didn't mention Dot, Aileen and me by name.

'There are two mortgages, repayable at £1,300 a month, two large, non-repayable loans and one of £69,000 pounds, a total of £300,000.'

This massive figure was beyond the normal reckoning of most comrades in the room. He proposed a solution.

'We are negotiating for Comrade Cowen to buy a section of the bookshops –'

A section? I thought they were proposing I buy all of them.

'– to get the £69,000 loan off the agenda. Although held by Comrade Cowen, the shops would be transferred directly over to the Party.'

Oh, really?

The meeting ran out of time. Re-registration of our 10,000 members had not been completed – only 2,800 had registered so far – so the deadline was extended till the next Central Committee. The *News Line* circulation report was referred to the Political Committee. Concrete discussion about our daily newspaper, the Party's *organiser,* to use Lenin's term, was always last on the agenda. Lenin must be turning in his tomb, I thought.

I woke Charlie.
  'Gerry's retiring.'
  'What?' He sat up straight. 'Surely he won't give up that easily?'
  'There's turmoil in the leadership, but the fault lines are still unclear to me. Sheila didn't like Dave's political attack.'
  Charlie guffawed.
  'I bet she didn't. Who the hell is Dave to challenge them? He should stick to technical work in his little office at the bottom of the alleyway and not meddle in political analysis, like they thought about me.'
  'Gerry's coterie has big differences with Sheila and her supporters, but they all disagree with Dave. I wonder what the next few weeks will bring.'

News Line report

I was confident of the conclusions in my report on *News Line* circulation. I had made thorough investigations into all the branches and I had worked out meticulous costings of overheads, printing costs, wages and vehicles.
  'The Party's monthly deficit of £20,000 does *not* centre on *News Line,*' I told the Political Committee, minus Gerry. 'The paper's monthly deficit is only £4,000.' Circulation had fallen from 85,000 a week four years previously to 66,000; an unknowable proportion was subsidised by branches paying in money to cover debts. 'This is a political, not financial problem.' Party branches saw sales as 'just another task' and almost everywhere, sales rested entirely on cadres, leaving the wider periphery and our 10,000 members uninvolved.
  'If every member read and sold one *News Line* per day we would immediately double our circulation. Bringing sales organisation to a higher political level needs the active, fighting support of the Party leadership.'
  The Central Committee should take more responsibility for writing articles so the paper didn't become 'divorced from the life of the Party'. I criticised the lack of a Party statement since the South African emergency. I proposed a properly planned, one-month circulation campaign with local rallies and canvassing. Each area should appoint a comrade with specific responsibility to follow *News Line* sales.

I had not anticipated the furore my report would unleash. Sheila led the charge, with the pained, irritated expression she often had in her dealings with me.

'A lot of this is just your opinion. You don't take into account the impact of the miners' strike, how the objective situation has affected the situation. We don't know if sales rest on a central group of cadres.'

Oh yes, we do. I've done detailed investigations.

' "Active, fighting support of the leadership"? What does that mean? Without the Central Committee we wouldn't have a paper. And *you* should have sent extra papers to Birmingham when the strike broke out.'

She looked at me angrily.

'You don't mention the struggles of the print union, you make no analysis of changes in circulation during this period. You say sales are considerably subsidised but that is not the case now.'

But no one can know which payments are subsidies.

Corin spoke next, with a kind of bored detachment.

'This is not a circulation report. You don't even mention new branches yet we're experiencing real improvements through taking the paper into new areas. These are impressions, followed by organisational measures.' He turned the pages disparagingly. 'This is neither a finance nor a circulation report. Paragraph one on page two is extremely tendentious.'

Mike Banda entered the fray.

'Some comrades say the circulation is more than 66,000 a week.'

For goodness sake, these are accurate figures.

'Your point number three negates points one and two. There is a dialectical relation between these matters, related to how the Party is directed and led, otherwise these statements are ultimatums and panaceas. Yours is an eclectic method – you need to integrate the circulation work with the whole question of branches, leadership and actualisation of our policy.'

Words, words. Mike's florid abstractions.

Vanessa waved my report in the air.

'These are just completely organisational proposals. We should proceed with the regional editions in Scotland, South Wales, and what about the North West?' Her intellectual-style glasses were slipping down her nose. 'The circulation remains static unless we build new branches.'

'In an idealist fashion, the comrade leaves out cadre training,' said Richard Price, London District Secretary. 'Obviously leading members play a leading role in sales because those on the periphery are unlikely to drive up circulation. We can only resolve the issue by fighting it out in the branches. Wrong political positions endanger circulation, it's an index of the development of cadres.'

Oh, God, the usual London District Committee-speak.

I writhed in my seat listening to all this nonsense. Who bullied branches to increase their *News Line* orders? Who harangued them to pay in the money, subsidies instead of increased sales? Sheila, of course. Why didn't she release the dozens of moped bikes stacked in the warehouse to help branches increase circulation?

Other comrades made useful comments. Sales at football matches were hampered by late delivery. Should we take distribution off the railways and cost truck-and-car delivery? What would the break-even circulation be? What about wholesale distributors?

Gerry had appointed me circulation manager 18 months previously. His absence today gave Sheila and the others who considered me politically inadequate an opportunity to rip into me. But I was not going to give way. If everything just depended on 'the political struggle' – dialectical, of course – then we didn't need to consider *any* organisational questions.

Dot intervened to bring some sense into the discussion.

'I propose the comrade does a further *factual* report, with the actual print run, charges, average payments and number of deliveries for each branch.'

She knew I had all these figures available.

'OK. Redo the report,' said Mike. 'That's all, comrade. You can go.'

I left the meeting, furious. They were living an illusion.

Mickie Shaw was waiting outside. The Political Committee had agreed she could present her concerns about Aileen's disappearance. I pulled a face and shook my head as I passed her.

While Mickie was in London, we met to assess developments, a warped reprise of the conspiratorial June gathering but with Aileen, the central player, missing.

I arrived first at Dave Bruce's flat. Sipping tea, I looked at the bookshelves crammed with Marx, Trotsky, Lenin, Kant, Hegel, novels, technical books. A window was ajar in the

▲ Mickie Shaw

final gasp of the summer's turbulent weather. Dot, Mickie and Charlie arrived and there was a moment's pause, as if waiting for someone to call the meeting to order.

'What happened at the Political Committee this morning?' I asked Mickie.

'They wouldn't believe I didn't know where Aileen was. Sheila was particularly insistent, quite rude.'

'The archetypal apparatchik Sheila dared to be offensive to you, a longer-standing member than anyone else on the committee?'

'I said they had no right to allege that Aileen had any association with the police or had misappropriated any Party funds.'

Dave laughed.

'They were rather ashamed about that and agreed to minute that the allegations were completely unfounded.'

'They told me to put in writing my request for a Control Commission inquiry into Aileen's disappearance, but they wouldn't show me her letter.'

'Ridiculous,' muttered Charlie.

Dot turned to him.

'The Control Commission request from the father of the first girl is now going ahead, despite Sheila and Mike trying for weeks to persuade him it would damage the Party. Today the committee agreed he should put it in writing.'

'And Sheila will tell the mother of the second girl to do so too,' Dave added. 'But the committee reaffirmed its opposition to a Control Commission, they'll still try and drag it out, render it harmless.'

We sat silently for a few moments.

'Who's on the commission now?' asked Mickie.

'Norman Harding, Jean Kerrigan and Liverpool docker, Larry Cavanagh. They won't stand for any nonsense.'

'Mickie, remind me how it works.'

'The three commission members take written and verbal statements from all the relevant people, completely confidentially. Then they report to the Central Committee and to Congress, without disclosing confidential details. In the interests of security and protecting the Party it's carefully managed.'

'So it could be a whitewash,' said Charlie.

'Not necessarily. Actions can be proposed to stop whatever is being complained of.'

'Could the commission just say that Gerry has agreed to "cease his personal conduct with the youth" and, because he's retired, the problem has been resolved?'

'The leadership will certainly pressure them to head it off so the membership never hears about Gerry's sexual actions,' said Dot. 'In the past Gerry has used the Control Commission to contain problems rather than bring them to light.'

I was beginning to realise we might not achieve what we wanted. Gerry and his acolytes had long experience in political manipulation.

'What if it leaks out? The father of the first girl has discussed with comrades in the Midlands. Won't that raise questions?'

'The trouble is, why should they believe him? Who is he, compared with Gerry's immense authority? Especially if the leadership backs Gerry.'

'Oh God, this is really depressing.'

'What does Gerry's retirement mean?' Mickie asked.

'We don't know yet. It's only days since the decision and he's gone to the school this week. He won't just give up, he'll fight to hang on to the reins.'

'But we have them on the run politically,' said Dave. 'My document has raised issues they can't sweep away. Sheila and Mike are preparing replies, and the discussion will continue.'

'Can we succeed in turning the Party politically?' I asked.

'The discussion must be taken into the membership. I can expose the absolute charlatanry of all Gerry's pseudo-philosophy. I'm working on another document now.'

I dunked a biscuit into my tea and only just managed to slurp the soggy mess into my mouth without dropping it.

'But when Alan Thornett raised questions ten years ago, all the leading members, including the intellectuals, rallied round and he was driven out with no real discussion inside the membership. Couldn't they do that again?'

'I've raised fundamental questions and Gerry is weakened.'

'Is he really?'

'Remember, they're divided among themselves. Sheila and Mike are defending Gerry together now, yet three months ago Gerry and Mike were plotting daily against *her*. And she opposes Mike's document. The Party can only go forward by resolving these major political questions.'

A train rumbled past. I felt a gnawing anxiety that Dave was over-confident. Party members saw Gerry as inheritor of Trotsky's mantle, a towering figure who had built our movement in Britain and worldwide. His political dominance was unchallengeable.

I turned to the morning's discussion on *News Line*.

'They blame the paper for the Party's financial problems. Can't they see the whole group needs reorganising?'

Dot shrugged.

'I don't know what they see. They're bumbling around, looking into files and bank statements and cash books they don't understand. They've brought Linda down from Runcorn to help. The finance office is an awful place at the moment.'

'What will happen about reorganising the finances?' Mickie asked.

Dot looked at her resentfully.

'I don't know. They don't trust me. Gerry is very nervous. When he's forced to face the full financial details he'll absolutely explode. At the moment it's coming drip by drip from the sub-committee. He calls me round to the flats to try and get information about what's happening in the Party.'

Mickie shifted in her chair, appalled.

'But why are you still going round there?'

'I've always been responsible for cleaning his flat. Aileen made his bed, cooked for him, washed his clothes, but I always did the hoovering and dusting. He still needs that.

I shivered in distaste. Mickie looked horrified.

'Dot, you're propping him up.'

'I need to follow his thinking, to know where things are going.'

The meeting ended inconclusively, on a slightly acrimonious note.

'We no longer share a clear direction,' I said to Charlie at home. 'Dave thinks the Party can be politically reoriented, Dot is worried about the Pandora's box of debts, unpaid bills, cancelled contracts. But Gerry's sexual practices – that's what the leadership really, really wants to conceal.' I felt bitterly frustrated.

'Party members would never accept that shit if they knew,' said Charlie. 'God knows what's going to happen.'

Challenges

Gerry was waiting for me in the anteroom to his office.

'Right, comrade. You're going to buy the bookshops.' His little eyes peered out above his fleshy jowls, his face expressed indifference towards me, even hostility. 'Book your trip to talk to your mother.'

'When should I go?'

'Late October, or November. The comrades will prepare the figures for you.' He dismissed me with an impatient wave of his hand.

I checked with the doctor that it would be all right for me to fly and then rang my mother.

'I want to put a business proposal to you, but it's also for a holiday.'

'I'm delighted.'

'And Mum, can I bring Charlie? I'd love him to see South Africa.'

I booked the flights for Friday 8th November, returning Sunday 24th. I wondered what would happen in the Party while we were away.

My written report on *News Line* circulation started with the actual print run: 71,850 copies per week. No one could argue with this figure, whatever fancy views they might have on new branches, cadre training, 'dialectical relations' and sales during the miners' strike. I attached multiple pages of figures for every branch in the country – weekly charges, average payments, weekly losses and the numbers of daily deliveries. I reported on arrival problems; I costed road distribution and provided a complicated diagram of how trucks and cars could link up all over the country at an annual fuel cost of over £60,000; I included the results of my visits to branches round the country. The final paragraph read:

> Accurate costing figures requested by Cde Banda: Having arranged with our accountant to come and help to do this, his superior spoke to me saying as insistently as he could that this was not possible without the financial re-orientation of the whole group. He emphasised that the "accurate" *News Line* costing would still be arbitrary while it did not take in the whole group's finances. Therefore I have not prepared any more accurate figures.

I heard nothing more. The pages of concrete figures may have defeated them. Maybe they didn't want to face up to reorganising all the companies.

The London District Committee was Sheila's power base. Southbank was short of potential candidates, so I had been selected unwillingly to attend the depressing Friday night meetings. Richard Price gave the opening report.

'The central question is the nature of this period: is it or isn't it a revolutionary situation? We need to drive the Party out on our analysis.'

Sheila referred to a 'dialectical approach' and 'grasping the essence'.

'There is a rightward drift on this committee. Comrades must put the class struggle *before* your individual requirements, do what's *necessary*, not what you think you can manage.'

Other delegates attempted to say what was expected, fearful of Sheila pouncing on them. She sat in front of the committee, picking her nose as she often did in meetings and cleaning the intricate joints of her glasses with little pieces of paper tissue. This rather disgusting personal housekeeping seemed to me contemptuous of the comrades in front of her.

My attention flagged as one of the prominent Young Socialists spoke about work in her branch. Suddenly, she changed tack.

'There are comrades requesting a Control Commission to investigate certain practices in the Party leadership –'

Sheila intervened immediately.

'Comrade, you have no right to raise these issues here.'

'This reflects political differences in the Party and affects all our work.'

A wave of surprise ran through the meeting. All faces were alert and attentive, puzzled.

'The discussion you are referring to is the property of the Political Committee,' insisted Sheila.

'I'm raising a serious issue which comrades need to hear –'

Richard interrupted, with self-important authority.

'Matters before the Control Commission are separate from political differences. You shouldn't be raising this here.'

Sheila took charge.

'This is completely inappropriate. You must withdraw your statement.'

The girl was defiant.

'Comrades have the right to know about these questions.'

'You will face disciplinary charges for raising matters that are before the Political Committee.' Sheila looked round the room. 'I propose that this comrade be removed from the meeting.'

'Include me too,' said another girl, looking straight at Sheila.

'And me.' A woman comrade spoke firmly from the back.

I looked round the room. The other comrades sat in silence, trying to fathom what was going on.

The three women gathered their papers, jackets and bags as Sheila called for the vote. I felt it still wasn't time to break discipline and voted for the resolution.

'That is unanimous,' Sheila said. 'Please leave the meeting.'

They marched out, heads held high, watched by everyone. I cheered them on silently.

Surely word would now leak out.

Gerry's retirement was in its second week. Phil Penn collected him each morning from his flat; a young comrade sat at Aileen's desk and did his running around. The advertisement for his lectures at the College of Marxist Education was removed from *News Line*, but no retirement announcement appeared. I was tense and alert, watching, listening.

I heard an altercation in the yard and slipped downstairs to Norman's dispatch bench where he was preparing bulk *News Line* wrappers.

'What's happened?' I whispered.

'The guard gave Gerry only the letters addressed directly to him. Someone has decided to separate the incoming mail.'

We both knew this challenged Gerry's daily ritual of opening all letters arriving at the Centre. Norman ripped a large sheet of brown paper from the wall-mounted roll and shook his head.

'I suppose he's complaining to the committee right now.'

He pasted a label on to the sheet and savagely tore off the next one.

The Central Committee meeting assembled, as always, in rows of chairs facing the main table. Gerry didn't attend, even though he'd been at Political Committee meetings all week. Peter Jones asked a simple question.

'If Comrade Healy has retired, on whose authority did he go to lecture at the school?'

Silence. Confusion. Alex, in the chair, looked at Sheila who looked at Mike.

'A number of comrades had signed up for Comrade Healy's course and he wanted to fulfil his commitment. The Political Committee didn't see a problem.'

Sheila rose to read her scorching document against Dave Bruce's analysis.

'The comrade is challenging the Seventh Congress decisions as well as the whole historic preparation of world Trotskyism, led by Comrade Healy, for the revolutionary situation which we are now in, which is deepening continually, and the turn, initiated by the Seventh Congress to the struggle to take power; i.e. for a Workers Revolutionary Government.'

Sheila's classic jumble of words.

'The retirement of Comrade Healy seems to have been the signal for every conciliator, every individual to come out of his hole, reflecting bourgeois pressure, to say to the Party – No! the struggle for power is "infantile leftism". It is years ahead. Our Party is too small, an insignificant force. Turn back towards the Labour Party and Parliamentarism.'

Dear me. This paraphrase of Lenin's 1901 condemnation of conciliators was meant to confer political authority. She interspersed her mediocre theorising with quotations from Lenin (*Dialectics of Nature*) and Trotsky (*Lessons of October* and *Where is Britain Going*), presumably selected by her husband, a shadowy figure not quite trusted by Gerry.

'We have entered into a revolutionary situation, the *most favourable possible situation* both nationally and internationally.' She sincerely believed this. 'The miners' strike did not end in stalemate. After years of preparation and colossal expenditure the Thatcher regime was hurled back because the undefeated strength of the working class proved too much.'

Mike Banda spoke next, dismissing her facile statements.

'We need a creative application of dialectical logic, not a *ritualistic*, simplistic, lobotomised version. There *will* be another Labour government because the working class hasn't exhausted that experience yet.' He ended with a stringent comment about 'plagiarisms from Lenin and others'.

Comrades stretched and moved about when he finished. Tony Banda welcomed Dave Bruce's document as 'a breath of fresh air'. Then the first girl's father spoke.

'At the Sheffield conference, Comrade Healy said if the miners went back to work fascism would follow.' I remembered that hysterical statement. 'We need to train cadres against a method that starts with subjective impressions and imposes them on the situation.'

His tentative attack on Gerry was reinforced by Cliff Slaughter.

'We have been proceeding from a mechanical and dogmatic version of the nature of the epoch. Our notion of cadre-training has become a collection of dialectical terms imposed arbitrarily and capriciously, with ultra-left talk of the immediacy of the revolution.' Surprisingly forthright. 'And there has been an individual arrogation of leadership: an unchallengeable, inspired leader has substituted personal decisions and prestige for collective leadership.'

I looked up, startled.

'The bullying, verbal, physical – and sexual – abuse cannot be separated from this.'

'*Sexual* abuse.' Most comrades weren't yet aware of it but Cliff, a senior member of the committee, had actually said it. The room was absolutely still; the leading cabal sat in silent fury; my stomach was tight with excitement.

'I recognise the powerful political intuition of Comrade Healy and his unequalled determination, but our practice has been distorted by a wrong philosophical position,' Cliff concluded.

Richard Price, Sheila's loyal lieutenant, took up the challenge.

'A practice is taking place in the Party of spewing guts, and in an unconstitutional way. The Political Committee took a decision on 1st July' – to ignore Aileen's letter – 'and it is distasteful that some people have changed their position. We made thousands of recruits in the miners' strike but some comrades want to return to being a small sect. Look at the events of the South African revolution and last week's riots in Birmingham's Handsworth area. Can comrades really say we are not in a revolutionary situation?'

'This apocalyptic view has to be completely nailed,' retaliated Robert. 'A wrong analysis of the period as *revolutionary* is irresponsible. The living perception we have to start from is that *News Line* circulation has fallen from 85,000 to 66,000 and by the previous Central Committee meeting only 2,800 members had been re-registered.'

The debate was refreshingly real, but Gerry's shadowy power hovered over it as Corin defended the official line.

'The decisions of last year's Seventh Congress have guided the Party in the most revolutionary period of its existence, with the greatest number of recruits. Why raise *now* a revision of our perspectives?' He looked round his audience. 'Is this related to Comrade Healy's retirement? Yes! If Cliff disagreed with the *Studies in Dialectical Materialism* in 1982, why was he silent then?'

The question disturbed me. Why, indeed, had Cliff and other leading intellectuals lent authority to Gerry's philosophical ideas through silence, or even support? I thought back to two incidents: the huge row with Jack Gale and his banishment to Australia before his death, and Cyril Smith being hounded in front of a Party Congress. Had Cliff been similarly attacked? Was Gerry's intellectual bullying akin to the physical violence he had used against Dot and Aileen?

Alex took the final item: 'Any other business?'

I raised my hand.

'What will happen about Comrade Healy attending the school?'

No one said anything. I sensed a vulnerability in the leadership that gave me sudden confidence.

'I propose that he should not go to the school any more.'

From behind me came a firm, clear voice.

'I second that.' It was miner Dave Temple.

I was thrilled. Alex had a hunted, frightened look. He didn't know what to do.

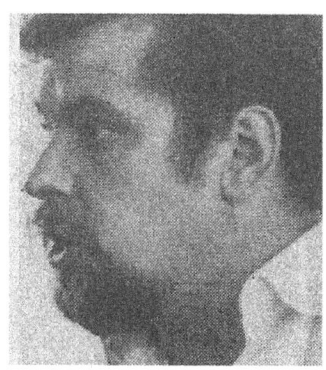

▲ Dave Temple

'Take a vote,' said Sheila dismissively from the front row.

There were five votes for my motion: Dave Temple, Peter Jones, the father of the first girl, Cliff Slaughter and me. Something had changed on the committee.

Brixton riots

I returned home from the Saturday night pub sale to find a note on the kitchen table: 'Going to Brixton to take photos. The radio says there are riots.'

The radio accounts reminded me of 1981 when heavy-handed, racist policing had provoked riots. This time the trigger was tragedy. Mrs Groce, the Jamaican mother of a suspect, had been shot during a police raid on her house. Anger was exploding on to the streets and the police appeared to be losing control.

The phone rang.

'It's me. Can you pick me up?'

'Where are you?'

'Brixton Law Centre. You need to take me to hospital. The fucking police beat me up.'

I parked in a back street. Blue-light police cars blocked the High Street near the town hall, crowds milled around the empty road in front of the Ritzy Cinema, a row of helmeted police blocked Coldharbour Lane, police vans were ranged behind them. At the far end a car was burning. The night was warm, the air smelled of smoke, I heard shouting voices and distant police sirens.

I rang the Law Centre bell and followed the man up to the first floor. Charlie sat there shirtless, forlorn, pathetic. I wanted to giggle. He was a strong man, he must be pretending. Then I saw his bruised, swollen back.

'My God, what happened?'

'I was down there next to the Ritzy, photographing the burning car, when about six riot police jumped on me. They threw my camera on to the ground and thumped me on my head and back with their truncheons. Then they reversed the van over my camera, several times, the fucking bastards.'

'We saw it all, from the window,' said the Law Centre man.

'The coppers had no fucking numbers on their shoulders. I was dazed, I didn't know what to do. I sat on the wall outside the cinema and a woman asked if I was OK. Then this man called to me to come up here.'

'You need to take him to hospital. And find someone to take photos of his back. I can certainly give a witness statement.'

Charlie was ushered into a cubicle at St Thomas' casualty department, but I wasn't allowed in. The waiting area was quietly chaotic and the atmosphere was tense. Vigilant hospital security staff stood by. Injured young black men and a few bleeding policemen were arriving all the time, accompanied by family or colleagues. Clusters of people discussed in low tones: youth, mostly black but also white, some young women, distressed mothers, angry fathers. New

▼ **Brixton, September 1985:** riots broke out after the police shooting of Mrs Groce, Jamaican mother of a suspect

arrivals limped in, one clutching a towel to his bleeding arm, another holding a bag of frozen peas against his head. Suddenly the wife of one of the *News Line* reporters came over to me.

'Ben was hit by a missile in Atlantic Road,' she said.

'Oh dear. Is it bad?'

'Well, his head is cut and it's bleeding. One of the photographers is there as well, attacked by youth who thought he was taking photos for the police.'

I was shaken. These were people I knew well. She looked at me.

'And why are you here? Oh sorry, I shouldn't have asked.'

I let her think it was because of my pregnancy. We talked quietly, watching the unabating flow of arrivals and gradual departures. It was hot in the crowded space; the atmosphere turned hostile and suspicious when several policemen arrived to inspect the situation. In due course, Ben emerged, bandaged, and left with his wife. I went into Charlie's cubicle.

'They're completing the paperwork and then I can go.'

'Nothing broken? No internal damage?'

'No. The coppers came in and looked at me and said, "They really had a go at you, didn't they?" so I said, "*Your* guys bloody-well did this to me," and they went away.'

Next morning at half-past eight we heard a knock at the front door. Two men wearing casual jackets were standing outside.

'We're from the CID.' He showed me his police identity badge. 'We understand there is a complaint.'

I looked at him in astonishment.

'Please wait.'

I closed the door firmly and went back inside.

'Police. They think you have a complaint. How did they know the address?'

'They must have looked at the hospital records.'

'Fucking cheek. What shall I do?'

He sat up painfully and wiped his eyes.

'I don't want to talk to fucking coppers.'

'Shall I send them away?'

'Well … I *do* have a complaint. They smashed my camera. It was deliberate. It took me months to save for it.'

'What do you want to do?'

'Maybe I should talk to them.'

'In our flat?'

'Well, I can't stand at the door discussing.' He took a deep breath. 'We'll have to let them in.'

He stood up gingerly and walked slowly to the bathroom.

I opened the front door.

'Please wait while he dresses.'

I closed the door again, dressed myself, and helped Charlie put his shirt on. His back was covered in purple and yellow blotches and he was very stiff.

'Don't offer them tea or anything.'

'Of course not.'

I led the two men into the living room and indicated the two armchairs. I sat on the sofa next to Charlie.

'Thank you for seeing us. Could you tell us what happened?'

With the help of a lawyer at the Stockwell legal advice centre Charlie took out a case against the Metropolitan Police. Many letters were exchanged and eventually he was offered a settlement of just over £1,000.

'I don't want a settlement. I want to fight all the way.'

'You're not guaranteed to win any more if you do and it could take years,' said the lawyer. 'Our advice is to take it.'

He accepted reluctantly, and never ceased complaining that he should have fought it further.

Finance report

Corin's 15-page finance report had few figures, no mention of accounting systems, company structure, the source of our debts, or how to stem the haemorrhage. Instead it was a bitter tirade against me and the others.

'Cde A. Jennings' letter to the Political Committee was a provocation' whose purpose was 'to cover up a conscious political manipulation of the Party's finances which was intended to bring the party to the brink of financial disaster'. It was the work of Dot, Aileen, me, Dave Bruce and Robert. We had 'manipulated the crisis in order fraudulently and illegally to buy, sell and mortgage Party property without permission of the appropriate committees of the Party'.

A litany of complaints followed: we had taken out mortgages on Dot's house, my building at the Centre, and my 'family property'; there were large loans from me; sales of Party properties to me. The report was peppered with words like 'illegal', 'fraud', 'forgery', 'deception', 'wilful and deliberate negligence', 'lies'. We were accused of 'concealing a mounting financial crisis from the leadership of the Party'. Bailiffs' visits had never been reported to the leadership; the Party's credit system had been 'virtually destroyed'; Dot 'did nothing' to settle the British Rail bill.

'It is impossible not to conclude that Cdes Gibson, A. Jennings, and in particular Cde Cowen were motivated by a high degree of self interest.'

As I read the muddled, incompetent report I became more and more furious. The bookshops, 'one of the most important sources of financial assistance to the Party', he claimed, 'had been turned into its opposite' by our actions. Priggish Corin had been shocked to discover a 'rumour throughout the book trade' that the bookshops were being used to finance the Party's debts; that bailiffs had taken 'walking possession' of contents of several bookshops and the printshop in Runcorn; and that British Rail had suspended credit facilities.

His greatest outrage was over a meeting with our accountant, Henry Hyatt of Richard Moss & Co., who had suggested 'streamlining' the group by closing down two uneconomic bookshops and selling some Youth Training properties. Corin had been shocked by Henry saying, 'I suppose you will have some problems persuading your committees to sell your assets.'

'Selling our assets, our sacred cows.' I muttered to Robert by the tea urn, under cover of the potato peeler rumbling noisily in the kitchen. It was a relief to snatch a moment's discussion.

'They're horrified at the conclusions of an experienced accountant,' he giggled.

'Corin is totally fucking deluded. Why in God's name doesn't he ask *why* the debts have arisen? Why doesn't he ask what Gerry's role was?'

'Or the company directors, Sheila, Tony, Janet.'

I flung my tea bag into the bin and slammed the lid shut. 'What about the "appropriate committees of the Party"? They never even *bothered* to inquire about the Party's finances, for years and years. Now Dot gets all the blame.'

Robert grinned.

'And us, don't forget. Charges under clause 9(a) of the constitution: "secretly and without authority" manipulating the finances and *causing* the financial crisis, or some such rubbish.'

'Yeah, they're proposing to ban us from the premises and then they're sending me to South Africa in a few weeks to try and raise £100,000 to buy the bookshops. It's fucking ludicrous.'

The boil bursts

When Mike returned from lecturing at the school he was edgy and restless, striding round the Centre with a distracted air. Next day, Dave North arrived unexpectedly on his way back to Chicago after visiting our sections in Europe. He discussed with Mike and the Political Committee and then left.

Sheila was on the phone berating someone.

'This is the Political Committee's responsibility, they shouldn't be discussing it with you,' she scolded. 'They're non-political allegations by forces who want to move to the right, they're succumbing to bourgeois pressure.'

Suddenly Mike burst into Sheila's office, waving his hands, ranting.

'Everything we're doing is compromised, soiled by this.'

'Mike, that's nonsense.'

'Retirement is not enough.' He banged her desk. 'He must be banned from the premises.'

'You're joining the capitulationists in the Party who're moving to the right.' Sheila was shouting too.

'I've given my whole life to this. I feel betrayed by this man.'

He stormed off, slamming the door into the library followed by the external one that led to his office. Sheila went into the canteen but returned shortly after and sat down to continue her phone calls as if nothing had happened.

While I was having lunch Mike barged into Sheila's office again, shouting, unconcerned that everyone in the adjacent canteen could hear his inchoate blusterings. Alex Mitchell stood up and went into Sheila's office to try and calm him, with little success.

'This is serious stuff, the Party's general secretary hollering at the assistant general secretary,' muttered one of the journalists.

Norman arrived in the middle of the uproar.

'What's going on?' he asked, looking around.

'Mike's very angry,' said a youth comrade.

Comrades exchanged glances and ate in uncomfortable silence.

Why had Mike suddenly become so volatile? I had no opportunity to speak to Dot or Dave Bruce and felt utterly frustrated. I phoned Aileen that night to ask if something had happened at the school.

'The first girl's father arrived unexpectedly to see Mike and spoke to him very frankly about the sexual abuse. He was quite shaken, and told Annabel afterwards.'

'But he's known about it at least since your letter.'

'Well, yes. He also spoke to Liz from west London, who was at the school too.'

'Had she also heard about it?'

'So it seems. She compared notes with Annabel and agreed to talk to Mike, but only by going for a walk because she was afraid to be alone with him in a room. She laid on the line what this sexual corruption means: abuse of the girls, abuse of power, destruction of cadres. She said that if they continued covering it up she would leave the Party, and so would hundreds of others. He was very shaken.'

'He's been rampaging around all day. Dave North's brief visit seems to have increased his fury.'

On Wednesday I arrived at work at lunchtime after a hospital check-up. Two members of staff stopped me at the bottom of the alleyway.

'Mike Banda and three others have withdrawn from the Political Committee, because' – he read a hand-written resolution on a piece of paper – ' "the Constitution of the Party is being grossly abused to perpetrate a cover-up of a scandal which seriously threatens the security and future of the Party". They've walked out to bring this to the attention of the membership. Comrades from most department have joined them.'

I needed no further elaboration.

'Where are they now?'

'At Mike's house in Orlando Road.'

Both excited and apprehensive, I walked to the nearby semi-detached Victorian house.

About a dozen comrades were milling between the front room and rear kitchen. Dave Bruce, Robert and a Young Socialist had left the Political Committee meeting with Mike. Also present were Paul Jennings and three other *News Line* staff, Tom Scott-Robson from the film department, a comrade who worked undercover on *Labour Herald,* and even Phil Penn, Gerry's loyal aide of recent weeks, an astonishing volte-face. There was a hubbub of voices, the kettle was boiling, cups were being washed, a cry of 'Somebody go and buy milk and sugar'. Mike was sitting on a well-worn sofa in the kitchen, talking to John Spencer from *News Line*. Dot was on the phone, coin-operated to avoid excessive bills. 'Give me some more change – thanks – hello? Could you ask the other bookshops to ring me back?'

Animated discussions were underway everywhere.

'They blocked the demand for a Control Commission.'

'How many women are implicated?'

'Where is Aileen now?'

'I've had serious differences with the political analysis for a long time.'

'Is this is why we've lost so many Young Socialist cadres over the years?'

Mike was holding forth in *mea culpa* fashion on his disillusion with his former mentor. Distaste and suspicion tempered my feverish excitement. Barely ten days ago he had been Gerry's leading defender, now he was chief accuser. But this change of position altered everything in the inner-Party struggle. His authority would have a huge impact.

'Listen, comrades.' Dot called for our attention. 'We have endorsement for our action from the two comrades in the Scottish office, comrades from five of the bookshops, the comrades at the school and Tony Banda, who's going to call a meeting in the printshop.'

Our enthusiasm was interrupted by an agitated comrade arriving from the Centre.

'Corin has removed boxes of documents from Gerry's office. A west London comrade helped load them into his car.'

'Didn't anyone stop them?'

'The security guard tried but they just opened the gate and drove out.'

There was consternation.

'It doesn't matter,' said Mike, with a contemptuous wave of his hand. 'It won't save him. He's done for now.'

Of course it mattered. The documents must have been important, even incriminating.

'Well it's too late. They've gone.'

'We shouldn't leave the Centre in their hands. Some of us should go back.'

The three Banda children came home from school, dropped their bags in the hall and took stock of the noisy gathering. They knew most of us quite well but meetings seldom happened in their house and we were an invasion. Janet came into the kitchen to prepare food for them but Mike was oblivious to the awkward family situation and carried on talking.

'He must be banned from the Centre. He can't participate in the Political Committee meetings. He'll destroy the Party.'

Dave Bruce and Robert were in the front room.

'OK, so Mike has changed his position,' I said. 'But what happens next?'

'We have to continue the discussion on Saturday at the Central Committee.' Dave was charged with tense excitement. 'We have to resolve the political errors that have dogged us for years, take the struggle to a higher stage. That's the only way to develop a collective leadership.'

'Mike has a lot to overcome politically,' said Robert languidly.

Dot clapped her hands and spoke loudly.

'Listen comrades, we must leave. The family needs their home.'

Mike stayed to discuss his next move with two or three others. The rest of us returned to the Centre in excited confusion.

OCTOBER
RUNCORN STRIKES

Mike was back at the Centre next day. He strode through the buildings after the Political Committee meeting.

'We're not a Trotskyist party. *News Line* should be closed down,' he bellowed angrily.

Furtive discussions took place in small groups as comrades, confused by Mike's histrionics, sought more detail. A dispatch driver questioned me and one of the girls in the canteen. We spoke quietly, unsure what details to disclose.

Sheila came out of her office.

'Comrade, I need that report on the youth conference.' She looked disapproving. 'It's all very well to stand here gossiping. Haven't you got work to do?'

We dispersed resentfully. I felt we were on the brink of something, but I couldn't visualise what. I expected Saturday's Central Committee meeting to be momentous.

Next morning journalists, typesetters and photographers were standing in the yard, discussing in low voices, restless, some smoking.

'What's going on?' I asked the guard.

'*News Line* hasn't arrived.'

I hurried over to the journalists.

'Some Runcorn comrades decided not to work on the paper, in support of Mike,' said John Spencer. 'The others completed it but Liverpool District

Committee members arrived and threw the bundles off the van to prevent distribution.'

'And the *News Line* office has been padlocked on Mike's instruction,' said a journalist who clearly disagreed with these actions. 'He has the keys and we can't get in.'

'There's a meeting for all staff at ten.'

We crammed into the canteen, some standing, not wanting to commit themselves, looking around distrustfully. Mike began speaking.

'Comrade Aileen Jennings left a letter stating that Comrade Healy had had sexual relations with a list of 26 women comrades. We have since found that the situation is even worse. We don't know how many cadres he has destroyed.'

A heavy silence filled the canteen. Everyone now knew why Aileen had disappeared. Mike continued.

'Dave North has brought shocking documents from two women comrades in international sections, detailing Comrade Healy's sexual actions with them. We'll circulate copies so you can see how foul his actions were.'

Alex and Sheila insisted angrily that *News Line* must be produced. But Paul Jennings intervened.

'It doesn't matter what we do here. The Liverpool comrades occupying the printshop say they will prevent further production until major political questions are resolved.'

'They're sending a delegation to tomorrow's Central Committee,' said Mike. 'All these matters will be dealt with then.' He put his hands flat on the table and looked round the meeting with a challenging glare.

The editorial office reopened, the Young Socialists returned to their upstairs office in agitated excitement, confused discussions about Gerry's sexual depravity swirled around the yard, warehouse and canteen. Sidelined theoreticians Geoff Pilling and Cyril Smith arrived to see Mike. Meanwhile the dispatch department answered continual phone calls.

'Serious allegations will be discussed at tomorrow's Central Committee,' Norman told one caller after another. 'No, there will be no paper tomorrow either.'

I couldn't bear to be in the same office as Sheila, so I went downstairs to talk to comrades arriving from London branches. Their incredulity at the details was followed by anger and distress.

Two comrades came through the warehouse from Mike's office, laughing contemptuously.

'Look at what Dave North has brought. This is dynamite.'

The first statement, from a comrade who had worked with us for many months, described in plaintive detail how Gerry had summoned her to his flat for a meeting. As she was leaving he had hugged and then kissed her. When she pulled back, he had admonished her and told her to take off her clothes. Shocked and unwilling, she had complied, sensing a threat. He had told her never to tell anyone, which had felt to her like blackmail. She had dreaded 'discussions' with him but had justified them to herself out of respect for the leader of the most important section of the Trotskyist movement.

I had known this comrade well and found her statement very disturbing.

The second document was a five-page account from a woman who had previously been a leader of her section. Years before, when Gerry had proposed sex with her she had agreed, because she had felt that knowing this important leader better would help the political struggle. But he had assumed a permanent agreement for sex, making it clear she must tell no one. He had insisted she attend four-weekly International Committee meetings, where she was in no position to confront him. Whenever she had tried to end the sexual relationship, he had reacted furiously, insisting it was a political relationship. She knew she risked being characterised as a class enemy and responsibility for her section had restrained her. The dreaded visits to England had affected her mental health and she had withdrawn from leadership of her section.

So that was why she no longer represented her section. She had often stayed in my flat and on one occasion had cried inconsolably, I had presumed over some political battle on the International Committee. Her document also included physical details to corroborate her claims: that Gerry had warts on his body, had potency difficulties, had erections but no ejaculation and simulated coitus interruptus.

Yes, warts under his armpits, potency difficulties. This was all true. I felt humbled at her courage in writing this full account, I felt bitter anger. But why had the two comrades laughed when they handed me the documents? At Gerry's sexual inadequacies? I went to speak to Mike.

'I don't think you should distribute these statements so freely. Some comrades are taking them lightly and laughing.'

'They're completely condemnatory of Gerry, they'll seal his fate.'

'They illustrate misery, a broken spirit, damaged lives. Laughter is absolutely inappropriate.'

'We need comrades to see them if we're going to deal with the old bastard.'

He was unrelenting and I had to accept it. Copies of the documents were already circulating.

A stormy Central Committee

The two international documents and Aileen's letter, minus the 26 names, were distributed to Central Committee members arriving at the Centre, eliciting furious reactions. Dozens of Party members who had come to lobby the meeting gathered in agitated groups in the yard, demanding to know if the allegations about Gerry's sexual crimes were true.

'This is monstrous. I always respected Comrade Healy.'

'How long has it been going on?'

'Were you involved?' they asked me and other women.

'Why didn't someone stop him?'

'What does Comrade Healy say about all this? Will he be at the Central Committee?'

'He's skulking away somewhere. He's been banned from the Centre since Tuesday.'

'The leadership must have known. They've been covering up for him,' a comrade said angrily.

'He's clever at hiding it,' I said. 'He has lots of meetings in his flat with comrades, but for the women, it led to something else.'

'Why did they let him?'

'Come on, he forced them, he intimidated them, he threatened them. You've seen the two international documents.'

'So he raped them?'

To call it rape troubled me. The scenario of widespread sexual intimidation over many years was so grotesque that people sought a straightforward explanation. I had to oppose this over-simplified view.

'It wasn't always rape. Some of us acquiesced because of his enormous authority. If the leader of the world revolution asks you for sex, if he seems to need some affection … well that's how I saw it.'

The comrade I was talking to dropped his eyes and shook his head. Maybe he was embarrassed at the thought of me and Gerry having sex, perhaps he found it all repulsive.

There were other concerns.

'These allegations could do serious damage to the Party,' said a journalist.

'And they haven't been proved,' stated a member of the London District Committee. 'There's a constitutional procedure, the Control Commission should investigate and report to Congress.'

The lobbying comrades arranged benches in the warehouse for an ad hoc assembly when the Central Committee meeting began upstairs. After reading Aileen's letter aloud, Mike proposed that victims of Gerry's sexual abuse should attend the meeting as observers. Several young women and three parents took seats at the back.

Political Committee members loyal to Gerry had met earlier that morning. Sheila presented their resolution, which demanded *News Line* production should recommence.

'A minority on the Political Committee, led by Mike Banda, has delivered the biggest body blow to Trotskyism and the international working class since Pablo destroyed the majority of the world movement after the second world war.'

Strong stuff indeed.

'Mike has mobilised misguided, misled and mis-informed Party members into actions which harm the Party and the working class.'

There was an affronted rustle.

'The comrades downstairs are creating an atmosphere of intimidation. The Political Committee *didn't* support the actions by Comrade Healy. He *did* abuse his leadership and took actions that could destroy the Party. But he carried out democratic centralism, this party *was* built – and the daily paper, and the youth movement. The Party was built from above by the leadership, not from below.'

She looked fiercely at Mike.

'Banning Comrade Healy from the Centre – we've never seen such methods since Stalin. The full Political Committee was not on the premises, it wasn't empowered to take such a decision. And no individual has the right to stop the paper. Why is there this mammoth attack on Comrade Healy?'

A voice called out from the second row.

'Because you did nothing to stop him when a youth comrade told you about his sexual bullying.'

Sheila looked disconcerted, but countered:

'She had a voluntary relationship with Comrade Healy. She wore see-through blouses.'

A shocked flutter ran through the meeting.

'Like the judge who says the rape victim "asked for it" with her sexy clothes,' someone else cried out.

Sheila continued defiantly.

'When Comrade Mike doesn't agree with decisions he just walks out. The more rapidly the revolutionary situation develops, the more frenzied the drive to break from democratic centralism and our history and traditions. We will not let him destroy the Party.'

Then an unexpected statement:

'I am claiming minority rights on the Central Committee.'

I looked up in surprise. I couldn't remember this constitutional right ever being claimed before. Things were moving fast.

Mike spoke next, outlining a new theory that Gerry was mentally ill with 'satyromania', an excessive sexual desire in a male, 'for which he should have had treatment'. Nonsense, I thought, that epithet better describes Alex. What Gerry has done is much darker, more sinister.

Mike ended with a momentous statement:

'I propose that Comrade Healy be charged under the constitution with actions detrimental to the Party.'

Several people called out to second his resolution. There was silence while we considered the situation, The most important leader in the Trotskyist movement was to be charged by his Party. My emotions were mixed. I felt anger, sorrow, triumph and even anxiety over what would follow.

Corin stood up to speak, sophisticated, patrician, cold as ever.

'Aileen Jennings' letter on 1st July was a provocation.' He linked it scornfully to Austrian psychoanalyst Wilhelm Reich's theory of a causal link between sex and politics. 'Bourgeois morality is quite different from *revolutionary* morality in the struggle for power. I too am claiming minority rights.'

Other speakers expressed shock at the sexual allegations, albeit cautiously. I had to remind myself that because Aileen's letter had been suppressed, most Central Committee members had learned about Gerry's sexual activity only three days before.

'I am very distressed by Aileen's revelations, but I don't support Mike's actions of the previous few days,' said one speaker.

'I do not condone what has happened and the Control Commission must investigate. But publication of *News Line* must continue,' said another.

One of Sheila's supporters complained that the father of the first girl had broken the rules of democratic centralism by telling comrades in the provinces about the sexual allegations. The father was unrepentant.

'What Comrade Healy has done is an attack on Trotskyism itself.'

Anger at the sexual revelations dominated the meeting, but other issues rose to the surface.

'A few months ago, Stuart Carter and Comrade Charlie were expelled in an unprincipled way,' said one comrade.

▲ Paul Jennings

'Our characterisation of Libyan leader Colonel Gaddafi as developing in the direction of a revolutionary socialist leader is wrong,' said another. 'And our silence in 1979 when Iraq's Ba'athist regime executed Communist Party members was criminal.'

Everyone listened carefully to Paul Jennings, who seldom spoke in Central Committee meetings.

'The freer discussion of the previous two Central Committee meetings has only become possible because of Aileen's letter. I knew she was being physically, mentally and politically abused. I didn't know about the sexual side. And I didn't know what to do.'

There was a sad silence as we measured the pain in his statement.

In the break we were besieged by the comrades downstairs.

'Will Healy face the membership?'

'Does anyone support him?'

It was clear that both upstairs and in the warehouse Gerry's Political Committee flag-bearers, Sheila, Corin and Alex, had less support than Mike. We resumed in a heightened atmosphere in the late afternoon. The heat in the crowded room was unbearable and the windows were opened.

It was my turn to speak. I squeezed along the third row to reach the front, clutching a wadge of papers. I was wearing a silky, red-and-black floral maternity smock, dangly red earrings, and red high-heel sandals. I knew I cut a striking figure and I was conscious of my unique position: I was widely known in the Party through long membership and my work on *News Line* circulation – and I was one of Gerry's sexual victims. Alex huddled warily at the window end of the front row. Sheila sat further along, haughty and impatient, in contrast to Corin's languid, lizard-like boredom. The Party I had joined 19 years ago, long before Alex and Corin, was represented by the comrades behind them and in the warehouse: trade unionists, Young Socialists and ordinary members who were closer to the working class than us apparatchiks ensconced in Clapham. I felt confident, determined to say all the things that had been building up inside me for so long.

'The miners' strike and international developments have compelled members to question our policies. Discontent is bursting out through a fissure. My own concerns began in the finance office when I came to understand how Comrade Healy dominated and distorted the Party's financial management. But the turning point came when I learned from Aileen 18 months ago that the youth were being sexually abused by Comrade Healy. I realised with a shock that I was not the only one.'

The silence in the meeting was absolute.

'I realised that a succession of women who had shared my flat, or stayed as visitors, had also been prey to Gerry's sexual demands. One of them made a suicide attempt. A woman of 27 who works at the Centre has to keep her relationship with another staff member secret because Comrade Healy would break it up if he found out.'

I checked my scribbled notes.

'Comrade Sheila has castigated Mike for individual decisions. But what about the individual actions by Comrade Healy? Remember when he stopped *News Line* production for a day? And remember – we gave him unchallengeable powers at the Congress a few years ago. Necessary, he said, because of the critical stage of the revolutionary situation. What happened to collective leadership when we took that vote?'

I looked round to emphasise my point.

'Comrade Healy didn't build the Party alone – we all built it.'

Sheila's gaze was fixed on the wall behind me, her glasses resting superciliously on her nose, her mouth pursed. Anger bubbled inside me at her years-long disdain for my political ability, mistrust of my class origins, contempt for my work on *News Line* circulation.

'What has Sheila's role been?' I looked at her directly. 'A youth comrade told you more than a year ago that Comrade Healy was abusing her. Earlier in this meeting you suggested that she had a voluntary relationship with him – an attractive young woman and a man old enough to be her grandfather. How could you think that? How many women comrades have been destroyed? You think Gerry's repugnant activities can just be tidied away, that the Party should remain ignorant of his shameful practices. You are wrong.'

I looked at Corin, at the far end of the front row, aloof, so remote from reality that he couldn't understand that Gerry's sexual bullying had *destroyed* comrades.

'You described the comrades downstairs as "mob rule". You express *contempt* for the membership. You have no confidence in their political judgement and you don't understand the frustration bursting through the dam walls. The membership will *not* dismiss Comrade Healy's sexual actions in the casual way you do.'

I was still groping towards a clear understanding of Gerry's sexual activities but I knew Mike's fancy theory was wrong.

'I disagree with Mike when he says Comrade Healy has an ailment called "satyromania". Gerry's sexual exploitation isn't some kind of excessive sexual desire. It's coercion. He has conned us. It's been *abuse,* connected with his power and domination over the Party, and over all of us women.'

I was struggling to develop my ideas.

'For Comrade Healy's victims it may have been rape in some cases. It was also something else. A background of violence runs through the Party against individual comrades …'

I faltered. I had never seen anyone oppose Gerry's occasional violence. Such questions were never discussed in the Party. I felt unsure of myself and I sat down.

The meeting ended in the early hours, to reconvene in the morning. Accommodation had been pre-arranged for out-of-London Central Committee members. The men lobbyists slept in the warehouse using camp beds and sleeping bags from the jailed miners' march. The handful of women lobbyists were billeted out to London comrades. Fortunately I wasn't asked to take anyone.

Back home in our secret flat I shook Charlie awake to tell him about the day's extraordinary events. I hardly knew where to start.

'Gerry is going to be charged under the constitution … Sheila and Corin and some others are claiming minority rights … comrades from all over the country came to lobby the meeting.

'It's the middle of the night. You're babbling. I can't understand what you're talking about.'

The charges

Comrades reassembled in the morning, tired, unshaven, tense, excited, gulping mugs of tea before the meeting started.

Four charges against Gerry had been drafted overnight: sexual abuse of female Party members; continual use of physical violence; violating his retirement agreement; and slander of an international comrade.

For the charge of physical violence four comrades had been selected as indicative of the problem. Committee members muttered angrily as they heard about Gerry's violent blows against Aileen and Dot. Next cited was Tom Scott-Robson, in charge of the film department.

'Comrade Tom was disabled as a result of childhood polio,' explained the comrade from the drafting panel. 'He can barely walk upstairs and is often in considerable pain. During a discussion about the department Comrade Healy struck him quite forcefully.' An angry murmur ran through the meeting. 'There were several witnesses.' Had Vanessa been present? The film department was her domain.

The fourth victim selected, to my surprise, was Charlie.

'Until his recent expulsion, Comrade Charlie had been a dedicated staff member at the Centre for seven years, in overall charge of security, on duty almost round the clock. On several occasions Comrade Healy kicked him in the shins, punched his head, hit his face, broke his glasses. He had to stand there, trying to block the blows, unable to retaliate because of Comrade Healy's authority.'

'We should stop calling him "Comrade",' protested someone.

Three months previously, this same committee had expelled Charlie on spurious grounds. Sheila, Alex, even Corin and Vanessa had always treated him contemptuously and would probably have turned a blind eye to podgy, bullish Gerry hitting nearly-six-foot Charlie. Now this power-crazed violence was deemed unacceptable. Yet when Gerry had hit Stuart Carter in the Central Committee meeting only a few months before, no one had protested. Violence was certainly not outlawed in the Party.

The third charge related to Gerry violating the retirement agreement, which had led to Mike's walkout. The fourth charge was over Gerry's unfounded accusations that Dave North of the American Workers League had involvement with the CIA. Inferring that someone might be an agent of the police or security services was an oft-used tactic in Gerry's political rows, part of his arsenal to pull comrades into line if they raised disagreements.

The comrade finished presenting the succinct, well-drafted charges. The room was quiet. This was a historic moment, the Party deciding charges against its founder and leader.

The newly declared Minority on the Central Committee protested.

'These charges pre-empt the Control Commission, which hasn't even begun.'

'The charges are completely constitutional,' ruled the chair. 'The comrade can defend himself at next Saturday's recalled Central Committee. The Control Commission is a separate matter. It will proceed to meet independent of our decision today.'

'Comrade Healy is the leader of our Party. Only Congress has the right to discuss charges against him.'

'If next Saturday's meeting votes to expel the comrade, he has a constitutional right to appeal to Congress, which will ratify or reject the decision.'

'Comrade Healy is also a leader of the Fourth International.'

'The International Committee too will ratify or reject our Congress decision.'

A few further points were discussed, with thoughtful silences in between. There wasn't much to say. A solemn vote was taken. I held my hand high, straight and firm. The votes were counted: 25 in favour, 13 against.

Dot went downstairs to type the charges. Corin was appointed to deliver them to Gerry.

'I won't do it.' He was adamant.

'How can Comrade Healy prepare his defence if he doesn't see the charges?'

'I refuse point blank to deliver them.'

The meeting was suspended while Dave Temple and another comrade took them to Gerry's flat. They reported on their return that there had been no reply so they had pushed the envelope under the door.

Further sweeping decisions were taken, underpinned by plans for a Special Congress in a fortnight. All votes reflected a split of 25 for our side against 12 or 13 for the Minority, whose supporters included some honest comrades, untainted by the Political Committee's corrupt cover-up, but worried about the direction of the Party and suspicious of Mike's sudden volte-face.

A resolution on Emergency Measures stated that the Central Committee took responsibility for 'regulating the chaotic position' created by the Political Committee. It called on comrades to return to their posts and to work under the direction of the Central Committee, which pledged full accountability to the Congress. The resolution included a stern warning:

'Any comrade who reveals details of the Party crisis to the bourgeois or revisionist press or anyone outside the Party will be charged immediately under the Constitution.'

The Central Committee Department would be closed down (hooray!) and all files handed to Mike. The Political Committee was dissolved (hooray!), the Central Committee would meet weekly as long as necessary. A Special Commission on Finance was appointed – three members not on the full-time London staff, under Mike as non-voting chair – to take control of the finances and 'to investigate the history and structure of the Party's income, expenditure and assets'.

'We have already circulated a finance report, which is before this Committee,' protested Corin.

'The new Finance Commission will take that into account as well,' ruled the chair.

A Security Committee was appointed to take control of all legal and company documents, and keys to all premises, before the meeting adjourned. *News Line* would be suspended for a week while the editorial board met to discuss its reconstitution. Aggregate meetings of members would be held in all districts in the next week.

It had been a tumultuous weekend.

Two London aggregates

Monday's staff meeting listened in shocked silence as Mike read the charges against Gerry. Minority rights were immediately proclaimed by Central Committee members and others who disagreed with the decision. The Centre was in disarray. The Press Association and Reuters tapes chugged away uselessly in the *News Line* office. Little money came in, but more bills arrived. Discussions took place everywhere.

'This could destroy the Party,' said a journalist at my lunch table. 'Gerry's been pivotal in building the movement. We need him for the continuity of the struggle.'

I shook my head.

'A party that covers up corruption isn't fit to lead a revolution.'

'OK, but we have to deal with these questions in a way that protects the Party.'

'Of course I want to protect it. But a party that covers up sexual exploitation has no place in constructing a new society.' I spoke slowly, still trying to understand the complexities of our situation. 'Look, we say communism will supersede the culture of bourgeois society. How can exploiting women and violence be called culture? You can't defend that.'

'I don't. We have to stop it. But we must protect the Party at all costs.'

A nearby Young Socialist comrade was impatient.

'I agree with Sheila. This moral stance is just a right-wing tendency that will destroy the Party.'

Yet her name was on Aileen's list of victims. She seemed to be clutching at some pathetic certainty, as if trying to convince herself that her sacrifice had been worthwhile. I felt deeply sorry for her.

With every discussion I felt more certain that the sexual exploitation was fundamental; all the rest was superstructure. Correcting the politics and financial issues on a totally corrupt foundation would be pointless.

A comrade rushed breathlessly into the Centre.

'Vanessa's removing stuff from Gerry's flat,' she reported.

'Is Gerry there?'

'No sign of him. They've parked outside and a comrade is helping her carry things downstairs.'

Two people went to investigate and returned half an hour later.

'We tried to stop them. Vanessa was cold and arrogant at first and then' – he spread his hands helplessly – 'she called the police.'

'Against you, her own comrades?'

'She told the coppers she was removing personal items and they told us not to impede her.'

'So Gerry's hiding somewhere.'

'Run away, more likely.'

Next morning a letter arrived from Vanessa's solicitors demanding the return of film department equipment and stating: 'Vanessa Redgrave will be unable to attend for very long at the Central Committee commencing at 2pm on Saturday next, October 19, owing to her engagement at the Queen's Theatre, Shaftesbury Avenue.'

Through a lawyer's letter Vanessa was effectively putting herself outside the Party.

The London aggregate meeting had been called for Tuesday. Sheila mobilised her supporters and so did Mike – intellectuals, trade unionists, members who had been sidelined by Gerry. Two different viewpoints emanated from the Centre, taking the turmoil to the branches.

I arrived for the meeting with two members from Vauxhall branch. Chairs and benches laid out in the warehouse were filling rapidly. The not-for-issue moped bikes were crammed against the back wall; the vehicle maintenance workshop was tidied on the opposite side, boxes of books were piled high in the far corner. In a clever move, Sheila and another comrade were already sitting at the speakers' table to ensure that they, the London District Committee, would run the meeting, not Mike.

The arriving comrades had learned of the Party crisis only when *News Line* had stopped the previous Friday. They appeared sceptical, even angry, and quietly questioned each other.

'What are these the sex allegations?'

'Are they true?'

The weather was chilly, but the industrial gas heaters fixed high on the walls remained off because the vast space would become hot with such a big crowd. Only standing room at the back was left. Alex sat next to Corin in the front row. Vanessa was absent.

Sheila called the meeting to order.

'The unconstitutional walk-out last week by the general secretary and other members of staff led to the suspension of the *News Line*. This is totally unacceptable. Production of the paper must recommence immediately.'

The crowd listened attentively.

'The Majority on the Central Committee have jumped on a morality bandwagon to avoid the political responsibilities facing the Party in this revolutionary period. We are a declared Minority on the committee and will fight inside the Party to become the majority at the Special Congress on Saturday week.'

Mike presented the Majority position.

'When the clique dominating the Political Committee allowed Healy back on the premises, breaking an agreement that he would retire, we walked out of the Centre to bring to the attention of the Party membership the serious cover-up of corrupt sexual practices that had been taking place.'

He described Aileen's letter and his subsequent realisation that suppressing it was wrong. He spoke with regret and bitterness about his own role in the events and became quite emotional. There was some uncomfortable shuffling, the occasional gasp. The general secretary, the second most important figure in the Party, was attacking the formerly unchallengeable leader.

But Corin defended Gerry's record as a revolutionary fighter and praised his role in building our movement.

'We in the Minority reject the vote to charge Comrade Healy, which is middle-class moralising. The Majority on the Central Committee has the mentality of the zealot Clean-Up-TV campaigner Mary Whitehouse.' He looked defiantly round the meeting. 'We are revolutionaries. We are neither for nor against corruption, we are for the socialist revolution.'

Uproar broke out with furious cries and shouts of 'Shame on you'.

'He just thinks it doesn't matter,' the comrade next to me spluttered.

The discussion continued, turbulent and angry, reflecting shock, disbelief, disappointment, yet concern to protect the Party. There was praise for Gerry's past contribution, sorrow that we had reached this point. Sheila's supporters reiterated the view that a right-wing tendency was bringing bourgeois consciousness into the Party.

'I'm disgusted that the paper didn't come out,' complained a particularly attractive young woman from north London. 'If it was a revolutionary situation 11 months ago, isn't it now? Has the working class been defeated?'

She's lucky she escaped coming into Gerry's orbit, I thought bitterly. He would have been very interested in her. Those speakers who discounted Gerry's sexual activities were loudly heckled but, despite high emotion, the meeting never disintegrated.

Another woman comrade came to the microphone.

'I heard three weeks ago about the sexual abuse from one of the youth comrades who risked discipline to tell me.' She pointed to Corin in the front row and then to Sheila at the top table. 'You have not stated that Comrade Healy's sexual activities did *not* take place, nor have you said that the revelations of these practices constitute a political frame-up of Comrade Healy. You just argue that his role in the Trotskyist movement puts him above criticism. But the sexual practice of a member can't be separated from his political and theoretical practices.'

Heartfelt applause broke out from some comrades. Sheila took the microphone.

'This moralising is a Trojan Horse for revisionism, a vehicle to smuggle major revisions to the Party position into our ranks. Look, the Political

Committee took a decision on 6th July. We demanded a written undertaking from Comrade Healy that such practices had to stop. We said that in view of his 49 years of outstanding leadership we would take action. The position of the Political Committee has been absolutely firm all the way.'

'You hid all this, and Aileen's letter, even from the Central Committee,' someone shouted. 'You just said he was retiring.'

The meeting ended inconclusively, with a decision to reconvene on the following Friday.

'If anyone takes this crisis outside the Party or speaks to the press, the Central Committee will bring charges against them,' Mike reminded us.

We dispersed with feverish chatter. Halfway down the alleyway, one of the young women caught up with me.

'Will we defeat the Minority?'

'We'll have to wait and see.'

I didn't feel completely confident.

In a secluded but unprepossessing room in the film department the long-demanded Control Commission began taking depositions on Gerry's sexual exploitation. The three elected comrades were Norman Harding and Jean Kerrigan, who both worked at the Centre, and Liverpool docker Larry Cavanagh, a leader in the 1970s docks strikes. When my turn came, I described how Gerry had inveigled me into succumbing to his sexual demands. They listened carefully, but Jean was sceptical.

'What do you mean, he "used his authority" to persuade you?' she asked.

I was distressed at having to justify my belief that I had been duped. I described how Gerry had broken up my marriage.

'Above all, we have to protect the Party,' Jean said at the end.

I realised Gerry had never tried to have sex with her. Why not? Aileen and I had discussed the exceptions to his wide range of victims: very intellectual women, unreliable ones whose commitment to the Party was still in question, some he was still working on, and those he feared would see through him. Perhaps Jean was in this last category. But surely she wouldn't disbelieve, or condone, his practices with the young women 20 years younger than us?

I was confident the Control Commission would find evidence that justified the charges against Gerry. But he was a skilled manipulator. Did he have a plan? What actions could Sheila, Alex and the Redgraves marshal to protect him?

Our day-to-day work was disrupted because we had no paper and more comrades from the branches came in seeking clarification. Febrile discussions took place in small groups in every corner of the Centre and in a more subdued way in the canteen next to Sheila's office. 'Were you one of them?' comrades asked women at the Centre, unaware how painful the question was. We affirmed or denied. I felt relief in having it all out in the open, a sense of new-found liberation, but I wondered how others felt. 'No, I wasn't one of them,' said one woman, 'but I had suspicions it was happening.' I didn't believe her on either count, but she had the right to deny the abuse; she had to deal with it in her own way.

A rather agitated comrade from a north London branch approached me.

'Sheila told the aggregate that Comrade Healy had signed a written undertaking to stop sexual affairs with the girls.'

'That secret statement was useless. They didn't know about it and he continued calling them to his flat.'

'But Comrade Healy's retirement will surely resolve the issue?'

'Look, it's a cover-up. These weren't "affairs". It was just bullying.'

'Surely they could have said no to Comrade Healy?'

'Well, I don't think so. You know how forceful he is.'

'There must be a way of sorting it out. Comrade Healy is our most important leader.'

A troubling view: find a compromise, smooth everything over, keep 'Comrade Healy' as nominal leader. A London District Committee member joined us. He was sceptical of Mike's change of mind.

'Mike must have known about this all along. I don't believe he has only just found out.'

'Well, none of us knew about the others,' I countered. 'None of us talked to each other.'

'He's worked closely with Gerry for years and he could have stopped it long ago. He's suddenly taking this moral position for his own opportunist reasons. He couldn't replace Gerry – it would destroy the Party.'

When Mike's position was scrutinised I felt great anxiety because I too had questions about his role in the past decades as Gerry's loyal henchman.

But changing his position was courageous and he had great political authority. His regular contacts with the Party's prominent trade union members enabled him to mobilise them now, along with the sidelined intellectuals, Cyril Smith, Geoff Pilling and Tom Kemp, respected as lecturers at the school, known for their theoretical articles in *News Line* and the journals *Fourth International* and *Labour Review*. But was Mike's authority adequate to carry the Party?

When the London aggregate meeting reconvened on Friday I realised I had underestimated Mike's political skill: he had brought Cliff Slaughter from Leeds to open the meeting on behalf of the Central Committee Majority. The atmosphere was sober as he began to speak.

'The flower of our movement, of every generation since the early 1960s, has been brutally attacked and many of them destroyed,' said Cliff. 'We are not talking here of promiscuity, but of organised abuse of the Party and its cadres in the interests of one individual's vile practices. The Minority's line of "rape doesn't matter" is alien to everything we stand for, contrary to the methods by which the working class will rise above bourgeois ideology and carry out its revolutionary role of transforming society.'

Comrades were listening intently.

'The mentality of fawning on the infallible genius, mostly by middle-class people who strayed into our movement in the late 1960s and 1970s looking for a guru' – a forthright swipe at the Redgraves and Alex Mitchell – 'became the method of the clique that has dominated the Party. They will not face up to the seething and explosive rage of hundreds of Party members who have sacrificed everything to build the Party, endangering their homes, families and children, only to discover now that Healy has turned this Party into his private brothel.'

No, no, no. 'Brothel' was not the right word. Healy's actions were something else. Cliff continued:

'Healy's sexual abuses were the most vile of the manifestations of subordination and use of individuals as objects with no rights. So acute and explosive were the internal political contradictions in our Party, stoked up by the tests we were put to by the miners' strike, that comrades were compelled to act unconstitutionally and secretly to expose the cancer eating away at the centre of the Party.'

There were protests from some quarters, but Cliff continued the attack.

'If Sheila Torrance were to come clean she would admit that, under great pressure from Healy in the first part of this year, she too worked outside the elected committees, even threatening to organise a split. After Aileen Jennings' letter she prepared to put Healy to one side on the basis of undertakings to cease the practices of sexual abuse and thought she could use Mike Banda and the Central Committee to persist in her own petty bureaucratic version of Healyite authoritarianism. Comrades fighting for a Control Commission investigation of Healy's crimes were obstructed for three months.'

'Yes, we were,' came a call from the middle of the meeting.

'But the cover-up was broken, so Torrance has run back to Healy, who has fled from the wrath of the Party.'

A comrade stood, demanding to speak from the floor.

'Comrade Healy joined the Fourth International before the second world war, when Trotsky was still alive,' he said angrily. 'He represents our continuity with the Russian Revolution. He fought against Pablo who would have liquidated the Fourth International. He built our Party. You're wrong to dismiss him like this.'

'Healy's past is on record,' agreed Cliff. 'But it ceased many years ago. Look at our relationship with the Arab countries. Our principled support in the 1970s for the national independence struggle gave way to a craven subordination to petty-bourgeois leaders and bourgeois governments. We moved away from the construction of Trotskyist sections in other countries.'

'Completely unprincipled,' someone muttered.

'Healy sought relations with bourgeois leaders like Saddam Hussein in Iraq, Gaddafi in Libya and Nkomo in Zimbabwe. Marxism was distorted in order to mislead on their class nature and Healy sought financial support, not just for this or that political purpose, but as a system. Despite Healy's past fight against Pablo this corresponds to Pabloite revisionism: abandonment of the revolutionary role of the working class.'

There was murmured assent. Our relationship with the Arab leaders had concerned many comrades.

'This achieved the most disastrous expression in Iraq,' Cliff continued. 'In 1979 *News Line* reported without comment the execution of Iraqi Communist Party members as "conspirators" by the Ba'athist government. Many were leading trade union officials.'

In the 1970s we gave principled support to the national independence struggle in many countries but we later abandoned the concept of building Trotskyist sections and subordinated our policies to nationalist leaderships

▶ Rhodesian Patriotic Front leaders Robert Mugabe and Joshua Nkomo

'One of them had spoken at our All Trades Unions Alliance conference,' someone called out.

'We now know more. A *News Line* photographer was sent to the Iraqi Embassy to take pictures of opponents of the regime. The comrade will tell you what happened.'

But the photographer sitting next to me declined to speak. It seemed he had lost his nerve. Suddenly, from the back of the meeting, a woman photographer stood up, jabbing her finger accusingly at Alex, yelling in her high-pitched voice.

'You sent me to the Iraqi Embassy to take photographs. When I realised this was to finger the demonstrators, supporters of the Iraqi Communist Party, I refused to take any and left.' She glared at Alex. 'I came back and told you never, ever to send me on an assignment like that again.'

Shouts and jeers rang throughout the warehouse. The chair called the meeting back to order.

'What about Iran?' asked one comrade. 'We praised Khomeini for using theory to lead the Iranian revolution – a travesty of Marxism. And since the Iran-Iraq war started, we have made no comment.'

◀ In 1978 marchers in London denounced the Shah's brutal, US-backed regime.

▼ By February 1979 Ayatollah Khomeini had returned to Tehran to establish the Islamic republic

'We never condemned Khomeini's suppression of the Kurds,' added Mike Banda, from the top table.

Corin attempted to put the Minority's position.

'The Majority are mobilising on the basis of lies. They have refused to discuss our investigation into the Party finances. They are hi-jacking the Party. They want to smash up the *News Line* and sell the Youth Training Centres –'

'Rapist.'

'You're corrupt.'

Corin struggled against the shouts.

'And now Comrade Healy fears for his life –'

'Rubbish.'

'Will he face tomorrow's Central Committee?'

The meeting's tone changed when one of Gerry's victims came to the microphone. Formerly a leading member, she had been sidelined. Her detailed description of the sexual abuse she had endured for 20 years was heard in horrified silence.

'He wore down my self-esteem. I had to separate myself from the abuse till my body didn't matter to me any more.'

Comrades listened compassionately. How brave she is, I thought. But Sheila was impatient with this very personal account and tried to return to the arid territory of documents and resolutions.

'The Minority's position is based on three documents: the resolution from last week's Political Committee, my September discussion document, and the report from the Finance Sub-Committee.' She pushed her glasses up her nose and looked round the meeting. 'There is a subjective wall here of emotionalism and hate. All sorts of tendencies reverberating in the Party have become an agency for the bourgeoisie by their unconstitutional actions.'

'Rubbish.'

'You've covered up for far too long.'

'On the allegations against Comrade Healy,' said Sheila, determined to be heard, 'let me tell you. A book was printed today about Yasser Arafat, alleging that he is homosexual and has been recruiting little boys into the Palestine Liberation Organisation for this purpose.'

The meeting exploded.

'What have slanders against Arafat got to do with Healy?'

'Are you saying the allegations against Healy are untrue?'

'Are they true or aren't they, comrade? Tell us.'

Things had changed since Tuesday. Members' festering disagreements with Party policies had been expressed. Some of Sheila's supporters were developing doubts. The groundwork we had laid months ago was bearing fruit.

Expulsion

The Minority didn't appear at the Central Committee meeting next day. The chair read out a letter stating that they feared violence would be used against them and thought it best not to attend, but would prepare for the following week's Special Congress.

'Who signed it?'

'Sheila and nine others, and three more who are not Central Committee members. Corin's and Vanessa's names have been typed in at the bottom. Healy is not among them.'

'They fear violence? Ridiculous.'

'They're scared of the Liverpool contingent downstairs.'

Comrades had arrived from all over the country to lobby the meeting. The Minority's absence nonplussed us, we had expected a meeting of stormy disagreement. A proposal was put:

'In this unprecedented situation the Central Committee accepts the request of comrades from the areas that they should all be visitors to this meeting, with the proviso that where security matters arise, the committee will ask them to withdraw.'

The visitors clattered into the back of the room with extra chairs, far outnumbering the 21 Central Committee members. We dealt with attendance – three others were absent through illness. We speedily went through the minutes of the previous meeting and matters arising.

'We come to the charges against G. Healy,' said the chair, looking slowly round the meeting. 'Every step has been taken to deliver them to him. The Minority, who are in touch with him, gave an undertaking last week to assist. We have to assume he has seen the charges.'

There were angry mutters from the lobbying comrades.

'I will read the charges again.'

It was a solemn moment. Most of the lobbyists had not heard them in full: sexual abuse, violence and slander. A comrade sitting behind me let out a deep sigh.

'Is there any discussion?'

Silence held for a while. We were about to formalise a momentous decision about the man who had inspired and dominated us ever since we had joined the movement. Finally someone spoke, slowly.

'The comrade has refused to appear to answer these charges. He has made no effort to be in touch. I propose we take the vote.'

It was unanimous, by committee members only. There was a further moment of tense silence and then the visitors broke into applause. No one indicated any support for Gerry, but surely at least one was present to report back to Sheila.

Rather than triumph I felt relief, tempered by exhaustion, cold anger, sadness for a lost era, and anxiety about the Party's future. As I looked around I saw mixed emotions on many faces.

We had other business to deal with, including an extensive backlog of correspondence. First was Vanessa's solicitor's letter demanding her film equipment, which we would have to surrender. We voted to charge her with acts detrimental to the Party and breach of the Emergency Measures passed the previous week, and to reclaim her Party car. Several letters calling for a Control Commission had been overtaken by events as it was already investigating. Then came Charlie's letter requesting pay in lieu of notice. Dave Bruce spoke about its background.

'Charlie came from the German section as a printer, then worked on security. He became a nark for Healy, but broke about 18 months ago. He was a constant victim of Healy's bullying and intimidation but retained his integrity and became more and more hostile to the clique in the Centre. In a

▶ As a result of Vanessa Redgrave's legal actions, film unit equipment was removed through the Centre's formidable metal gates at the top of the alleyway

moment of frustration he told Alex Mitchell he was going to investigate him – a mistake. Part-time guards were set up by Mitchell to report on him and Healy became determined that he had to go. This devoted comrade, on duty almost 24 hours a day, for six days and most of the seventh, was charged by the Political Committee. His appeal to the Central Committee was dismissed in ten minutes.'

There was an angry reaction.

'We should apologise as humbly as we can and exonerate him of all charges.'

'It's not only Healy. We too are responsible for what happened,' someone said regretfully. 'The procedure was a parody, a disgrace to this committee. I propose we rescind all decisions relating to the comrade.'

This was agreed unanimously. I sat very quiet, marvelling at how things had changed, thrilled at this vindication of Charlie.

Phil Penn, an alternate member of the committee like me, came forward to speak. His tousled hair and distress made him seem older than his early 30s. As well as maintaining the Centre's car fleet, he had been Gerry's trusted bodyguard and driver for the past few months. But he had queried an anomalous philosophical statement in one of Gerry's last lectures at the school, and the unsatisfactory reply had contributed to turning him.

'Aileen's letter was burned on 1st July,' he began. 'Immediately afterwards, a secret faction was set up consisting of Gerry, Alex, me, the Redgraves, Mike Banda, and a youth comrade, but not Sheila.'

He paused and wiped his face with his hand.

'It had five purposes.' He enumerated them on his fingers: 'First, to frame Aileen, Dot and Clare on the finances. Second, to protect Comrade Healy. Third, to sack the female comrades who were making sexual allegations. Fourth, to get rid of Comrade Charlie. Fifth, to persuade the youth comrade to retract her letter supporting Aileen.'

He wiped his face again.

'About Charlie. I too was involved with Alex. We asked the guards to report anything he said about Gerry.

▲ Phil Penn

One of them reported that he had said I was being used by Gerry' – he faltered in distress – 'which was true!'

He sat down and put his face in his hands, quietly weeping. A visitor comrade from the eastern region leaned forward and comforted him by putting her hand on his shoulder, a poignant gesture of compassion. Of course Phil had been used without realising it at the time, like so many of us, on big and small issues.

The meeting rescinded several suspensions, reinstated Stuart Carter, and arranged Majority report-backs to regions which had not yet held aggregates. Then we came to the *News Line*. A new editorial board was formulated, without the Minority, with a view to recommencing production. But first came the report from the Runcorn printshop occupation committee, which consisted of both staff and north-west members. One of the machine crew had been delegated to speak.

'In the past week we have had a new regime where we could actually *think*. There is no support in the north-west for the Minority position. At the Liverpool aggregate the vote was 85 against four full-timers and one girlfriend.'

He looked at the meeting.

'Printing will be resumed only when the Central Committee has convinced the occupation committee, whose decisions are pending next weekend's Congress.'

He made a wide gesture to include everyone in the meeting.

'There is a standing invitation for any member who has not declared support for the Minority to come to Runcorn and have full voting rights. OK, for London it might seem that the Healy regime has gone, but I personally wouldn't support production of *News Line* on the terms proposed here.'

A cameraman gave a further explanation.

'The occupation committee is not prepared to be taken for granted. Comrades on the Central Committee are going to have to fight for their position in the Party, just as the Party has to fight for its position in the working class. The only support for the Political Committee clique in the north-west has been via a handful of staff in the printshop who support the Minority and in Manchester it's only five.'

A delegation was appointed to travel to Runcorn to ask the occupation committee to allow the paper to be printed again: two trade unionists from London and Wales, a leading youth comrade who was one of Healy's victims, and a journalist.

A draft statement on Gerry's expulsion, to appear once the paper restarted, was presented by Paul Jennings and agreed by the meeting.

News Line appeared again on Wednesday 23rd October with the front-page headline: 'G. HEALY EXPELLED – Unanimous vote by WRP Central Committee'.

▲ *News Line*, 23 October 1985

All efforts now focused on the Congress scheduled for 26th October, which would ratify or rescind Gerry's expulsion. Branches hurriedly met to elect delegates and Sheila rallied her cohorts to visit branches who had not heard the Minority's defence of Healy, but they usually got short shrift. Gerry's expulsion was now public knowledge and we could openly discuss the sexual abuse. Irish Mrs Feeny was sceptical.

'Surely everyone realised the old goat was making advances? I can't believe no one knew.'

I was distressed by her reaction. But another woman, a council worker on Dorset Road estate, steadied my confidence.

'I completely understand how people could be taken in. It happened to us at work over something else. They can be so skilful.'

Vauxhall branch meeting assembled, including several Young Socialists, Mavis and Mullins, the Jamaican couple who lived alarmingly close to my secret flat, and Owen, a long-standing Jamaican member who was in the throes of a serious mental breakdown, sitting silent in a heavy coat and dark glasses.

'He shouldn't even be here,' a Minority supporter said angrily.

We elected her as a congress delegate along with Bob, a member of the London engineering union executive. One each for the opposing views, as specified in the Party constitution. I had an automatic right to attend as a Central Committee member.

Independently of Sheila we checked that branches were holding meetings and electing delegates. Phoning round the areas, I heard different reports. What happened in Scotland was particularly revealing.

'Corin spoke for the Minority at our aggregate meeting,' said journalist Simon. 'He opposed charging Healy on the grounds that it would damage the revolutionary leadership. Then a veteran member said to him: "Can you look me in the eye and tell me, honestly, that these charges are without foundation? That they shouldn't be brought because they're false?"'

'What did Corin say?'

'He cited the Party's achievements – the daily paper, big youth movement, influence in trade unions and so on. Then he said: "If this is the work of a rapist, let's recruit more rapists."'

'Fuckin' 'ell.'

'Yeah. The meeting was deeply shocked. We only just managed to continue in good order.'

Congress confirms

I arrived early for the Special Congress, tensed for a sharp political battle. As delegates registered they were issued with folders containing documents from both the Minority and the Majority, including Aileen's letter with the list of names replaced by '[26 individuals]'. Extracts from the Political Committee minutes documented how both her letter and requests for a Control Commission investigation had been suppressed. Comrades leafed through their folders, discussing solemnly.

Bridget from east London arrived.

'I went to pick up a delegate who told me she was not coming. She handed me her own membership card and two more from comrades who felt the same.'

This was unexpected. Looking round we realised that other comrades were missing. Then news arrived that the Minority was organising a breakaway conference.

'They're splitting the Party,' someone said scornfully.

'Cowards.'

The standing orders committee discussed the Minority's absence and decided the Congress should begin. Dave North, leader of the American Workers League, addressed the Congress on behalf of the International Committee. Confident, in his prime, he made a powerful impression as an untainted leader.

▲ Dave North

'The political situation in the Workers Revolutionary Party has produced the most serious crisis in the International Committee of the Fourth International since it was formed in 1953 through the British comrades' struggle against Pabloite revisionism's attempt to liquidate Trotskyism.' The spectre of Pablo again. 'The present crisis erupted with the exposure of the corrupt practices of Healy and the Political Committee's attempt to cover them up. At the root is the prolonged drift of the WRP leadership away from the strategical task of building the world party of socialist revolution and towards an increasingly nationalist perspective and practice.'

The problems arose from our *nationalist* drift? I wasn't sure.

'A bogus report of the WRP's financial crisis was used to obtain pledges from the international sections totalling £82,000 to assist the WRP.'

A comrade near me shook his head, muttering to himself.

'Overcoming the crisis in the WRP requires the closest collaboration with its co-thinkers in the International Committee. Political differences must be openly and fully discussed. The present crisis can be overcome, and bring gains for the International as a whole.'

'That's the way forward,' someone murmured.

'Our British comrades work under enormous class pressures generated by the ruling class of the oldest capitalist country. These can be surmounted only with a truly internationalist practice. We propose re-registration of the membership of the WRP on the basis of an explicit recognition of the political authority of the International Committee and the subordination of the British section to its decisions.'

Gerry's authority had pervaded all past Congresses. He had intervened in the discussions, he had always made a powerful speech at some point to orient and inspire our work with incisive analysis, compelling perspectives, skilful oratory. But now his control had been rent asunder, the clique surrounding him had been unmasked, their misleadership exposed. Today his *absence* dominated as the Party felt its way in an unprecedented situation. All our policies and perspectives were open to re-examination and Dave North seemed to offer a clear way forward.

Not everyone was convinced.

'We've been under the control of a corrupt clique for so long. Why should we rush to subordinate ourselves to the "political authority" of another body?' a comrade asked. But Congress voted by a majority to support Dave North's resolution.

Larry Cavanagh and Norman Harding of the long-fought-for Control Commission came before Congress. Jean Kerrigan was absent, presumably at the Minority's breakaway conference. Norman read out the interim report.

'We have met for the last eight days. We have interviewed nine comrades who appeared on the original list in Aileen's letter. Seven say that the accusations are true. One said that it was true but nothing happened to her. Another said that advances were made on many occasions but she always managed to put him off.'

He looked up from his notes.

'Healy either broke down the will to resist his advances or he was able to keep the comrades under his domination. I will now read anonymised extracts from some of the youth comrades' statements.'

Shocking statements described regular visits to Gerry's flat, where he began by discussing any political problems the comrades were encountering, spoke encouragingly about their development as revolutionaries and suggested passages they should read. But in due course the political discussion was followed by an attempt to kiss and fondle them. If they resisted he reacted with

▲ Larry Cavanagh

▲ Norman Harding

anger and the next day called them into his office to harangue them about their 'refusal to be trained as a revolutionary'. There would be shouting and drama for days on end until they eventually gave in, often in tears.

One statement recounted that he had said it was useless to complain to the Political Committee, because they wouldn't believe her. 'I am the Political Committee,' he had said. Another reported that Healy had been angry to hear that she had a black boyfriend. 'You shouldn't go with black men,' he had said. 'They have diseases.'

The working life, friends and, in some cases, even family of some of these young women were intricately tied up in the Party. The threat of discipline, even expulsion, meant breaking with everything. Working on that side of the Centre I had become accustomed to shouting sessions emanating from Gerry's office without realising what was at play. He was attacking their resistance to his sexual approaches with pseudo-political attacks on their 'opportunism' and, most forcefully, the threat of expulsion.

There was a troubled silence as Norman finished reading. I saw some comrades wiping their eyes, others had their faces in their hands or were shaking their heads angrily, muttering, swearing. I couldn't work out who had made the statements but wondered whether this public reading made them feel better or worse. Norman continued:

'Although the investigation will continue, we already have enough evidence of the anti-communist activities of Gerry Healy, involving the grave abuse of his authority and position in the movement, to say that the decision of the Central Committee on 19th October to expel Gerry Healy was correct.'

The Congress formally endorsed the Central Committee decision with a unanimous vote. The Party had fractured but we, the Majority, had expelled Gerry.

The Minority splits

Who were our leaders now? Mike Banda had a history of political errors to overcome before he would be credible. Cliff Slaughter and other intellectuals who had been sidelined would have to re-establish trust. Dave Bruce and others had been fighting politically in recent months. Who would be up to the task? Who would manage all the Party property, the resources, the debts?

The Majority now controlled the Centre. Relations with the Minority were on a war footing and they kept away. The Congress reconvened a week later because so much was still to be resolved.

'Why don't you come?' I said to Charlie.

'To risk attack from Healy's thugs?'

'They won't be there.'

'But his spies will be.'

'Probably. Come on, comrades have been asking about you.'

'They asked you?'

'Not me, of course not. They don't know about us.'

Four months of exclusion had crystallised his thoughts.

'I don't want to go back to that madhouse. Our souls were sold, we were owned. I now have a job where I'm treated with respect.'

Dot's financial report to Congress tackled the incompetent mumbo-jumbo in Corin's report. She explained the violence, humiliation and autocratic methods Gerry had used in the Centre, the first time most members had heard about it. She gave examples of expenditure on equipment, much of it unused – moped bikes, trucks, mobile radios, Gerry's secret BMW car, the Solna web-offset press. Comrades struggled with the incomprehensibly large figures.

She described our group of five who had organised the 'conspiracy'. This had not been openly mentioned until now. I looked across at Dave Bruce, but he was watching Dot.

'Aileen's letter was designed to bring everything to a head. We had concrete evidence that Healy had abused our youth. The Party was at bursting point. Everywhere there was opposition to Sheila Torrance's method of organising, to the method of "training" by Healy, and to the line being printed in *News Line*.'

There were murmurs of agreement.

'The Political Committee never discussed the financial crisis in the Party, leaders and members were kept in the dark. Corin Redgrave was put into the Finance Office. Vanessa and Gerry were presented as saviours of the Party as they tried to raise money, desperate to hide the scandal of Aileen's letter.'

She turned to Mike Banda, who was looking down at the floor.

'When Comrade Mike decided to stand up and be counted it was a turning point. That's when Healy went into hiding.'

A sigh flowed along the rows.

'In the last two weeks we have been facing writs, solicitors' letters, attacks on our banking procedures, and threats to wind up our companies. We have spent hours with our accountants and solicitors to offset these attacks and save the Party's property. Vanessa has set in motion winding-up proceedings on Astmoor Litho for the return of the £50,000 she now says was not a donation but a loan.'

'Fucking cow,' someone muttered.

'We have to be clear. If Healy and this anti-Party clique cannot have the Party themselves, then they will do everything in their power to smash it.'

'Gold, South African gold! The Party has been financed by apartheid gold.'

Mike Banda's wife Janet and his brother Tony, both directors who had never previously taken responsibility for the companies, reacted furiously when they discovered that I had made loans and had purchased Party properties.

'The loans are scandalous, they're *tainted*.'

Their angry cry greeted me in mid-November when I returned from South Africa, where political crisis was visible everywhere: military and police

▼ Pregnant during a visit to South Africa shortly after Healy's downfall

controls; grenade attacks in city centres; bombings of industrial and military targets; strikes, boycotts and rebellions in the townships. A mass movement was appearing in widely separated places. The proposal to buy the bookshops had been rescinded so Charlie and I had gone simply to visit my mother.

The International Committee's investigation into the Party's crisis was in full swing. Their financial report was much more competent than Corin's travesty and included material from Gerry's files, including reports of visits to the Middle East; handwritten drafts of letters requesting payment of money promised; sales of Vanessa's film *The Palestinian* (£315,000); printing (£237,000); donations to Youth Training and such-like (£524,000). Much of this was for legitimate commercial transactions, but I was shocked to realise how much Gerry had relied on large funds from Arab governments.

The Centre exuded optimism, a kind of post-revolutionary fervour. A flurry of political discussion took place as comrades from far and wide came to seek clarification, declare support or offer help. Others, who had left the Party or had been expelled over the years, came to re-evaluate their own experiences. I found the situation exhilarating for a while, but we also had things to sort out and it became tiresome until a more formal operation was established.

Our own finance commission, made up of comrades from outside the Centre, grappled with financial reorganisation. Dot was a new woman – confident, enthusiastic about the ceaseless political discussions, determined to find ways to resolve our financial problems. But she faced bitterly critical questions from some members who felt she bore responsibility for the financial errors.

Dave Bruce and others discussed with intellectuals whom Gerry had sidelined or excluded and met former members such as Alan Thornett to investigate what the real issues had been 11 years before when he and over 100 others had been expelled. Discussions were arranged with other Trotskyist groups, the 'revisionists' we had always spurned, to investigate points of agreement and reexamine our history. We were learning how to have comradely political discussions even where there were big disagreements.

▶ Healy, now expelled

▲ Vanessa Redgrave   ▲ Alex Mitchell   ▲ Sheila Torrance   ▲ Corin Redgrave
Leaders of the clique supporting Healy, also nicknamed "The Rump"

We had control of the Centre and all the assets, and now faced the task of clearing up the past, rationalising the company structures, dealing with huge debts, disposing of unnecessary assets. Moped bikes were issued to delighted branches. The erstwhile Minority clique around Gerry now also called themselves the Workers Revolutionary Party, raised money from wealthy supporters, and announced that they would print their own daily version of *News Line* by February 1986. Intent on destroying us, they launched multiple legal actions over items of property. On 16th December receivers arrived to close down the Runcorn printshop, Astmoor Litho. As the company had never had any assets it was a Pyrrhic victory for them, but it complicated our rationalisation plans and prevented us printing *News Line* or any other publications. Our small London printing press printed a single sheet explaining this to our readership. The huge web-offset presses, state-of-the-art cameras, computer typesetters and all other production equipment were auctioned off in poor market conditions to pay creditors. An ignominious end to Gerry's hubristic vision.

All sections of the International Committee of the Fourth International, except the Greek and Spanish, supported the break from Healy. But Dave North's insistence that our Party should subordinate itself to the International Committee was overturned at a further Party Congress and a new minority faction was declared to support him. The International Committee suspended us as the British section of the Fourth International. Tom Kemp, a previously sidelined intellectual, was scathing.

▲ A sticker attached to our 1985-1986 membership cards affirmed the Special Congress decision on the subordination of the WRP to the International Committee of the Fourth International. Bernard Franks never signed his. A later Congress overturned the subordination decision

'Who is the International Committee?' he asked. 'There were only three sections in the 1960s. Establishing the others – Australia, the United States, Latin America and so on – took place around the British section.'

We were now isolated internationally, although discussions were supposed to continue. Groups from other Trotskyist Internationals in several countries contacted us for discussions. We hoped to find agreement but it was rarely fruitful.

Two leading Young Socialists, supporters of the new minority faction, went to our bank at Clapham Junction and emptied the Young Socialists' account of several thousand pounds in cash. As signatories to the account, they were entitled to do this, but the bank rang Dot immediately afterwards to inform her. The minority group soon split from us to align themselves with Dave North and the remaining international sections.

Charlie and I had a secretive Christmas dinner in a pub near Tower Bridge with Paul Jennings. The landlord looked at me.

'Don't worry about anything, my dear. Should you need it, the barman' – he pointed to the right – 'was a qualified midwife in his former life.'

I had to wait another six weeks for the baby. On the seventh floor of St Thomas' hospital I had a splendid view of the Thames and Westminster. Our accountant, Richard Moss, sent flowers and many comrades visited me. Dave Bruce looked at the tiny baby and whispered with a giggle:

'He has Charlie's feet.'

Although Charlie had by now been warmly welcomed at a Party conference, too much of the past hovered over us to feel confident of disclosing that he was the father. He came during visiting hours like any other visitor and left early to wander in distant corridors before using his father's right to return after hours.

The baby's arrival changed our lives more than I had anticipated.

1986 AND BEYOND
THE WOMEN'S QUESTION

Reorganising the Party fell to a team of Party comrades, and included Dave Bruce and Dot. Financial and legal issues were tackled; projects and companies were closed, sold or restructured. Publication of a new weekly *Workers Press* began. I was preoccupied with a new baby and escaped the turmoil, although from time to time I brought him to finance discussions or even to political meetings.

Aileen chose to remain in hiding. Although I had some idea of her difficult situation and I understood her fear of Healy's thugs, I barely grasped the traumatic effect of the 20 years of physical and psychological abuse she had suffered. Charlie too chose to stay disengaged from the reorganisation.

Former members of the Robertson group, a Trotskyist organisation in the United States, contacted us to discuss the women's aspect of the split. The two women described abusive sexual practices by the leadership in their organisation, not unlike our experiences.

'We decided to tackle the problem politically rather than on sexual grounds,' they told us. 'In the end we were expelled. Today things go on as before inside the organisation.'

'We think the sexual questions *are* political,' I said.

This discussion reinforced a line of thought that had troubled me for some time. Comments at Party meetings or in documents on Gerry's sexual abuse sometimes jarred: Healy was guilty of 'byzantine, bacchanalian and bureaucratic violence and intrigue'. He had 'run a brothel'. He was a 'serial rapist'. He was like the 'Lord of the Manor exercising his right of the first night'. His 'sexual and other arbitrary and bureaucratic activities' were 'appalling', but 'his major crimes were *political*'.

All these comments missed the point that Gerry's actions had nothing to do with sexual desire, 'bacchanalian' or otherwise. His sexual actions were about subjugation, humiliation, control – and these were political issues.

This led me to new trains of thought. While Gerry's practices constituted the most destructive abuse of women, the top leadership of the Party had acquiesced at other levels. Capable women had been excluded from leading political roles or had been discarded, like a woman delegate to the International Committee or the national agent for General Election candidates. Prominent women in the Party were kept as activists; we came to believe we weren't capable of anything else. For Gerry's own opportunist ends, Vanessa had been artificially elevated; leading women from the international sections were brought to London for 'cadre training'; young women in the Young Socialists were promoted into leading positions. Sheila's years-long leadership was anomalous – she had some unfathomable hold over Gerry, possibly some information that could destroy him.

Our Party had never discussed the 'women's question'. It didn't exist for us. Single-issue politics like women's liberation, Black Power, or gay rights were considered ill-conceived because no single group could be liberated except through the working class taking power. The 'women's question' was unfamiliar territory, but I discovered that Liz Leicester from west London had similar concerns to mine. We began discussing tentatively, feeling our way.

By now Dave North and the breakaway faction supporting him were concluding that the sexual-abuse issue was secondary. Our 1986 Congress mentioned Gerry's sexual actions less and less in evaluations of the Party's political errors. Liz and I decided a contribution on the 'women's question' was needed. We nervously prepared some notes for her to speak.

'We expelled Healy and his supporters. But it was not political or theoretical differences, agent-hunting or violence that evoked the powerful and rapid reaction from the Party membership. It was the revelation of his sexual abuse.'

She quoted Engels' characterisation of class society and private property as 'the world historic defeat of the female sex'; Trotsky had pointed out that the first attacks by the triumphant Stalinist bureaucracy were on abortion, divorce and childcare measures brought in by the October revolution.

▲ The determined and inspiring struggle of women during the miners' strike signified a massive change in society

'The British miners' strike represented a historic leap, particularly for miners' wives and women's support groups. The determined struggle of women during the strike was the most dramatic sign of massive changes in society, in the relations between men and women, and in the family. These developments provided the material conditions for Comrade Aileen's letter to expose Healy.'

No one referred to Liz's points. But towards the end of the conference discussion Cliff Slaughter supported and developed what she had said. I was relieved and excited. As a result, we set up a Women's Commission to try and deepen our understanding. It consisted mostly of women but included theoretician and former leading member Cyril Smith, at his own request.

A programme on daytime television caught my attention as I fed my baby. The interview guest was Richard from the Incest Crisis Line.

'As a child I was sexually abused by my father, a Guardsman. By chance I discovered that my sister was being abused too. We decided to tell our mother, who took immediate action. She bolted the front door and phoned the police.'

This shocking story established Richard's credentials.

'We define incest as any sexual contact between a child and an adult in a position of trust. It happens in every layer of society and it doesn't just happen within a family. Sexual abuse by anyone in a position of power and trust is incest.'

I had never heard anything like this before. I scribbled down the telephone helpline number at the end of the programme and, after some thought, I phoned Richard.

'Ah yes, I read about Mr Healy in the papers,' he said. 'It's to the credit of your organisation that you brought it out into the open instead of hushing it up, as other organisations have done when paedophilia has been uncovered.'

'Would you characterise what happened in our organisation as incest?'

'Yes, I would. Rape happens at a given opportunity but incest is abuse of someone the abuser has control over, in order to further compound that control. It is never the fault of the victim, though they are always made to feel responsible and guilty.'

I told him how Gerry had operated. He listened and corroborated my conclusions. He was not surprised that some of our members had supported Gerry even after his exposure.

'Families often split when incest is uncovered. Even victims sometimes defend the abuser. And, you know, some abusers are very puritanical.'

'Well, yes. Mr Healy always seemed moralistic on the outside, with strict rules about the girls being out late, for instance. Some people can't understand why none of us realised that others were being abused. They don't believe we didn't know.'

'That too is a pattern of incest. Multiple victims in one family *never* discuss the abuse with each other, even if they are aware of it. They feel that this will exclude them from the family. This will have been a factor in why victims in your organisation didn't discuss it.'

Richard offered to hold a meeting with us. About 30 people assembled in a pub function room, a motley group of members from London branches, several of Gerry's victims, but few leading members. Richard arrived, informally dressed, slim, with his Guardsman father's stature. His easy-going manner quickly relaxed my nervousness.

'I've never met Mr Healy,' he said. 'But I'll describe an average sexual abuser. He is very practical and accomplished at his abuse. He always transfers responsibility for the sexual actions on to the victim. Physically he's likely to be not very tall, paunchy, losing his hair. He wears glasses, possibly has bad breath, he's insecure emotionally, has no real friends who are close to him. He is always worried about losing his position of power. It's not sex, but power and domination that motivates him.'

I was amazed. This description accurately fitted Gerry.

Somebody asked what the long-term effects on victims might be.

'Each victim will need to confront the problem some day, even symbolically. For instance, they could write a letter to the abuser, even if it's not sent. You should insist with victims: "You didn't *let* it happen. He *took advantage* of you. You have done *nothing* that you have to feel guilty about."'

I was enormously encouraged by the meeting. I felt Richard understood what we had been through.

'Never ask a victim what the abuser did to them. Let them feel free to talk about it – if they want to. Concern for the victims should be the main issue and their feelings of guilt and shame must be challenged.'

Loose ends

I last saw Healy in 1986 near Stockwell station when I came upon him walking with Corinna who, I guessed, now assisted with his menial tasks and acted as his secretary. He was rather disconcerted; I felt quietly triumphant. The man who had dominated my life for 20 years no longer intimidated me.

In December 1989, when I was in South Africa, Charlie rang me.

'Have you heard? Healy has died.'

Strangely, I felt no great emotion. Gerry's influence on my life had already been terminated. His supporters had dwindled to the Redgraves, a handful of others, and a few contacts from Gorbachev's Soviet Union. I would have liked to attend his funeral in exotic, colourful clothes, perhaps wearing a theatrical, flower-laden hat. But I was thousands of miles away and I would have been excluded anyway.

New Park Publications, our flagship company, owned most of the Centre and had substantial book stocks of Marxist and Trotskyist classics and our more recent publications. But New Park was no longer viable. A new company was set up to buy the remaining book stocks and two surviving bookshops

◀ Entrance to the WRP's former headquarters. We knew it as 21b Old Town, although the alleyway entrance led to Units 5 and 7. By 2018 the entire complex had been converted into '24 stunning, loft style apartments, set around a beautiful landscaped courtyard'

in London. Smaller premises were found for the Party and the Centre at 21b Old Town was put on the market. I was only peripherally involved in the restructuring and escaped the mammoth task of clearing the premises and selling or otherwise disposing of the contents.

New Park Publications went into voluntary liquidation in 1988. The administrator, Mr Souster of Baker Tilley, a stern accountant in a dark, pin-striped suit, presided over a bitter creditors' meeting. Large book wholesalers, suppliers of greeting cards, paper merchants and the Church Commissioners, who owned the warehouse storing the book stocks, gathered in a hotel in Bloomsbury. I sat on a bench at the back, with my second baby in his buggy. I had a clear view down the central aisle.

'The largest creditor is Mrs Clare Cowen,' said the administrator. 'Is she present?'

I was breastfeeding at that moment, an unlikely occurrence in a liquidation meeting. I raised my hand. Mr Souster looked down the aisle at me, taken aback, disapproving.

The small supplier of greeting cards from Brixton was very distressed at his losses. The Church Commissioners' representative was particularly belligerent. It was a sorry day.

Gerry's son Alan Healy died in early 1991. I had known him since joining the League, his sister Mary to a lesser extent. I scarcely knew their mother, Betty. She had ceased political activity before I joined the movement and Gerry had moved out of their house in Streatham to the flats on Clapham High Street soon after my arrival in London. Betty occasionally came to the Centre in later years, perhaps to discuss Alan's psychiatric treatment with Gerry. She and Dot knew each other from the old days, but I had never really understood how she fitted in.

Alan was an intelligent but troubled man whose life had been complicated by being the son of a powerful leader. Quite a crowd assembled in the crematorium chapel to bid him farewell, all past or present members of the Party, warring fractions in the bitter struggles of the preceding five years. Some nodded acknowledgement to Dot and me, others studiously avoided recognition; none of us wished to talk to each other. The air was tense with hostility but we all observed the convention of manners expected at a funeral.

Betty conducted the proceedings courageously, explaining that Alan had died of an overdose of his anti-psychotic medication.

'He was very depressed about the war in Kuwait and the winter's bitter cold really distressed him. The overdose may have been accidental, or it may have been intentional. We'll never know.'

Somebody read a T.S. Eliot poem, *Macavity: The Mystery Cat*, which Alan had liked. Corin gave the eulogy, a dignified, eloquent account of Alan's life, mentioning his love of music, that he played piano and guitar, and enjoyed playing chess on Clapham Common. When he referred to Gerry I glanced round, marvelling that some in the gathering still revered his memory. I looked at Betty and remembered something Aileen had told me. Betty had warned Mike and Tony Banda years before: 'You're tied to a madman.' How different things might have been if they had heeded her advice.

We were invited to pay our last respects at the open coffin. As the mourners filed past, Vanessa lingered for a long moment. I stayed in my seat, noting who was present. I counted eight splinter groups of our former Party. The Healy-Redgrave-Torrance Minority had split into four grouplets, to my knowledge. Three groups, including Mike and Tony Banda, had broken away from our organisation, which remained the largest fraction. All were represented in the chapel.

Betty closed the proceedings.

'It's the first day of spring and the sun is shining. Let's go outside and enjoy the flowering trees in the gardens.'

Afterword

When the dust had settled after the 1985 expulsion of leader Gerry Healy from the Workers Revolutionary Party (WRP), I set about consolidating my family life, buoyed by the awareness that I had contributed to bringing down a corrupt and abusive leader. For 15 years I ran a small typesetting and printing business, working on political publications and numerous books. I later worked in the voluntary sector in the London Borough of Southwark. After retiring I embarked on an MA in Creative and Life Writing at Goldsmiths, University of London. Although actively involved in my local community, I am not a member of any political party.

I have written this memoir to tell my story, to record the little-known inner workings and secret preparations that brought down Healy, and to acknowledge and celebrate fellow members who campaigned in the working-class movement to build our Party, sacrificing so much over many decades. I am deeply proud that hundreds of members rose up to expel Healy when his sexual abuse was uncovered. I know of no other case where a sexual abuser has been dealt with in this way, *by his own organisation*.

A position of power or trust over women or men passionately engaged in a cause does not confer a right to abuse them violently or sexually. Sexual abuse has been exposed in churches, corporations, governments, sports clubs, political organisations, the film industry and charities. Although never acceptable, it has been going on for years but after becoming headline news it is now widely condemned. We didn't go to the police about Healy because we believed nothing was worse for him than expulsion from the organisation in which he had spent 49 years, most as its leader.

I do not regret the fascinating and amazing experiences I had in the Party. My world encompassed the widest layers of society from the most exploited sections of the industrial working-class and unemployed to professionals, artists, academics and – always – young people. The skills and inner-confidence I gained have been invaluable since. My political background colours everything I do. But I do not hanker after the Party of yesteryear. Socialism was never going to come via an organisation self-proclaiming its leadership of the struggle for capitalism's revolutionary overthrow.

I don't have answers for today's turbulent times, but truth still rings through Lenin's 1916 words*: 'The epoch of capitalist imperialism is one of ripe and rotten-ripe capitalism, which is about to collapse, and which is mature enough to make way for socialism.'

Over years, and particularly in 1984-85, I took extensive notes in political meetings, both to keep awake and because the discussions seemed important. These notes, and the many documents I kept, are reflected in verbatim accounts in this memoir. We considered the oppression of women in only the most general way, believing women's and black liberation could only be achieved through the liberation of the whole working class. Since we opposed 'sectional' struggles, the feminist movements of the time passed us by.

I am lucky. My life after Healy's expulsion in 1985 has been rich and varied. Our two sons have given Charlie and me great joy and we have been able to build a stable life. But it has not been so for everyone. Many of Healy's victims were unable to move on easily or speedily. Some lost jobs, homes or both. Relationships broke up in agonising fashion. The mental and physical health of some victims has not healed with time and some have not managed to rebuild their lives.

In a small way I hope my book may help some achieve closure on regretted or bitter experiences. Healy's secretary Aileen Jennings has encouraged me throughout to write this account:

'The sexual abuse story has to be told, warts and all. Yours will be the only voice we ever have.'

---

* V. I. Lenin, Opportunism and the Collapse of the Second International. Marxists Internet Archive

GLOSSARY

Political terms

Central Committee (CC) Under the constitution, this was the highest committee of the Workers Revolutionary Party, elected by National Congress, with full powers between congresses.

Control Commission Independent regulatory body consisting of three non-Central Committee members, elected by Congress, with the power to conduct investigations that the Central Committee or Congress considered necessary, or to inquire into the complaint of any individual member. It reported to Congress.

Democratic Centralism A method of leadership in which political decisions reached by the party (through its democratically elected bodies) are binding upon all members of the party. Lenin described it as 'freedom of discussion, unity of action'.

Fourth International The Communist international founded in 1938 by followers of Leon Trotsky after his expulsion from the Soviet Union. Opposed Stalin's view that 'socialism in one country' could be built in the Soviet Union alone.

International Committee of the Fourth International Formed in November 1953. Favoured building independent revolutionary parties against the policies of Michel Pablo (see below) of working within the communist or socialist mass parties.

Minority rights Clause 8(b) of the WRP constitution stated that minorities had 'the right to express dissenting opinion and organise within the Party'. 8(c) laid out the procedure for establishment of a minority right.

National Congress Highest body of the Party, convened at least once a year, with delegates from local branches.

Political Committee (PC) Elected by Central Committee with full powers between CC meetings.

Socialist Labour League (SLL) Forerunner of the Workers Revolutionary Party (WRP), which was launched in 1974.

Party publications

Keep Left Young Socialists' newspaper during the fight inside the Labour Party in the 1960s. Continued afterwards; later renamed *Young Socialist*.
Newsletter Weekly paper of Socialist Labour League, 1957-69.
News Line Party's daily paper 1976-85.
Workers Press Party's daily paper 1969-76.
Theoretical journals *Fourth International* (1964-1979) and *Labour Review* (1977-85).
The left-Labour weekly newspaper *Labour Herald* 1981-85 was typeset and printed by WRP print companies

Party premises and companies

186a Clapham High Street 'The Centre' – Socialist Labour League's headquarters. Used as Young Socialists' offices after the move to Clapham Old Town. Subsequently kept for accommodation.

180b Clapham High Street Print shop in the 1960s, later a warehouse for books. Access to a Party flat overlooking the high street; entrance via the back alley.

155a Clapham High Street Eight Party flats on second and third floors.

Accommodation for Healy, two married couples and generations of young women Party members.

21b Clapham Old Town The Party printshop and headquarters moved to this large industrial site in the late 1960s. The address was technically 7b Old Town but was always known as 21b. No frontage on to the street; very secure, intimidating to some.

Astmoor Litho, Runcorn The Party's modern printshop was set up in 1975, behind the back of the NGA print union and staffed by Party members who were in the print unions. Enabled the Party to benefit from advanced high-tech photo-typesetting and printing processes.

Bookshops (six) owned by New Park Publications Known as Paperbacks Centres in London (Charlotte Street, Upton Park, Brixton) and Norwich, Merseybooks in Liverpool, and Hope Street Book Centre in Glasgow.

College of Marxist Education Party's school near Parwich, Derbyshire; also known as White Meadows or the Red House.

Copsecroft Ltd Owned our Youth Training Centres.

Grafton Litho Small printing company based in its own premises next to the Centre.

New Park Publications The Party's biggest company; owned the bookshops and many of the premises.

WRP Film Department Produced Party films. Run by Tom Scott-Robson; worked with Hogarth Films and Vanessa Redgrave Productions.

Youth Training Centres Seven centres were run by the Young Socialists in Brixton, Newcastle, Manchester, Nottingham, Liverpool, Glasgow and Merthyr Tydfil. Buildings were owned by Party company Copsecroft Ltd.

Party members who recur

To simplify my account I have used names sparingly and I have excluded any I believe may have been Healy's sexual victims. Absent are the names and pictures of the numerous young women, leaders of the Young Socialists, who gave vitality and energy to our vibrant youth movement. Two people are referred to by their initials only, to conceal their identity.

Banda, Janet SLL national organiser until circa 1970; latterly worked in the finance office. Married to Mike.
Banda, Mike CC member and Party General Secretary
Banda, Tony CC member, politically in charge of Runcorn printshop. Mike's brother
Bruce, Dave CC member, in charge of printing and technical equipment at the Party Centre in London
Carter, Stuart CC member from Manchester
Cavanagh, Larry Liverpool docker, longstanding Party member. Elected to Party Control Commission
Charlie Seconded from the German section; in charge of security at the Party Centre
D Involved in Young Socialists' fight against Labour Party bureaucracy in the 1960s; London area secretary; had international responsibilities. My first branch secretary in London
Fryer, Peter Author of *Hungarian Tragedy*. Broke with Communist Party in 1957; became editor of *The Newsletter* until his 1959 break with Healy
Gale, Jack Party theoretician and journalist, formerly on the CC. Died after a period in Australia
Gibson, Dot CC member in charge of finance office.
Gibson, Peter CC member, Dot's husband
Harding, Norman Longstanding member, in charge of *News Line* dispatch. Elected to Party Control Commission
Harris, Robert CC member, worked in finance and technical offices
Healy, Gerry Party leader
Jennings, Aileen Involved in Young Socialists' fight against Labour Party bureaucracy in the 1960s and editor of youth paper, *Keep Left* until 1970. CC member, and Healy's secretary for 15 years
Jennings, Paul CC member. Sub-editor and later editor of *News Line*. Aileen's former husband

Jones, Peter CC member; lecturer at the Party's College of Marxist Education
Kemp, Tom Party theoretician, formerly on the CC.
Kerrigan, Jean Longstanding member. Elected to Party Control Commission
Linda Efford Long-standing member, worked in finance office. Married to printshop manager Ray
North, Dave Leader of the Chicago-based Workers League, in 'political solidarity' with the International Committee of the Fourth International
Mitchell, Alex Journalist and CC member. *News Line* foreign editor and sometime editor
Penn, Phil Responsible for Party's vehicle fleet. Latterly a CC member
Pilling, Geoff Party theoretician, formerly on the CC
Ray Efford Manager of Runcorn printshop, Astmoor Litho
Redgrave, Corin Actor, CC member
Redgrave, Vanesssa Actor, CC member
Scott-Robson, Tom Film editor; responsible for the Party's film units
Shaw, Mickie Veteran member, joined during second world war. Aileen Jennings's mother
Slaughter, Cliff CC member and Party theoretician. Left the Communist Party after 1956 Hungarian uprising to join the SLL
Smith, Cyril Party theoretician, formerly on the CC
Temple, Dave Durham miner, CC member
Thornett, Alan Shop steward at Cowley car plants. CC member who led opposition to Party policies. Expelled in 1974 with many supporters
T My husband for four years
Torrance, Sheila Involved in Young Socialists' fight against Labour Party bureaucracy in the 1960s. CC member and WRP Assistant General Secretary

Brief bibliography

Harding, Norman *Staying Red, Why I remain a Socialist.* Index Books, 2005
Lotz, C and Feldman P *Gerry Healy: A revolutionary life.* Lupus Books, 1994
Mitchell, A *Come the Revolution,* Alex**,** UNSW Press 2012
Redgrave, Vanessa *An Autobiography.* Arrow Books, 1992
Shaw, M *Fighter for Trotskyism Robert Shaw 1917-1980.* New Park Publications. 1983

Historical and political figures

Arafat, Yasser Chairman of the Palestine Liberation Organisation (PLO)
Cliff, Tony Leader of the International Socialists, another Trotskyist organisation
Gaddafi, Colonel Muammar Leader of 1969 revolutionary coup against western-backed Libyan monarchy; leader of Libyan Jamahiriya (state) until 2011 assassination
Heath, Edward UK Conservative prime minister 1970-74
Hussein, Saddam President of Iraq, 1979-2003
Khomeini, Ayatollah Leader of the Islamic Republic after the 1979 Iranian Revolution
Lenin, Vladimir Ilyich (1870-1924) Russian communist revolutionary, politician and political theorist. Leader of the Bolshevik Party and 1917 Russian Revolution
Marx, Karl (1818-83) German philosopher, economist, historian, sociologist, political theorist, journalist and socialist revolutionary
Mugabe, Robert Leader of Zimbabwe African National Union (ZANU), a leader in the war of independence. Prime Minster of Zimbabwe from 1980
Nkomo, Joshua Founder of the Zimbabwe African People's Union (ZAPU), a leader in the war of independence
Pablo, Michel (1911-96) A leader of the Fourth International who argued in 1953 for adapting to the mass social democratic and communist parties. Disagreements led to a major split, and formation of the International Committee of the Fourth International, in which Gerry Healy played a leading role
Pinochet, General Augusto US-backed dictator of Chile, 1973-90
Smith, Ian Prime minister of Southern Rhodesia, 1964-79. Declared unilateral independence from Britain, which led to a 15-year civil war
Stalin, Joseph (1878-1953) Dictator of the Soviet Union, 1929-53. Ruled by terror; millions of Soviet citizens died during his brutal reign
Thatcher, Margaret UK Conservative prime minister, 1979-90
Trotsky, Leon (1879-1940): A leader of the 1917 Russian Revolution who led the Red Army's defence of the revolution during the 1918-20 civil war. Expelled from the Soviet Union by Stalin after Lenin's death. Assassinated in exile in Mexico in 1940 on Stalin's orders
Tshombe, Moïse President of secessionist State of Katanga 1960-63, prime minister of Democratic Republic of the Congo 1964-65
Wilson, Harold UK Labour prime minister 1964-70 and 1974-76

Chronology 1964-87

1964	Labour government elected under Prime Minister Harold Wilson. Soviet leader Nikita Khrushchev removed from office
1965	Unilateral Declaration of Independence by Ian Smith's white Rhodesian government. US sends troops to Vietnam
1966	Labour government wins larger majority in election. Prime Minister Hendrik Verwoerd assassinated in South Africa
1967	Six-Day War between Israel and neighbouring states of Egypt, Jordan and Syria. Greek colonels establish a military dictatorship that lasts for seven years
1968	May-June: student revolt in Paris links up with general strike of 10 million workers throughout France. Martin Luther King Jr. and Robert F. Kennedy assassinated in US. Prague Spring ended by a Soviet invasion. Protests across Europe against the Vietnam War. My Lai massacre in Vietnam
1969	British troops sent to Northern Ireland in a 'limited operation' to restore law and order. Libyan monarchy overthrown, army officer Muammar Gaddafi heads government. September: Socialist Labour League launches daily paper *Workers Press*
1970	Conservative government elected with Edward Heath as prime minister
1971	February: Decimal currency replaces 'pounds, shillings and pence' in UK. August 15th: dollar taken off gold standard. Bangladesh liberation war gains independence from West Pakistan
1972	January: Miners' national strike. January 30th: British army kills 14 on 'Bloody Sunday' in Londonderry, Northern Ireland. July: Pentonville dockers jailed. Ugandan Asians expelled by President Idi Amin, many settle in UK
1973	Yom Kippur War between Israel and Arab states. Oil Crisis caused by Organisation of Petroleum Exporting Countries' embargo. Chile's socialist President Allende overthrown and dies in a coup led by General Augusto Pinochet. November: Socialist Labour League transforms into Workers Revolutionary Party
1974	Conservative Heath government brought down by miners, leading to 'hung parliament' under Labour Prime Minster Wilson, who

	wins a tiny majority in October election. 'Carnation Revolution' in Portugal against fascist regime. Richard Nixon resigns as US president while facing impeachment charges. WRP stands candidates in October general election
1975	April: Vietnam War ends with fall of Saigon and unconditional surrender of US-supported South Vietnam regime. End of Portuguese colonial war in Angola and Mozambique, followed by civil war in Angola and interventions by apartheid South Africa in both countries. Lebanese civil war begins, involving both Israel and the Palestine Liberation Organisation, and endures till early 1990s
1976	Prime Minister Wilson resigns, replaced by James Callaghan. Two-year strike for union recognition begins at Grunwick Film Processing Laboratories in Willesden, north-west London, by a workforce predominantly of Asian women. June: Soweto uprising; estimated 700 black school children killed by South Africa's security police. February: WRP closes *Workers Press*; begins production of new daily paper, *News Line*, on 1st May
1977	South African anti-apartheid activist Stephen Biko murdered in police custody. Spain's fascist dictator Franco dies after 39 years in power
1978-79	'Winter of discontent' in UK. Widespread strikes against Labour government's pay freeze
1979	Following strikes and demonstrations which paralyse Iran, Shah flees into exile and revolution takes place; power concentrates in the hands of the Islamists led by Ayatollah Khomeini, who establish the Islamic republic of Iran. Oil crisis occurs due to fall in Iranian production. Saddam Hussein becomes president of Iraq. May: Conservative government elected under Prime Minster Margaret Thatcher. December: Lancaster House agreement signed to end Rhodesian civil war. May: WRP stands 60 candidates in general election and qualifies for a party political broadcast on television. July: First colour issue of *News Line*
1980	Severe global recession begins. Iraq invades Iran and an eight-year war ensures. Ronald Reagan elected US president. Zimbabwe, formerly Southern Rhodesia, officially becomes independent

1981	April: Riots in Brixton and other inner-city areas. October: Hunger strike by Republican prisoners in Northern Ireland ends after ten deaths
1982	Economic recession. Unemployment tops 3 million. April: Britain defeats Argentina in war over isolated Malvinas Islands. Israel occupies southern Lebanon
1983	Landslide election victory for Margaret Thatcher's conservative government
1984	March: Miners' national strike over pit closures begins, involving 142,000 mineworkers
1985	March: Miners' strike ends after one year. April: Former-WRP member Bernie Grant becomes the first black council leader in Labour-controlled London Borough of Haringey. Inner-city riots in Birmingham and London. December: unemployment 3.16 million. October: Gerry Healy expelled from WRP
1986	Soviet Nuclear reactor at Chernobyl explodes, causing release of radioactive material across much of Europe. Greater London Council and other metropolitan county councils are abolished by Tory government. British Gas Corporation privatised
1987	Thatcher government elected for a third term

INDEX

Allan, my younger brother, 9-11, 20, 47-8, 152
Annabel, College of Marxist Education manager, 197, 261-62, 287-8
Arafat, Yasser, 140, 216, 310, 312, 342
Arden, John, 81
Banda, Janet, 46, 120, 154, 159, 187, 217, 229, 250, 286, 289, 323, 340
Banda, Mike, 35, 51, 58-60, 65, 69, 79-80, 91, 96, 113-114, 154, 158-59, 162-63, 165, 169, 174-75, 196, 199-201, 209-210, 212, 217, 224, 229, 231, 233, 237-44, 246-52, 256-57, 259, 264, 266-70, 272-75, 279-80, 287-93, 295-302, 304, 306-309, 312, 315, 321-23, 334, 340
Banda, Tony, 113, 115, 117, 128, 130-1, 267, 280, 286, 289, 323, 334, 340
Battle of Lewisham, 123, 193
Bevan, Jim, 243
Birnberg, Benedict, 163
Black People's Day of Action, 145-6
Bruce, Dave, iv, vii, 101, 117, 119, 162, 170, 173, 178, 200-201, 209, 211-212, 220, 224, 227-31, 235, 237-39, 250, 257, 264, 266-67, 269-71, 273-76, 279-80, 285, 287-89, 314, 321-22, 324, 327-28, 340
Calder, Dave, 101, 235
Campbell, Cartoon, family, 136
Carter, Stuart, 224, 297, 300, 316, 340
Castle, Barbara, 52, 55
Cavanagh, Larry, 274, 306, 320, 340
Charlie, responsible for Party Centre's security, vii, 152, 154, 156, 162, 163, 186-88, 190, 197, 201, 203-205, 208, 210-212, 217-220, 226-231, 235-37, 239, 242-45, 248, 250, 254-55, 264-65, 271, 274, 276-77, 282-85, 297, 299-300, 314-315, 322, 324, 326-28, 332, 336, 340
Cliff, Tony, 63-64, 342
College of Marxist Education, 108-109, 131, 180, 187, 197, 214, 217, 260, 279, 339, 341
Cowley, British Leyland plants, ix, 105-106, 157-59, 163, 174, 188, 190, 252, 341
Cromwell, Oliver, 156, 224
D, my SLL branch secretary, 61-62, 67, 69, 75-76, 90, 106, 340
Devlin, Bernadette, MP, 56
Devlin Plan for the docks, 41

Efford, Linda, 90, 99, 161, 276, 341
Efford, Ray, 112-114, 179-80, 341
Engels, Friedrich, 176, 215, 329
Euro-Marches, 147
Fabrizio, 21-26, 29, 34, 39
Falklands war, 158, 345
Firemen's strike, 1977-78, x, 124-6
Flynn, Kevin, 4
Fourth International, International Committee, 1, 5, 7, 166, 172, 174, 215, 264, 301, 309, 319, 325-26, 337, 341-42
Fourth International, theoretical journal, 139, 308, 338
Fredericks, Lisa, 97
Fryer, Peter, 36-7, 198, 340
Gaddafi, Colonel Muammar, 118, 122, 216, 297, 309, 342-3,
Gale, Jack, 62, 140, 281, 340
Gelfand, Alan, 170-2,
Gibson, Dot, iv, vii, 90, 93, 95, 98-99, 157-69, 171, 173-74, 178-81, 187-90, 192, 198-201, 203, 206-207, 209-11, 213, 219-21, 223-228, 230-32, 235-241, 244, 246, 248-50, 253-54, 258, 260, 263-64, 266, 270, 273-76, 281, 285-90, 300-301, 315, 322, 324, 326, 328, 334, 340
Gibson, Peter, 137, 148, 170, 230, 243, 266, 340
Greenham Common, 143
Hamilton, Betty, 62
Harding, Norman, 6, 109, 132, 153, 208, 228-29, 231, 265, 274, 279, 287, 292, 306, 320-321, 340-41
Harris, Robert, 159, 164, 169, 174, 178, 209, 211, 226-28, 232, 235, 240, 245, 250, 264, 266, 269, 281, 285-86, 288-90, 340

Healy, Alan, 334
Healy, Betty, 334
Healy, Thomas Gerard (Gerry), v, vii, 1-2, 4-7, 31-32, 36, 38-9, 45-50, 54, 57-60, 62-65, 68-73, 76, 84-5, 87-88, 90, 93, 96-99, 102, 107-109, 111-12, 115-17, 119, 121-22, 124, 126, 128-29, 131-32, 139, 149-50, 153-171, 173-74, 176-80, 185, 187-88, 190-92, 196-204, 206-220, 222-52, 254, 256-65, 267-71, 273-76, 279-82, 286, 288-89, 292-309, 312-325, 328-332, 334-336 339-42, 345
Heath, Edward, 100, 192, 342-43
Howard, my older brother, 15, 20, 29, 43, 48, 106, 155
Hussein, Saddam, 309, 342, 344
Incest Crisis Line, 330-32,
International Socialists, 63, 95-96, 342
Jennings, Aileen, v, vii, 34, 36, 39, 49-50, 63-65, 71, 111, 117, 119, 128, 152-5, 165-72, 178-81, 188-90, 196-98, 200-203, 205-206, 208-20, 222-24, 227-31, 233, 235-45, 247-50, 254-56, 258, 261, 263-64, 266-67, 270, 273-74, 276, 279, 281, 285-89, 292, 294-98, 300, 303-304, 306, 309, 315, 318, 320, 322, 328, 330, 334, 336, 340-41.
Jennings, Paul, 49, 119-120, 122, 128, 130-131, 155, 157, 198, 206, 223-24, 230, 235, 237, 240, 288, 292, 297, 316, 326, 340
Johns, (Hammond) Steve, 28-29, 33, 39, 64, 140
Jones, Peter, 217, 243, 260-2, 266, 268-69, 279, 282, 341
Justice for Jailed Miners March, 221, 224, 228, 230-32, 239, 241, 243, 256, 258

Keith, branch comrade in Dagenham, 91
Kemp, Tom, 64, 308, 325, 339
Kempinski, Tom, 81, 101
Kerrigan, Jean, 42, 51-52, 232, 235, 274, 306, 320, 341
Khomeini, Ayatollah, 311-312, 342, 344
Knight, Ted, 168, 206-207, 234
Labour Herald, 206-207, 248, 288, 338
Labour Review, 160, 308, 338
Leach, Bridget, vii, 180, 318
Leicester, Liz, vii, 113, 288, 329-30
Lenin, Vladimir Ilyich, 30, 63-64, 69, 176, 192, 215, 271, 273, 280, 336-37, 342
— *What is to be Done?* 64, 192, 260,
— *Volume 14,* 226,
— *Volume 38,* 126, 174, 176,
Livingstone, Ken, 18, 206-207, 257, 269
Lotz, Corinna, 1, 6, 128, 332
Lumumba, Patrice, 23
Marx, Karl, 30, 34, 43, 63-4, 174-75, 215, 235, 273, 342
Mendelson, Vivian, 93, 95
Militant tendency, 63
Miners
— 1972 strike, 76, 78-81, 84, 343
— 1973-4 work to rule, 99-100, 343
— 1984-85 strike, x, 3, 182, 186, 191-196, 200-202, 209, 215, 220-21, 224, 233, 249, 258, 262, 269, 272, 277, 280-81, 298, 308, 330, 343, 345
Mitchell, Alex, 6, 121-22, 124, 152, 199-201, 208-210, 213, 220-21, 224, 229, 237-39, 241-43, 270, 279, 281-82, 287, 292, 296-98, 300, 304, 307-8, 311, 315, 325, 341
Mopeds, 191, 259, 273, 304, 322, 325
Moss, Richard, 161, 252-53, 286, 327
Mugabe, Robert, 141, 310, 342
Myers, Bob and George, 139
New Cross Fire, 145-6
Newsletter, 25, 29, 31-33, 41-2, 45, 49, 57, 64, 133, 198, 338, 340
News Line, iv, x-xi, 1, 5, 115-16, 118-19, 121, 124-26, 128, 132-33, 135, 140, 151-52, 157, 160-65, 183, 188, 190-92, 196, 203, 208, 210, 212, 219-21, 228, 230, 233, 235, 238, 246-47, 249-50, 253, 255, 257, 259-61, 266-68, 270-71, 273, 275, 277, 279, 281, 284, 288, 291-92, 295-298, 302, 304, 308-9, 311-12, 316-17, 322, 325, 338, 340-41, 344
Nkomo, Joshua, 11, 141, 309-310, 342
Norah, my sister, 10, 20, 48
North, Dave, 167, 170, 173-74, 263, 287-88, 292-93, 300, 319-20, 325-26, 329, 341
Observer, The, 109-110, 131-32, 259-60
O'Brien, Tony, branch comrade in southeast London, 74
Pablo, Michel, 295, 309, 319, 338, 342
Peach, Blair, 135
Penn, Phil, iv, 201, 207, 230, 237, 240, 279, 288, 315-316, 341
Pentonville Five dockers, 88-89, 343
Perrier water, 64, 70, 174, 200, 220
Pilling, Geoff, 30, 58, 64, 69, 292, 308, 341
Pinochet, General Augusto, 269, 342, 343
Pirani, Simon, vii, 138, 194, 318
Price, Richard, 238, 257, 272, 277-78, 281
Ram John Holder, 79, 85
Read, Peter, 28-9, 33, 64
Redgrave, Corin, 2, 97, 108-109, 131,

199-200, 209, 224-25, 230, 236-38, 246, 248, 250, 254, 257, 259, 261, 264, 266-70, 272, 281, 285-86, 289, 296-302, 304-305, 307-308, 312-315, 318, 322, 324-25, 332, 334, 341

Redgrave, Vanessa, 2, 4-6, 79, 100-102, 131, 149, 153, 165, 177, 199-203, 209, 217, 227, 230, 237-39, 242, 248, 255, 272, 300, 303-304, 307-308, 313-15, 322-5, 329, 332, 334, 339, 341

Reich, Wilhelm, 22, 296

Rhodesia, Southern, ix, 2, 8, 11, 13, 15, 17, 19, 21, 23, 25, 27-29, 31-33, 36, 55, 82-3, 106, 122, 141, 215, 310, 342-4

Roach, Colin, parents, 136

Robertson group, US, 328

Ruddock family, 145

Sands, Bobby, 144

Scargill, Arthur, 192-94

Scarman Inquiry, 146

Scott-Robson, Tom, 288, 300, 339, 341

Security and the Fourth International, 5, 7

Shaw, Mickie, 111-13, 117, 131, 240, 250, 264, 273-76, 341

Shiraz, security guard, 201, 206

Shrewsbury Two, 104

Simmance, John, 79-80, 86

Slaughter, Cliff, 25, 29, 63-5, 244, 268, 280-282, 308-9, 321, 330, 341

Smith, Cyril, 34, 177, 281, 292, 308, 330, 341

Smith, Ian, 27, 141, 342-43

Smith, Roger, 81, 101

Smith, Sean, *News Line* photographer, 203

South Africa, 2, 13, 19, 21, 23, 27-28, 36, 48, 59, 83-84, 97, 107, 119, 140, 149-51, 170, 182-83, 185, 252, 254, 256, 259, 270-71, 277, 281, 286, 323, 332, 343-4,

South West Africa, x, 182-85

Soweto, 119, 151, 182, 185, 344

Spencer, John, vii, 140, 249, 288, 291

Stuart, Calvin, 137

T, my husband, ix, 36-40, 42, 46-51, 53-4, 60, 62, 68, 70-4, 341

Temple, Dave, vii, 3, 195-96, 242, 268, 282, 301, 341

Thatcher, Margaret, 141-42, 145, 158, 234, 256, 342, 344, 345

Thornett, Alan, 100, 157, 198, 275, 324, 341

Tomlinson, Ricky, 104

Torrance, Sheila, 29-30, 34, 58, 64, 68, 74, 76-77, 80-81, 84, 90, 93, 97-9, 106, 108, 119-21, 125, 128, 152-53, 155, 157, 164-65, 169, 171, 174, 179, 187, 191-92, 195-96, 198-200, 205, 209-10, 217, 221, 224-25, 227, 232-33, 235, 237-43, 246-50, 257-60, 262, 264-65, 268-69, 271-75, 277-82, 286-87, 291-92, 295-300, 303-305, 307, 309, 312-15, 317-18, 322, 325, 329, 341

Treacher, Karen, 41

Trotsky, Leon, 2, 7, 23, 30, 62, 63, 88, 96, 105-107, 138, 158, 171, 212, 215, 261-62, 269, 273, 275, 280, 309, 329, 337, 342

Tshombe, Moïse, 16, 23, 342

Ulli, a leader of our German section, 167

Unilateral Declaration of Independence (Southern Rhodesia), ix, 27, 342-43

USDAW, shopworkers' union, 93, 95

Warren, Des, 104, 139
Wilson, Harold, 27, 33, 37, 100, 342-44,
Workers Press, ix, 53, 64-67, 72, 79, 84, 88-89, 91, 93, 107, 109, 111-15, 118, 133, 328, 336, 341-42,

Youth Training Centres, 159, 179, 181, 237, 286, 312, 324, 339
Zambia, 15
Zimbabwe, 141, 182, 309, 342, 344

MY SEARCH FOR REVOLUTION

Clare Cowen was born in 1945 in South Africa and moved to Southern Rhodesia, now Zimbabwe, for her teenage years before going to Europe and to Bristol University. She was a member of the Workers Revolutionary Party and its predecessor, the Socialist Labour League, from 1966 until its demise in the 1990s. She lives with her partner in south-east London. They have two adult sons.